卡尔·波普尔
理性与传统

KARL POPPER

[英]菲尔·帕尔文——著　莫昕——译

华中科技大学出版社
http://www.hustp.com
中国·武汉

Major Conservative and Libertarian Thinkers:*Karl Popper*

Copyright © 2010 by Phil Parvin

First published in 2010 in UK by Bloomsbury Publishing Inc.

Simplified Chinese edition copyright:

Huazhong University of Science and Technology Press

湖北省版权局著作权合同登记图字:17-2018-283 号

图书在版编目(CIP)数据

卡尔·波普尔:理性与传统/(英)菲尔·帕尔文著;莫昕译.—武汉:华中科技大学出版社,2019.1

ISBN 978-7-5680-4799-9

Ⅰ.①卡… Ⅱ.①菲… ②莫… Ⅲ.①波帕尔(Popper,Karl Raimund 1902—1994)-传记 Ⅳ.①B561.59

中国版本图书馆 CIP 数据核字(2018)第 288800 号

卡尔·波普尔:理性与传统　　　　　　　　　　　[英]菲尔·帕尔文　著
Karl Popper:Lixing yu Chuantong　　　　　　　　　　　　莫昕　译

策划编辑:薛　蒂　　　　　　　　　　封面设计:三形三色
责任编辑:薛　蒂　　　　　　　　　　责任校对:张会军
责任监印:朱　玢
出版发行:华中科技大学出版社(中国·武汉)　　　电话:(027)81321913
　　　　　武汉市东湖新技术开发区华工科技园　　邮编:430223
录　　排:华中科技大学惠友文印中心
印　　刷:湖北新华印务有限公司
开　　本:880mm×1230mm　1/32
印　　张:11
字　　数:303 千字
版　　次:2019 年 1 月第 1 版第 1 次印刷
定　　价:45.00 元

序言

　　卡尔·波普尔(Karl Popper)是 20 世纪最重要的和极具争议的思想家之一。如今,他最为人所知的思想是他对科学哲学和观念史所作出的贡献。在前一领域,波普尔主张,仅有可证伪的科学理论才能对知识增长作出贡献,不可被证伪的命题不能促进人类对世界的了解。在后一领域,波普尔将 20 世纪极权主义的起源追溯到柏拉图和黑格尔的观点,他认为,他们的理论为要求个人权利服从于追求集体目标的法西斯主义和纳粹主义政权提供了思想基础。

　　因此,波普尔思想中的一些元素有着明显的自由主义或保守主义的特征:波普尔拥护个人自由,采取方法论的个人主义方法来进行他的学术研究;他信仰充满活力的、世界主义的"开放社会",以思想自由、表达自由为特征,并将这种理想社会与为了便于共同追求由政治精英们所确定的社会目标而组织起来的"封闭社会"进行对比;对于旨在实施预先确定的社会结构设想而发生的剧变,他持怀疑态度。

　　然而,在其他方面,波普尔的思想并不能简单地归入自由主义或保守主义的阵营。波普尔的政治学是显而易见的社会民主政治学,他信仰旨在改善社会中最贫穷者命运的渐进式社会改革,对西欧战后的社会福利制度极为支持;他主张市场的作用范围应该被限制,他坚信从民主审议中产生的公共理性的力量,能引导国家有效改善社会问题。因此,波普尔的开放社会并非一个自由市场的乌托邦,而是一个政治共同体,各色各样的人们在其中进行建设性的对话交流,寻求解决共同问题的政治方案。

拉夫堡大学的菲尔·帕尔文(Phil Parvin)在这本著作中出色地阐述了波普尔的研究工作,表明波普尔对自由主义和保守主义传统作出了重要而长久的贡献,因而不加鉴别地给他贴上保守主义者或自由主义者的标签是错误的。事实上,波普尔作为学者,并没有被某一个特定的视角或方法所束缚,他在相当范围内的不同领域都作出了贡献。我们正应该从这个背景来理解波普尔对自由主义和保守主义思想的贡献。

本书是《大思想家政治哲学》丛书之一,以浅显易懂、令人信服的风格,阐释了波普尔的思想。这本杰出的作品全面讲述了波普尔的生平和著作,研究了波普尔作品在其同时代人中引起的反响,也展示了波普尔思想的持续的相关性,特别是对于21世纪英美政治哲学而言。本书对不熟悉波普尔思想的读者,甚至更为资深的研究者,都是不可或缺的参考资料。

约翰·梅多克罗夫特

伦敦国王学院

目录

学术生涯　1

　　早年生涯　3

　　教育学院　9

　　维特根斯坦和维也纳学派　13

　　"战斗书"　21

　　后期生活　27

波普尔的思想　35

　　波普尔的认识论　37

　　从科学到社会科学　50

　　从社会科学到政治学　67

　　开放社会　86

波普尔哲学的反响和影响　95

　　波普尔、伯克，以及推理的易谬性　105

　　激进的政治学、激进的哲学　111

波普尔与新右派的兴起　**121**

关于意识形态的最终结论　**129**

波普尔哲学的当代关联性　131

结论　**149**

参考文献　**152**

名词索引　**158**

英文原著　**187**

卡尔·波普尔

学术生涯

卡尔·波普尔是 20 世纪最重要的哲学家之一。他的影响跨越诸多学科,著述涵盖多个复杂的门类,如数学与科学哲学、音乐、历史、心理学、政治学、逻辑学和认识论等。他不是一个严格意义上的政治哲学家,尽管他针对柏拉图、黑格尔等思想家所谓的极权主义倾向,为个人自由进行了著名的捍卫,长期以来为西方政治思想作出了重要贡献。他将对历史主义的批评作为一种理解方法,不仅包括对哲学、社会和政治的理解,也包括对音乐、科学和历史本身的理解。对于在这些领域内如何进行辩论也产生了巨大而持久的影响。他对自然科学和社会科学的适当行为的观点,仍然是 20 世纪对认识论和科学哲学作出的重要贡献之一。他将这种方法应用于包括政治学在内的人类探究的各个方面,为理解政治和社会,以及哲学的适当目标,提供了一种崭新的具有启发性的方法。

尽管如此,波普尔仍然是政治思想史上的一个边缘人物。当代政治理论家们很少提及他的观点,甚至也很少鼓励学生们研究他。

波普尔是具有争议性的。《开放社会及其敌人》(*The Open*

Society and Its Enemies)与《历史决定论的贫困》(*The Poverty of Historicism*)两本著作是他对社会和政治理论所作出的最著名的贡献,引起了许多哲学家的愤慨,也招来其他哲学家的嘲笑。他的书被批评为缺乏学术精神,因为他诋毁了西方文明史上一些最受尊敬的思想家的名声,他为简单化的自由主义民主的资产阶级霸权辩护,反对更激进的社会和政治观点。波普尔的政治思想源自一种与当时的许多政治哲学都不相容的深厚的哲学理性主义,也发源于一种信仰,即相信我们需要社会和政治理论对立法者和政策制定者起到实际的帮助。这种理论与众多分析性的政治哲学家中流行的理想理论化,以及许多后现代主义者和后结构主义者的抽象主义背道而行(如今仍然如此)。但是,他的思想也发源于深刻而清晰的道德意识。《开放社会及其敌人》写作于第二次世界大战期间,欧洲正濒于落入法西斯主义的魔爪,该书完全代表了对西方文明及其得以建立的价值观的哲学性捍卫。它代表了对自由、平等和民主的价值观的辩护,代表了对那些以民族团结、稳定或全民利益为名而否认这些价值观的人发起的一场毁灭性的、直击要害的攻击。波普尔的语言往往是犀利的,他的论证无法以学术界的传统标准来衡量,他的攻击是有针对性的、破坏性的。他的开放社会承诺清晰有力、坚定不移,对于古往今来那些他认为给纳粹、法西斯提供了哲学工具,为他们的罪恶辩护的人,他的仇恨是显而易见的。那么,他的著作问世时引起如此争议,这么多的当代哲学家面对他的著作不知如何回应,这也就并不奇怪了。他的政治药方无法轻易地与任何政治意识形态相联系,尽管政治领域内持各种观点的思想家都试图把他归为自己一派。他的认识论观点也将他置于了解社会和政治的众多主流方法之外。波普尔对政治思想的贡

献是具有独创性的、有争议的、有缺陷的，却是十分重要的。它经受住了时间的考验，却仍然被社会和政治理论家所忽视。在下面的章节里，我们将更加清楚地看到波普尔对政治、社会和哲学的论述，他所引发的争议，以及他的主张对当代社会及其问题研究的持久的影响。

早 年 生 涯

卡尔·波普尔的一生始于接近哈布斯堡王朝尾声的维也纳。当时，这座城市是一个庞大的多民族帝国的首都，民族主义正成为奥地利政治中一股日益显著和重要的力量。在 1867 年至 1879 年间，奥地利自由主义完成了大批积极的社会和政治改革措施，包括经济现代化和公共教育推广，这将深刻地塑造波普尔后来出生时的社会和政治环境。然而，它也遗留下了一个将会笼罩波普尔世界的黑暗传统。奥地利自由主义具有同化主义和民族主义的特征：完全的公民权仅限于那些"展现了德国公民的坚实品格"[1]的人。维也纳当时是"欧洲同化比率最高的城市"[2]，"在欧洲城市中犹太人归信基督教的比例最高"，部分原因在于许多犹太人普遍感受到反犹太主义的存在。[3] 随着时间的推移，奥地利自由主义沦为德国民族主义，因为自由主义者试图将日益支离破碎的中产阶级在一个源自种族划分的崭新而本能的政治愿景下统一起来。这个愿景变得越来越强大，对像卡

---

[1]　Hacohen, 2000: 32.

[2]　Edmonds & Eidenow, 2002: 72.

[3]　Edmonds & Eidenow, 2002: 72.

尔的父母西蒙和珍妮这样的犹太人——特别是像他父亲这样的犹太移民（珍妮·波普尔出生在维也纳）——的生活和利益则越来越不利。与众多生活在这个城市里的其他犹太人家庭一样，波普尔一家与犹太社区断绝了关系，并在 1900 年转为路德教派。但尽管如此，尽管他们也接受了德国文化的职业道德和价值观，波普尔一家和大多数犹太人一样，仍然从未真正被主流社会衷心接纳。早期的自由主义观点认为，一个人通过文化适应和努力工作，可以获得"好公民"的品质。然而这种思想似乎已经被新近对种族划分的诉求所取代。于是，犹太人闭关自守，生活、工作、社交、婚嫁，都在一个具有广泛凝聚力和普遍排外的社区之内进行。

当时的维也纳也是激进的进步运动的发祥地。波普尔一家与其中许多最重要的成员在相同的圈子里活动。甚至在波普尔出生之前，激进的进步派就已经"背弃了主流自由主义的社会保守主义，为工人寻求出路。他们在开明的官僚主义的支持下选择了一个资产阶级-无产阶级的联盟，促进社会立法、经济现代化和科学教育"①。他们寻求新的左派议程，向奥地利自由主义挑战。他们相信科学和"社会技术"能够解决贫困和贫富之间资源分配不平等的问题。因此，他们认为，社会公正需要对这些问题（及其解决方法）的科学理解。他们于 1891 年成立了维也纳

---

① Hacohen,2000:24.

费边社①,1896 年又成立了社会政治党,并利用这些组织及其他论坛来倡导全面男性选举和福利改革,反对天主教、反犹太主义。

因此,1902 年 7 月 28 日卡尔·波普尔出生时,正是处在这样一个在政治、社会、经济和宗教方面各自分野的帝都,在这样一个刚刚归信基督教的家庭,他的父母为了获取成功放弃了自己的宗教、接纳主流文化,却仍然被在很大程度上反犹的主流社会疑心猜忌。尽管如此,波普尔的父母仍然成功地爬上了维也纳社会的上层。西蒙·波普尔(Simon Popper)是一位高薪的律师,他和妻子、两个女儿及刚出生的儿子住在一套有 20 个房间的宽敞公寓里。这里足够容纳他们一家五口、他汗牛充栋的藏书、他的秘书和仆人,以及他所经营的各个慈善机构。在他的自传中,波普尔形容他的父亲"更像是一个学者,而不是律师",父亲对诗歌、历史和哲学都很感兴趣,他的藏书浩若烟海,书房里摆不下,只好摆放在公寓里的其他房间,多达 14000 册书籍,包括柏拉图、培根、笛卡儿、斯宾诺莎、尼采、洛克、康德和密尔的作品,以及"德国、法国、英国、俄国和北欧文学经典作家"②的作品;还包括大量的历史文献、古典著作、当代哲学和文学以及最近的维也纳政治、社会改革和心理分析出版物;还有查尔斯·达尔文(Charles Darwin)的著作。

学术生涯

---

① 费边社(Fabian Society)是英国的一个社会主义团体,成立于 1884 年,由一群中产阶级知识分子所发起。奉行的思想被称为费边主义(Fabianism),又称费边社会主义(Fabian Socialism)。费边社的传统重在务实的社会建设,倡导建立互助互爱的社会,其实质在于把资本主义社会传统的自由民主政治与社会主义相结合,从而推行和平宪政和市政社会主义的道路。主张通过渐进温和的改良主义方式来走向社会主义,并强调通过教育的途径让权力回到知识精英的手中。译者注。

② Popper,1974/2002:6.

波普尔的家人以及他父母所参与的进步运动的成员，对他多加鼓励，令他很小就开始学习知识、学问和文化。他形容自己是一个"书呆子"，"相当死板"和"多愁善感"。从很小开始，卡尔就迷上了哲学问题，他对这些问题的探寻也得到了鼓励。他写道，在 8 岁时，无限性就令他穷思竭虑。在 12 或 13 岁时，他开始探究"达尔文留下的关于生命起源的问题，以及生命是否仅仅是一个化学过程等问题"[①]。他声称在 15 岁时，偶然发现了一个后来预示他最重要、成熟的哲学体系的观点："本质主义的问题"（problem of essentialism）。

波普尔形容他的学校生活"无聊透顶"。尽管他的老师尽了最大的努力，他还是发现那些课程只不过是"好几个小时的酷刑"和"浪费时间"。出生于重视批判、思考传统智慧的家庭和社会环境，波普尔讨厌教师"填鸭式"的教学方式。他寻求一种更具反思性和互动性的学习方式，这样的方式允许学生培养出批评和鉴别的能力，而不是不加批判地接受老师教导的一切。在第一次世界大战期间和之后的几年，这个观点得到了强化，因为他开始对自己当时所持的许多观点提出了质疑。

战争爆发时他 12 岁。他清楚地记得那一天。家里的一位朋友亚瑟·阿恩特（Athur Arndt）是个社会主义者，经常带他去参加一元论者协会的会议。这是一个进步社会主义者的协会，致力于"哲学、教育和法律的科学化改革"。卡尔在这里了解到了进步派的事业，参与讨论政治改革。[②] 波普尔与那些一元论者们在一次远足时，第一次听到了弗朗兹·费迪南德大公被暗

---

① Popper,1974/2002:12.
② Hacohen,2000:42.

杀的消息。一周后,在他的生日那天,战争爆发。这场战争对奥匈帝国和波普尔都具有深厚的、不可逆转的影响。战前的社会、政治和经济分歧(存在于贫富、犹太人少数派和基督徒多数派、自由派和进步派之间)进一步恶化,并成为政治问题。其结果是,维也纳社会变得更加四分五裂,反动加剧。战争开始变得白热化,移民(其中许多是犹太人)涌入奥地利。反犹太主义兴起,犹太难民被大众视为寄生虫。严重的粮食和燃料短缺加剧了社会的紧张局势,最终导致了罢工和示威。社会和经济混乱,加上前线的巨大失利,共同造成了局面的动荡。到 1918 年 10 月签署停战协议(标志着哈布斯堡王朝的结束),维也纳社会已经发生了根本性的变化。

当时的年轻人变得越来越政治化,卡尔·波普尔也不例外。几乎就在波普尔反抗奥地利学校制度所代表的权威的同时,他也对那些主导当时政治话语的思想发起了反抗。1918 年,波普尔离开了学校(违背了父母的意愿),在维也纳大学成为一名不在册的学生。他也开始参与学生和青年政治活动,衷心支持以共产主义为手段来终结冲突、贫穷和普遍的社会动荡。然而,他对共产主义的这种同情注定将是短暂的,在 1919 年一次由像他一样的共产主义者组织的学生示威中熄灭了。在这次示威中,一些学生被警察枪杀。在《无尽的探索》(*Unended Quest*)中,他写到他"被警察的暴行震惊,也被我自己震惊。因为我觉得,作为一个马克思主义者,我也负有部分责任——至少在道义上。马克思主义理论要求深化阶级斗争以加速社会主义的来临。其论点是,尽管革命可能会牺牲一些人,但是与整个社会主义革命相比,资本主义会牺牲更多的受害者"①。枪杀事件发生在波普尔 17 岁生日前几天,他声称到 17 岁时他就成了反马克思主义者。"我意识到了其信念的教条化和它惊人的知识分子式的傲慢。"他写道,"妄称自己具有某种知识,称这种知识使自己为了一个不加辨别而接受的教条,或者一个在当时的条件下可能最终不可实现的梦想,而有义务以牺牲他人生命为代价,这是一件可怕的事情。这对于一个勤读多思的知识分子来说尤其是一种压抑,因为陷入这样一个陷阱令人非常沮丧。"②波普尔开始"厌恶"他的"一些马克思主义者朋友和同学的知识分子式的自以为是,他们几乎想当然地认为他们就是工人阶级的未来领袖"。他说,他们"没有特殊的知识才能,他们所能声称的理论只是基于对马克思主义著作的某种熟悉——尽管甚至算不上是完整的认识,当然也不是批评性的认识"③。

在这些话语中我们或许可以窥见他未来思想的影子。在《无尽的探索》中,波普尔赞扬了维也纳的工人和他们的政治运动,同时否定了"他们的社会民主领袖的极端错误的历史主义观点"④。他们的领袖能够在他们心中激发出一种感觉,即他们要履行的使命的重要性不啻要把人类从贫穷、饥饿和压迫中解放出来。这个运动以工人受教育为前提——提供个体"解放自己,从而解放全人类"所必需的知识资源。⑤ 将教育建立起来,使之成为全民都可以获得的东西(无论贫富),这一直是波普尔所持

---

① Popper,1974/2002:33.

② Popper,1974/2002:34.

③ Popper,1974/2002:35.

④ Popper,1974/2002:35.

⑤ Hacohen,2000:36.

卡尔·波普尔

有的进步目标。他在《开放社会及其敌人》中主张国家提供全民教育。因此,自由和平等可以由国家制度来保证,使人民有能力将自己的生活(和政治命运)掌握在自己手中,这个观点继续存在于他后来的著作中,并形成了他对极权主义和法西斯主义,以及他认为它们凭以建立的历史主义学说的批判中的一个重要主题。通过知识解放自我,通过人类能动性——对贫穷、不公正和压迫的憎恨——进行社会改革,波普尔认为,在他反对马克思主义的同时,仍然保有以上这些观点。

教 育 学 院

这之后波普尔开始寻求自己解决社会问题的办法,同时也寻求一个具有实用性、专业性的职业,一个对他的知识分子朋友来说似乎有些异类的职业。1922 年,波普尔 20 岁,他通过了会考(即毕业考试),这使他成为维也纳大学的正式在册的学生。两年后,他又通过了一所师范学院的第二次会考。与此同时,他也正在给一个木匠当学徒,学习成为木工。当时的教职岗位很少,木工活也不适合他,于是他转行做了一段时间的社工,照顾被疏于照料的儿童。波普尔的生活飘忽不定。战争和革命带来的社会、政治和经济动荡摧毁了过去的安定性,在这种环境下,稳定的生活方式遭到破坏。这种新出现的不确定感反映在当时的知识界和艺术界的运动中。随着社会和政治冲突而来的是既定传统的解体,维也纳成为产生了恩斯特·马赫（Ernst Mach）①及自我起伏无常的理论、弗洛伊德（Freud）及潜意识的力量、勋伯格（Schoenberg）及传统声调系统被十二音制所替代的城市。在这里，仅仅在一段时期内，就出现了阿瑟·施尼茨勒（Arthur Schnitzler）②关于内心独白和性欲作为人际关系原动力的文学作品，出现了阿道夫·卢斯（Adolf Loos）③及在建筑中去除以装饰之名而装饰，……以及卡尔·克劳斯（Karl Kraus）④和他对掩盖了政治和文化现实的语言形式——陈词滥调、隐喻——的攻击。⑤

不确定的社会新秩序给波普尔带来了一种不断发展的政治意识，他认识到需要如何按照更具人性化、更公正的路线来重建社会，但是这对于他的生活之路该何去何从却没有什么可贵的指引。与此同时，他对政治和哲学的兴趣也在持续并加深。影响他的有受人尊敬的社会理论家卡尔·波兰尼（Karl Polanyi），他主张非马克思主义的社会主义形式；激进的康德学派哲学家、世界主义者伦纳德·纳尔逊（Leonard Nelson），他主张建立一个国际法律体系，支持采用"苏格拉底式的方法"来教育年轻人。

---

① 1838—1916，奥地利-捷克实验物理科学家和哲学家。马赫的物理科学研究课题主要包括光的传播规律和超音速现象。他大力强调了经验主义和实证主义在科学研究中的重要性，为科学哲学的发展奠定了基础。后来出现的逻辑实证主义借鉴并发展了马赫的科学哲学。译者注。

② 1862—1931，奥地利剧作家、小说家。维也纳现代派的核心人物。第一个把意识流手法引入德语文学中的奥地利作家，以表现心灵、下意识和内心情感为宗旨的心理艺术风格使他成为德语现代派文学最杰出的代表之一。译者注。

③ 1870—1933，奥地利建筑师与建筑理论家，现代主义建筑的先驱者。他提出著名的"装饰即罪恶"的口号，主张建筑以实用与舒适为主，认为建筑"不是依靠装饰而是以形体自身之美为美"。译者注。

④ 1874—1936，20世纪早期最著名的奥地利作家之一。他是记者、讽刺作家、诗人、剧作家、格言作家、语言与文化评论家。译者注。

⑤ Edmonds & Eidenow，2002：76.

波兰尼和纳尔逊都对波普尔产生了深远的影响。波兰尼指出，对社会公正的承诺与资产阶级经济学并不矛盾（因此社会主义不一定要是革命的，也不一定要以劳动力的社会化为目标）；纳尔逊关于康德的著作以及他关于"批判哲学"的观点，认为苏格拉底和康德是理性哲学探究的典范（被黑格尔、费希特、谢林等人背叛），这为波普尔的知识和政治哲学的发展提供了关键要素，并为自由和平等主义（egalitarianism）之间的关系提供了新见解。

1925 年，维也纳市建立了教育学院——一个与维也纳大学相联系的自治机构，旨在鼓励中小学系统的改革。波普尔是该学院聘入的几位社会工作者之一。在那里的几年，他描述为致力于学习、阅读、教学和不以出版为目的的写作。他讲授心理学课程，并因此遇到了维也纳大学的心理学教授卡尔·布勒（Karl Buhler）。第二年，他遇到了维也纳大学的哲学教授海因里希·冈珀茨（Heinrich Gomperz），冈珀茨关于认识论的著作将对他产生极大的影响；还有朱利叶斯·克拉夫特（Julius Kraft），他与波普尔同样对社会主义抱有非马克思主义的认识，经常和他一起讨论马克思思想的问题。在学院里波普尔也遇见了约瑟芬·亨尼格（Josephine Henniger），后来成了他的妻子。

正是在教育学院，波普尔开始对心理学和认识论产生了兴趣。通过与布勒、冈珀茨和克拉夫特的讨论，波普尔产生了他早期对当时维也纳儿童受教育方式的普遍担忧。他对这些问题越来越感兴趣：个人该如何获取关于世界的知识？这种知识是什么样的形式？要获得这种知识会受到哪些限制？他 1927 年的论文《习惯和法律经验》（*Habit and the Experience of Lawfulness*）——是为完成学院的两年工作而提交的——探索了逻辑与心理学之间的关系，主要侧重于探索儿童获取知识的方式。他认为，儿童天生因循守旧，因为他们喜欢秩序，讨厌无序。因此，他认为儿童会尽可能地通过了解世界的规律而对世界施加秩序。这个观点——即人类试图通过推断（自然、历史、传统、民族的）总体规律从而对他们的生活及他们所处的世界施以规则——后来在波普尔成熟的政治哲学中占有举足轻重的地位。波普尔把这篇论文看作是"对科学教育法的局限性的一种康德式批判"，通过这篇论文，他批评了当时在教育改革中占主导地位的诸多趋势（而该学院的成立，正是出于对这些趋势的鼓励）。结果他发表了另一篇文章，质疑儿童可以被教育成能进行批判性思考的人，并试图通过使用科学探究的标准归纳法（而非心理学）为儿童获取知识的过程提供一个一般性的描述。在一年后提交的博士论文中，波普尔对这些论题进行了扩展。这篇题为《关于认知心理学的方法论问题》(*On the Methodological Problem of Cognitive Psychology*)的论文力图通过为认识论和心理学之间的"划界"提供某种标准，从而解决"心理学、逻辑学和认识论之间的界限问题"[①]。波普尔声称对自己的论文并不满意，并在自传中称它是"一件临时抱佛脚的作品"[②]。尽管如此，他的论文考官（卡尔·布勒和莫里茨·石里克）以优异的评分通过了他的论文。无论波普尔是否满意，这篇论文标志着波普尔与心理学决裂，转向了逻辑学与科学。波普尔获得博士学位，代表着他与心理主义(psychologism，即认为所有知识都可以按照主观思维过程得到理解的观点)的对抗，发展了布勒的

① Hacohen, 2000:63.
② Popper, 1974/2002:87.

主张,即"我们不是在想象中思考,而是思考问题及其尝试性的解决方案"。① 这个主张——即人类在根本上是问题解决者——在波普尔后来的作品,包括《历史决定论的贫困》和《开放社会及其敌人》中再次出现。波普尔转向科学的过程大约在一年后完成,1929 年他 26 岁时,波普尔获得教师资格,可以讲授中学水平的数学和物理科学。他的论文(毕业论文)内容是关于几何的历史和基础,包含了他关于科学理性和进步的一些最早期的思想。

维特根斯坦和维也纳学派

尽管并非学术界的一员,波普尔却继续出入于欧洲一些最有才华的学者圈子,特别是在认识论、科学和数学领域。两次大战之间的维也纳是一片知识分子的乐土,活跃着来自学术圈内外的众多不同学科的学者,他们生气勃勃、热情洋溢。早在第一次世界大战爆发之前,维也纳就以环城大道沿线上的咖啡馆和聚会点里随处可见的文学、学术和文化生活而久负盛名。知识分子和激进分子们在这里会面、辩论,"一杯咖啡、一杯水、一块果馅卷的工夫,就写好了一篇文章,重整了一场论证,评论了一部戏剧,完成了一番引荐"②。对于这么一幅知识火花迸发的场景,波普尔的态度虽然称不上是嗤之以鼻,至少也是将信将疑的。他视其为有钱人的自我放纵,被知识界昙花一现的时尚潮

---

① Popper,1974/2002:86.

② Edmonds & Eidenow,2002:58.

流所左右。波普尔曾说，维特根斯坦的《逻辑哲学论》（*Tractatus*）(他厌恶这本书)"就散发着咖啡馆的气味"。

波普尔或许不是维也纳咖啡馆的常客，但他受到了许多其他学术聚会的深刻影响，特别是在他准备博士论文期间和之后的一段时间。例如，海因里希·冈珀茨组织了一个关于观念史的非正式讨论小组，来自不同学科的学者聚在一起讨论历史和哲学问题。通过冈珀茨，波普尔受邀参加这些会议。事实上，或许正是他在一次会议中的表现，令他未能成为地位更重要、影响更深远的维也纳学派的成员，该学派的召集人正是他的博士学位考官莫里茨·石里克。石里克也偶尔参加冈珀茨的讨论小组聚会，他对波普尔素来不怎么赞赏(他以优异的评分通过了波普尔的博士论文，显然更多是出于他对布勒的敬重，而与波普尔的论文无关)。波普尔在会议中激烈攻击路德维希·维特根斯坦——石里克的偶像，也是维也纳学派的理论之父。会议尚未结束，石里克就一脸厌恶地离开了，并谴责波普尔的批评是小丑作秀。无论这一事件是否起决定作用，总之波普尔从不曾获邀加入维也纳学派。

被排除在维也纳学派之外似乎令波普尔沾沾自喜，他始终为自己未被接受为其成员而感到得意。学派的一位成员奥图·纽拉特(Otto Neurath)曾形容波普尔是学派的"反对党"，这个角色波普尔倒是很喜欢。波普尔学术生涯的大部分时间都用来攻击维也纳学派的哲学基础，发动论战反对学派中多位极具影响力的成员。这些成员确实影响力十分强大。石里克创办的维也纳学派，是两次世界大战之间欧洲最重要的学术团体之一，汇聚了哲学、逻辑学、数学、社会科学、自然和物理科学等领域最重要的思想家。正式成员中有赫赫有名的鲁道夫·卡尔纳普

（Rudolph Carnap）、奥图·纽拉特、汉斯·汉恩（Hans Hahn）、库尔特·哥德尔（Kurt Godel）、弗里德里希·韦斯曼（Friedrich Waissman）和赫伯特·费格尔（Herbert Feigl）。时常列会的国际人士有美国的威拉德·冯·奥曼·蒯因（V. W. O. Quine）、英国的阿尔弗雷德·艾耶尔（A. J. Ayer）、波兰的阿尔弗雷德·塔斯基（Alfred Tarski）、柏林的卡尔·亨佩尔（Carl Hempel）。学派的会议名单就是一份不折不扣的哲学和科学界的英才名人录。学派之所以存在，这个杂糅了各领域思想家的团体之所以能被凝聚一堂，就是因为他们拥有一个共同理念，即物理科学的研究方法应该被运用于哲学研究。他们的立场明显是针对德国观念论——其思想主要体现在黑格尔、费希特、谢林和康德的著作中。德国观念论主张，世界的某些方面不能通过观察而了解，因此，科学方法不能产生关于世界的正确的或完整的认识。由此，德国观念论学者认为，哲学和科学是两门不同的研究学科，世界上存在着科学无法回答的根本性问题（如形而上学、本体论、伦理学和神学问题），而哲学是唯一适合解决这些问题的学科。然而，维也纳学派的成员认为，哲学应该向科学学习，哲学作为可以有意义地追寻、获取关于世界的知识的手段，应永远从属于科学。因此，他们的主要目标是从"形而上学"（即不能被科学地了解的学科）中区分界定"物理科学"（即可以被科学地了解的学科）。界定的标准则来自维特根斯坦的《逻辑哲学论》（1921），该书就成了维也纳学派的"圣经"。

在《逻辑哲学论》中，维特根斯坦探讨了语言与现实之间的关系。他论述道，这二者的关系是一种描述性的关系：世界是我们周围存在的所有事实的总和，我们使用语言来描述这个世界。因此，可以有两种方式来确定一个陈述是否具有意义：它或者必须是能通过观察而得到验证的(即它有意义地描述了世界上可以被观察到或体验到的某样东西),或者是"分析性的",即它的意义完全来自所使用的特定词语间的逻辑关系。如果既不能令人理解地描述世界上的某个事实,也不能从其本身的内部结构得出其意义的逻辑性陈述,那么这样的陈述或话语就是无意义的。例如,"长方形有四条边"这个陈述是分析性的(因而也是有意义的),是因为它的含义来自按此顺序排列的特定词语,而不是因为它一定要告诉我们关于世界的某个正确的事实。这是一个同义反复,它的意义源自陈述本身的逻辑。同样,"鞋盒是长方形的",这个陈述之所以有意义,是因为它可以通过观察和体验得到验证。然而,如"上帝创造了那个鞋盒"这样的陈述就不具有分析性或可验证性,因而是无意义的。

由此看来,哲学对于维特根斯坦(及维也纳学派)而言,不是寻求真理,而是寻求意义:寻求关于世界的陈述,要么凭自身的逻辑而具有意义,要么通过验证而获得意义。因此,形而上学的陈述,如"思想和身体截然不同"或"上帝是宇宙的根本推动者",就被认为是无意义的。它们并不是"不正确的"或"错误的",而只是超出了哲学的解决范围。科学确定什么是正确的,而哲学应该关心如何确定词语以及它们所构成的话语的意义。这种方法被称作"逻辑实证主义",它体现了了解哲学的目的和局限的一种激进的方法。因为如果界定一句陈述有意义与否的首要标准是它是否可以通过观察真实世界而得到验证,或者它自身的内在逻辑是否能赋予其意义,那么,被弃于垃圾桶里的就不仅仅是形而上学的陈述了,还包括所有的美学、伦理学、政治学和神学的陈述,因为它们都无法通过验证的测试。"贝多芬作为作曲家比莫扎特优秀""全人类都应该道德高尚""上帝赋予人类权利"，这样的主张都是无意义的，因为它们都不是分析性的（在维特根斯坦看来），也不是在经验上可以验证的。因此，维也纳学派认为，维特根斯坦的语言哲学已经揭示了哲学真正的内容和目的，并提供了凭以确定问题或陈述是否重要、合理，是否无意义、多余的标准。

波普尔同意逻辑实证主义者的总体主张，即科学和哲学可以相辅相成。毕竟他和逻辑实证主义者一样，也致力于理性、推理和知识探究。他认为，区分真正的知识和主观的看法十分重要。举例来说，他支持卡尔纳普对"理性，（以及）更强的知识责任感"的呼吁。他说，卡尔纳普"要求我们学习数学家和科学家的研究方法，他将其与哲学家令人沮丧的研究方法进行对比：哲学家自恃才高，独霸知识，他们将知识展现给我们时仅提供极少的一点理性的或批评性的论证"。[①] 我们可以再次感觉到波普尔对咖啡馆里的哲学家的鄙夷，他们中许多人都觉得他们可以对现实的本质加以断言，而不必费神为自己的主张提供证据。逻辑实证主义者的态度是"启蒙主义的态度"，而波普尔则声称自己与维也纳学派的主张高度一致，即认为哲学家（与其他人一样）应该将自己的观点限定在推理和理性论证所能建立的范围之内，人们对不能经受住理性批判的关于哲学真理的妄自断言应该予以质疑。

但波普尔并非一个逻辑实证主义者，也不像许多人认为的那样是维也纳学派的成员。事实上，他热衷于和维也纳学派脱离干系。波普尔反对逻辑实证主义者的信条，因为他们的目的是揭露形而上学、美学、伦理学和其他哲学分支是无意义的、多

---

① Popper,1974/2002:100.

余的。他们试图从形而上学中划分出物理科学,旨在把形而上学置于无用之境地。但是波普尔对这种观点表示强烈的批评,主要是因为他觉得许多在历史上最具创新性的科学发现最初都是以形而上学的陈述出现的。他论述道,"如果……在时而模糊的理论观点中没有'形而上学的'信念,科学研究很可能是无法实现的。"[①]他还论述道,"所有的观察结果都需要根据我们的理论知识来进行解释……纯粹的观察性的知识如果不掺杂理论的话,即便可能获取,也是完全空洞无用的"[②]。他认为,形而上学并非无用,相反,它是许多将继续发展成为科学主张的言论的基础。他认为,科学知识比形而上学知识更高级,科学家们可以"通过可检验性对其进行区分,逐个排除理论中剩余的形而上学成分"[③]。因此,形而上学并不是无意义的,而是科学发现的一个重要方面。波普尔因而认为,逻辑实证主义者试图把形而上学弃入垃圾桶,却"没有意识到自己把科学理论也丢弃在了'无意义的'形而上学理论的同一个垃圾桶里"[④]。因此,我们的任务不是从形而上学中划分出物理科学,而是从"伪科学"中划分出"科学";也就是说,要弄清楚哪些知识领域属于科学的范畴,哪些不属于科学的范畴。

所以对波普尔来说,维也纳学派的逻辑实证主义存在的问题在于他们为了错误的目的而试图去划分错误的东西。不仅如此,他还认为他们使用了错误的划分标准。这个学派被维特根斯坦搞糊涂了,他们在集会时逐字逐句地阅读(不止一次)《逻辑

---

① Popper,1935/2007a:38.

② Popper,1963/2007b:30.

③ Hacohen,2000:247.

④ Popper,1963/2007b:349.

哲学论》，长达一年时间；他们仔细研究每一处细节、每一丝差别；莫里茨·石里克与学派的其他几名成员一起，与维特根斯坦建立起个人联系，组成了一个非正式的讨论小组，从这位伟人的智慧中获益。波普尔厌恶维特根斯坦，认为他的整个哲学体系都是错误的，更糟的是，他的哲学与哲学的本意完全相悖。维特根斯坦成了波普尔的死敌。维氏的主要主张不存在哲学上的"问题"，而只有从语言运用中产生的哲学"谜题"；哲学是对意义的追寻，而不是对真理的追寻。这种主张全面体现了波普尔所憎恨的哲学家的自我放纵。对于一个在被反犹主义、贫穷和冲突四分五裂的城市中长大的人，对于一个经历了第一次世界大战并直接目睹了哈布斯堡帝国的倾覆、粮食和燃料短缺以及革命的人，所谓没有哲学"问题"、只有哲学"谜题"的说法，实在是太过明显地散发着咖啡馆的宠溺世界、上流富裕阶层以及有钱有闲之人不负责任的高谈阔论的气味。波普尔认为真正的哲学问题是存在的，哲学家的任务就是寻求解决这些问题的方法。他认为哲学是寻求真理，而非意义的。这个观点——即哲学家们应该关心如何解决世界上存在的具体问题——表达出了波普尔哲学的方方面面，从他认为重要的问题到他寻求解决问题的方式。关键不在于区分什么有意义、什么无意义，而在于区分究竟是什么提供了知识的基础。

早在他的博士论文和 1929 年关于几何学的论文中，波普尔就开始了这项工作。然而直到 1934 年，随着《研究的逻辑》（后被译为英文版《科学与发现的逻辑》，*The Logic of Scientific Discovery*）出版，波普尔才广泛地概述了他的另一种划分理论，并批判了逻辑实证主义得以建立的根基。波普尔提出将科学重新解释为一个演绎过程，而不是归纳过程。他声称，逻辑实证主义者的问题并不是他们试图将物理科学的方法应用于哲学,而是在于他们对于科学是什么以及该如何理解有着错误的认识。波普尔认为,许多科学家也犯了这个错误,他们基本上都坚持牛顿的观点,即我们有可能从特定的实验或测试中推断出普遍的自然规律。波普尔批评了这种观点,批评了它建立的基础——归纳法,并将其完全颠覆。他将休谟的怀疑论应用于归纳法本身,将科学定义为一个演绎过程。以他认为科学发现往往从形而上学的主张开始这个观点为基础,波普尔论述道,发现的归纳过程(科学家从事实到普遍理论)应该被颠倒过来:科学发现始于被事实或其他理论证实或证伪的理论陈述。从这个观点来看,任何特定理论(无论如何令人信服)的正确与否总是推测性的、假设性的,从来不是无可辩驳或坚实固定的。科学理论是关于世界的某个方面的主张,因此,它要求他人来检验和证伪其核心论点。如果它经得住这些检验和证伪,那么它对其正确性的主张就仍然是有效的(但依然是假设性的,因为它可能在将来被证伪)。如果它不能经受住检验和证伪,那么它就会被摒弃。因此,科学发现就是一个通过试错法来建立理论、证伪理论的过程。其结果是研究科学哲学的一种全新的方法,对于追寻科学领域以外的知识也具有启发意义,并有可能使哲学家和社会科学家(以及科学家)能够采用同样的方法来解决根本问题。其要点并不是确定什么是科学的,什么不是科学的,目的在于抛弃后者;而是提供一个认识论的总体理论,利用这个理论可以确定什么应该属于科学领域,什么不属于科学领域。因此,波普尔的方法将非科学形式的哲学重新认可为有效的追求。它也为解决维也纳学派所面临的许多问题提供了一种"实证的而非归纳的,可检验可证实的而非必然的,按可证伪性从形而上学中划分出来却不认为形而上学是无意义的演绎科学。该种科学为认识论、方法论和'非科学的'哲学留下了空间。"①

"战斗书"

在自传中,波普尔宣称逻辑实证主义已经被他亲手扼杀了。他说,逻辑实证主义在"不可克服的内部难题"的压力下崩溃了。"这些难题大多在我的《研究的逻辑》中已经被指明。维也纳学派的有些成员感受到他们迫切需要改变,于是就这样播下了种子。经过许多年时间,这些种子的成长渐渐导致了学派的理论分崩离析。"②但是,波普尔也指出,维也纳学派甚至在其宗旨崩塌之前就已经逐渐开始瓦解了。两次大战之间的维也纳对知识分子,特别是那些对左派抱有同情或本身就是犹太人的知识分子,变得越来越不友好。1929年开始的经济衰退将本已极度紧张的社会进一步分化,迎来了一个右翼极端主义的新时代。工业生产的急剧缩减、工会运动的衰微,同时1929年到1932年间的失业率翻番,令许多人陷入了经济困境,给联合政府带来了新的政治挑战。战后的通货膨胀达到前所未有的水平,将人民的长期储蓄一扫而空,使许多家庭陷入贫困(波普尔的父亲就是这样失去了所有积蓄)。反犹太主义已经成为维也纳社会的一股显著的力量——并变得更加邪恶和广泛。所有奥地利政党都在宣传中使用反犹太主义的形象,一旦出现经济动荡,犹太人就在

---

① Hochen,2000:199.

② Popper,1974/2002:99.

公众的恶意行动中首当其冲。如哈科恩所说,"在资产阶级的想象中,犹太人同时代表了资本主义、社会主义和共和政体"①。

20 世纪 30 年代初,民族社会党崛起,因为"德国中产阶级白领、公务员、德国知识分子、非犹太裔专业人员和小资产阶级",全都成了纳粹事业的支持者。② 1933 年 1 月 30 日,德国民族社会党在柏林上台,不到三个月,奥地利联合政府(反对纳粹)的领导人就废除了议会民主制,宣布总统制。这一举措伴随着一系列镇压措施,包括新闻审查、规定罢工非法、禁止公共集会和示威。社会党没有回击,这显然表示此时已经到了千钧一发的时刻。1934 年,恩格尔伯特·多尔福斯(Englebert Dollfuss,总理兼联合政府首脑)创立了一党制国家,同年 7 月 25 日他被纳粹暗杀。

政治和经济上的紧张局势已经是一触即发,被德国占领的威胁迫在眉睫,维也纳学派的哲学家、科学家和数学家们加入了医生、银行家、艺术家、制片人及其他人的行列,纷纷逃离奥地利。卡尔纳普移居布拉格,然后到普林斯顿投奔了哥德尔;门格尔搬到印第安纳州圣母大学;亨佩尔取道布鲁塞尔和芝加哥去往纽约;费格尔穿过爱荷华州去到明尼苏达州;弗里德里希·瓦斯曼移居剑桥,后至牛津。学派中在政治上最活跃的纽拉特,离开维也纳前往荷兰,之后在英国度过了余生。

波普尔于 1937 年离开维也纳前往新西兰,在坎特伯雷大学学院获得了第一份全职讲师职位。随后他在英国进行了一次长时间的巡回讲学,在讲学期间遇到了许多英国学术界的领军人

① Hacohen,2000:294.
② Hacohen,2000:296—297.

22

物,包括阿尔弗雷德·艾耶尔、以赛亚·柏林(Isaiah Berlin)、吉尔伯特·赖尔(Gilbert Ryle)、伯特兰·罗素(Bertrand Russell)、理查德·布莱斯维特(R. B. Braithwaite)和乔治·爱德华·摩尔(G. E. Moore),并在许多大学就《研究的逻辑》中的论题发表了讲话。他最关键的一次会面——尽管在当时他可能并没有意识到——是与奥地利流亡经济学家、伦敦经济学院教授弗里德里希·冯·哈耶克(Friedrich von Hayek)的会面。哈耶克邀请波普尔在伦敦经济学院由他组织的一次研讨会上发言。正是在这次会议上,波普尔决定进一步发展他一直没有太认真考虑的一些关于社会科学方法论的想法。这篇题为《历史决定论的贫困》的论文,后来成了同名书,在其中可以看到波普尔将许多在《研究的逻辑》中提出的关于科学和认识论的论证,应用到了社会和政治研究中。哈耶克读过《研究的逻辑》,对其印象深刻。波普尔对社会、经济和政治规划的反对令哈耶克感到意气相投,哈耶克独创的自由放任的自由市场经济正是源于他对认识论的不确定性的担忧。哈耶克和波普尔忧虑的是相似的事情:乌托邦政治意识形态对个人自由产生的威胁;人类知识的不确定性;推理的易谬性;对他人利益的了解不可能比他本人更全面或更理性;而也许最重要的是,我们需要确保国家不逾越其界限,不声称存在一个适合所有人的目标。哈耶克和波普尔给彼此都留下了深刻的印象,哈耶克对波普尔的好感一直持续到战后,使他协助波普尔到伦敦经济学院任职。

波普尔在英国旅居后回到维也纳,准备前往新西兰,到这个时候,他几乎已经准备好了为政治哲学作出重大贡献。各方面几乎都各就其位。出生在一个知识分子的城市里,被进步的社会主义者所包围,经历了曾经被他视为理所当然的一切,在战争、革命和内讧的破坏性力量下崩塌瓦解之后,波普尔走向开放社会的过程是缓慢却不可阻挡的。奥地利马克思主义者的傲慢自大令波普尔怒不可遏,他们没有意识到两次大战之间的经济冲突并没有带来社会主义革命,而是导致了法西斯主义,以及一个充满仇恨和分裂的反动政治。波普尔认为,奥地利社会主义者自我蒙蔽,他们没能根据 20 世纪 30 年代所发生的各种事件而改变策略,而是一直被自己的意识形态和马克思关于资本主义将会终结并被共产主义所取代的预言所麻痹。他们没有面对现实,而是不顾后果地继续下去,将所有事件和进展都解释为通向共产主义之路的必经阶段。然而,他们的希望是徒劳的。波普尔认为,他们的失败不仅是奥地利社会主义的失败,也是当时更广泛意义上的社会主义的失败。波普尔落足新西兰时,他与维也纳的分离还只是地理上的,他的心里还挂念着留在身后的政治和社会环境。1938 年 3 月,纳粹占领奥地利,波普尔听说许多家人和朋友落入了新政权的魔爪。许多人遭到逮捕、审讯,然后音信全无,被带到集中营或监狱。他母亲于 1938 年 5 月去世,妹妹 6 月逃到巴黎,身无分文且没有护照。"其他亲戚朋友也仓皇离开该国,到了英国、法国,还有别的地方,甚至新西兰"。① 据哈科恩说,波普尔和友人奥托·弗兰卡尔(Otto Frankael)尽其所能为奥地利人赴新西兰办理移民许可证,但受到了诸多阻碍。

面对如此巨大的恐怖和动荡,波普尔的思想从自然科学转向了政治学。维特根斯坦认为,哲学对于政治或社会问题无话可说,而波普尔却不这样想。他认为,他所理解的哲学可以为反

---

① Hacohen,2000:345.

对暴政、反对法西斯主义浪潮的斗争贡献自己的力量。随着第二次世界大战爆发,波普尔将《历史决定论的贫困》的草稿置于一旁,开始着手撰写另一本书,其中将用到《历史决定论的贫困》一书的许多主要论题。这些书一起代表着波普尔的"反战努力",特别是《开放社会及其敌人》,他称其为"战斗书"。

由于当代政治哲学家们对《开放社会及其敌人》的忽视,我们很容易低估这本书在出版之时的激进程度和重要性。波普尔的目标正是追溯当时占领了世界政治并制造了人类历史上极恶的极权主义意识形态的起源。他的结论是,这些源头可以追溯到西方文明史上最著名、最可敬的一些人物。如在《开放社会及其敌人》成书之前,古希腊在很大程度上被古典学者和历史学家视为开明的民主和文化所在地,其最引人注目、最为雄辩的代言人柏拉图,则被视作理性和人性的化身。黑格尔——他的哲学被认为是极有争议、晦涩难懂的——仍然被认为是非常重要的哲学家。波普尔认为他们全都为存在于法西斯主义和纳粹主义核心的残暴和邪恶铺平了道路,如柏拉图被描绘成一个种族主义者,一个憎恨自由、自我膨胀、背叛了苏格拉底的人;黑格尔是一个小丑、一个愚人,给他那荒谬而可恶的思想披上了一件复杂多变、令人迷惑、刀枪不入的斗篷,为了金钱而迎合当时的政治领袖;马克思的学说鼓动一代人相信他们是不自由的,并且在势不可挡的历史力量面前是无能为力的。这本书的主题思想清楚明了:在这些伟大人物以及与他们观点相同的人的著述中,我们找到了为暴政、杀戮、种族政治、部落制、罪恶的辩护——我们找到了那个封闭社会。在他的回应中,我们可以窥见可追溯到他在维也纳的童年时代的那些想法,我们可以看到波普尔因为排他性和"封闭性"而反对民族主义是受到了进步派的影响,他相

学术生涯

25

信个人有能力改变他们身处的社会,国家的目标应该是通过实施人道的社会政策来减轻贫困,科学和社会技术可以被视为理解社会问题并对其做出回应的手段。我们可以看到他认识个人能力的立场,认为个人有能力对他们的生活以及他们所生活的世界进行富有成效的理性分析,国家(和教师)承认并鼓励这种能力是十分重要的。最明显的是,我们可以看到在《研究的逻辑》和无数其他文章及演讲中表达出的他关于知识——个人了解他们所生活的世界的过程,关于这个过程的局限性——这些局限性为国家能够做什么设定了必要的限制——以及国家可以如何为其行动提供正当理由的思想。

《开放社会及其敌人》立刻给波普尔带来了关注,有褒有贬。许多人嘲笑他的学术水平,指责他讽刺和歪曲马克思、柏拉图和黑格尔等著名哲学先贤的观点。尽管他支持国家为了缓解贫困、提供全民可享的公共服务和教育(无论收入如何)而干预经济市场,尽管他反对社会、经济或政治特权,他公开支持所有人可以参与的民主审议形式,尽管他坚信可通过对基本政治设想进行辩论和批判来进行社会变革,许多人仍然谴责他是一位当权派,是资本主义的辩护人。然而,哈罗德·拉斯基(Harold Laski)等国家社会主义者支持波普尔的结论,还有许多别的社会主义学者和活动家,包括伯特兰·罗素(他对波普尔和维也纳学派而言都是理论导师),他宣称波普尔对柏拉图哲学的攻击"精彩绝伦"。波普尔的目的是"弥合分裂各个左翼阵营中理性与自由的人的虚幻的、形而上学的鸿沟",把这些迥然不同的群体凝聚在一起,共同进行反对极权主义的事业。[①] 但是他的书在右翼阵营中也流行起来。其中最重要的一个拥护者是波普尔的朋友哈耶克,他深受触动,凭借这本书为波普尔在伦敦经济学院谋取了一份教职。波普尔捍卫零星的社会工程,以其取代乌托邦式的社会规划,他批判政治学和社会科学中的历史主义,这与哈耶克对认识论确定性的普遍怀疑以及他关于社会和政治制度的自发性的观点都不谋而合。波普尔关于经济干预主义和社会规划的论辩不如哈耶克那么犀利,但哈耶克还是对波普尔将科学理论应用于社会和经济问题的观点印象深刻,认为他是教授逻辑和科学方法教师的完美人选。哈耶克的努力见了成效,在欧洲的战争结束之后,波普尔于 1946 年 1 月 5 日抵达英国,开始在伦敦经济学院任职。1949 年,他被任命为逻辑和科学方法教授,任职长达 23 年。

后 期 生 活

波普尔在伦敦经济学院的最初几年"令人振奋。他如一颗冉冉升起的新星,《开放社会及其敌人》一夜之间将他抛入了公众的视野。在伦敦经济学院,他吸引了大量的听众,与拉斯基竞争知名度"[②]。请他演讲的邀请络绎不绝。尤其是一次具传奇性的会议。1946 年 10 月 25 日,波普尔在剑桥大学道德科学俱乐部的一次论坛上演讲了一篇论文,参会者中有一些著名的哲

---

① 波普尔 1943 年 12 月 12 日致阿尔弗雷德·布兰安哈尔(Alfred Braunthal)的信。Hacohen,2000:449.

② Hacohen,2000:523.

学家,包括伯特兰·罗素和路德维希·维特根斯坦。波普尔应邀演讲一篇关于"某哲学谜题"的短论文。波普尔决定讲一篇主题不是那么单一的论文,题为《哲学问题存在吗?》(*Are there any philosophical problems?*),并利用这次讲话对维特根斯坦的观点——哲学是在语言学的谜题中寻找意义,而不是寻求具体问题的解决方案——提出了尖锐而持久的批评。在会议中到底发生了什么,一直是众说纷纭(波普尔个人对此事的回忆已被证明并不可靠),但从当时在场者的证言中可以推断,维特根斯坦向波普尔提出挑战,要求波普尔举例说明哲学问题怎么不是谜题。波普尔提出归纳法、无限性、道德规范的有效性以论证。维特根斯坦驳斥了这些示例,在不快中,他摆弄起了他从房间里的壁炉边拿来的拨火棍(这显然是他的习惯)。当波普尔被要求给出一个道德规范的例子时,波普尔说:"不要拿拨火棍威胁访问讲师。"这时候(据波普尔及其他一些人说),维特根斯坦扔下拨火棍离开了房间。这一说法的准确性很难得到证实,但是显然,波普尔很满意有这个机会,能直面论敌并批判他的哲学观点。这可不是维特根斯坦听惯了的评论。

《开放社会及其敌人》跨越了意识形态的分水岭,将许多自由主义者和社会主义者联合起来,反对民族主义、部族主义和暴政,并支持个人自由、平等和理性。这本书成了人们所知的"冷战自由主义"——略带贬义——的一个经典文本。波普尔与战后的其他自由主义者一起,试图使工会和社会主义者相信,资本主义已经被极权主义所取代,成了人民的敌人。冷战时期,与共产主义的敌对是自由主义者、社会主义者和自由至上主义者与共产主义的敌对状态,使它们构成了反对共产主义的统一战线。波普尔对零星社会工程和民主的辩护为此提供了一个集结点。

然而,随着时间的推移,波普尔对民主的态度开始转变。世界各地的法西斯主义和非自由主义政党受到民众的大量支持,令他(和其他战后的自由主义者)担心自由与民主互不相容。战后自由主义者越来越怀疑民主是否是保障个人自由的最好方式。波普尔仍然是民主的倡导者,但他决定将它重新定义为一个空泛的、不具有实质性内容的概念。他认为民主的基础并不应该由多数人来决定,决策权或者应该移交给公民团体,或者公民团体一定要参与政治活动;实际上,波普尔认为舆论是一种"不负责任的权力形式","如果不受到强有力的自由主义传统的约束,它就是对自由的威胁"①。舆论只是一个允许和平推翻暴君的检查和制衡机制。因此波普尔似乎认为民主应服从自由主义。由此,评论家们认为波普尔正在转向政治右翼(哈科恩)。

　　这个看法也许由于波普尔后来关于自由主义宽容的声明而得到了强化,他认为自由主义的宽容规定了非自由主义的、不宽容的团体要噤声。他主张,"任何宣扬不宽容的运动都是非法的",因此可以被合理镇压。② 然而,这种镇压被认为是最后的手段,战后自由主义者普遍赞成以公开对话作为解决分歧和代表不同利益立场的途径。批评者认为,这种观点是理想主义的,而且也再次代表了保守主义的倾向,因为占优势的大多数总是会使少数群体的需求边缘化。波普尔在《开放社会及其敌人》和后来的文章中所展现的民主图景,被有些人认为太过抽象,且对多数群体掌握权力、少数群体权力不足的现象不够关注,因此少数群体无法影响政治议程,无法为自己的利益发声。而且还有

---

① 　Popper,1963/2007b:476.
② 　Popper,1945/2006a:292—294.

一个更根本的问题：波普尔的知识和发现理论，以持续的反驳、辩论和批判为前提，这使得产生政治上必要的共识与和解何以可能？卡尔·施密特（Carl Schmitt）等保守主义思想家曾经提出，面对无法解决的分歧和永无休止的民主对话，真正的决策实际上是由具强权的精英暗中作出的。波普尔为理想化的审议式民主进行的辩护，并没有针对这一指控提出有说服力的反驳，因此，他对民主的辩护被有些人认为事实上是为精英统治辩护。

1950 年，波普尔搬到了伦敦郊外白金汉郡的佩恩乡村。尽管继续研究政治问题，特别是自由主义和社会主义之间的关系，波普尔的思想却回到了科学哲学。他的生活变得深居简出，波普尔建立的政治观点也显得更为保守了。尽管要给波普尔的政治观点贴上意识形态的标签并不容易，这一点我们接下来就会看到。之前引用过的他在 1954 年的文章《舆论和自由主义原则》（*Public Opinion and Liberal Principles*），就表明了这一点，他的文章《宽容与知识分子的责任》（*Toleration and Intellectual Responsibility*）和《西方相信什么？》（*What Does the West Believe in?*）也同样如此。他在文中赞扬了自由主义民主作为有史以来产生最好政府的形式的各种优点。他对哈耶克 1960 年出版的《自由宪法》（*The Constitution of Liberty*）不吝赞美之词。这本书迫使波普尔在自己的文章中直面他对零星社会工程的辩护和对有限国家的支持的矛盾。他的回应是要对国家干预抱以更加怀疑的态度，要更强烈地坚持民主和自由的解放力量，以此作为零星社会改革的基础。

《开放社会及其敌人》出版后的几年是他获得学术成功并发生个人转变的时期。他于 1958 年被选为英国科学院院士，1965 年获封爵士。同年，维也纳市政府授予他精神科学奖，之后以研讨论会和颁奖的形式为他庆祝 80 岁诞辰。1976 年他当选皇家学会会员。然而，波普尔变得更加脱离其他哲学家了，他认为他们许多人关注的是旁枝末节。他在伦敦经济学院露面越来越少，但他的影响力依然巨大。1962 年托马斯·库恩（Thomas Kuhn）的开创性著作《科学革命的结构》（*The Structure of Scientific Revolutions*）出版后，波普尔用《框架的神话》（*The Myth of the Framework*）作出回应，文章中他对库恩的"论题之不可通约性"的论述进行了强烈的抨击，对文化和政治相对主义提出了尖锐的批评，并为政治审议和理性进行了辩护——这在后来的自由主义思想家如约翰·罗尔斯（John Rawls）、杰里米·沃尔德伦（Jeremy Waldron）和约书亚·科恩（Joshua Cohen）的著作中都得到了响应。

波普尔不仅与伦敦经济学院越来越脱离，与整个世界也是如此。他对批判理论的激烈批评，对尤尔根·哈贝马斯（Jurgen Habermas）、西奥多·阿多诺（Theodor Adorno）和麦克斯·霍克海默（Max Horkheimer）等理论家的愤怒谴责，似乎进一步促使他向右派的转变，并使他远离了许多在 20 世纪 60 年代和 70 年代开始与左派政治相关的东西。同样，他声称人们需要与现存的政治制度和实务合作，以便从内部发起改革而不是发生正面冲突，这似乎也与左派支持者越来越倾向于采取更直接、更激进的社会变革方式（如组织抗议运动或参加示威活动）相左。20 世纪 70 年代的政治和社会大环境激起了他更加明显的保守主义情感，他经常对"新左派、英国公共卫生体制等，以及英国工会的自杀策略"表示愤怒。[①] 然而，波普尔对世界事务的了解显然

---

　① Hacohen，2000：540.

是模糊的。"在晚年时他看了一点电视节目,就被节目和媒体的力量所惊骇,他建议以违反自由原则的方式来对其加以控制。"①20 世纪 70 年代英国社会主义的失败似乎是压在波普尔身上的最后一根稻草,哈耶克等人早已令他越来越相信在个人自由原则和平等原则之间存在着潜在的矛盾。到 1974 年,或许还更早,在众人眼中,波普尔从进步社会主义者转变为共产主义者,再到社会民主主义者,最后成为保守的自由主义者,这个过程明显已经完成了。在他的自传中波普尔回顾这段旅程,他极生动地阐述了他为什么放弃了社会主义及其对平等的承诺。他写道:

> 我身为社会主义者多年,甚至在我抛弃了马克思主义之后。如果能够把社会主义和自由相结合的话,那么我还是会成为社会主义者的。因为没有什么比在一个平等的社会中过一种适度、简单和自由的生活更好的了。我花了一些时间才认识到这不过是一个美丽的梦,自由比平等更重要,想要实现平等的企图会危及自由,而如果失去了自由,那么在不自由的人中间就不会有平等。②

从表面上看,这段话似乎佐证了普遍存在的一个观点,即波普尔结束了自己作为一个自由至上主义者——或者像撒切尔夫人、罗纳德·里根和新右派那样的保守主义者——的思想旅程。但是事情没有那么简单。波普尔的政治哲学(在早期和晚期)的特征是寻求自由和平等可以共存的社会。诚然,他捍卫个人自由、有限国家、理性讨论,认为它们是解决文化和种族差异的手

---

① Hacohen,2000:540.
② Popper,1974/2002:36.

段;诚然,他认为反对非自由主义的团体、否认某些无理的主张或观念需要被排除在公共辩论之外、否认自由主义和民主不可能完全相容,这些观点也许有其存在的理由。但是,它们现在被众多当代平等主义的自由主义者所认同,他们却既不是保守主义者,也不是自由至上主义者。在政治话语正在被团体、运动和社会行动主义的言论所支配的时代,波普尔可能仍然是一个坚定的个人主义者。但是声称个人(而不是团体)应该被视为民主国家的主要活动者却不一定意味着保守主义,虽然这样的立场完全符合非社会主义者对平等的理解,也被许多自称有意支持自由和平等的自由主义者加以发展。波普尔在上述论证中对平等的摒弃令人好奇,尽管他担心社会主义建立平等的能力,但他似乎并没有放弃平等这个观点本身。在他早期或晚期的政治哲学观点中,他从不曾捍卫过一个把个人自由视为唯一优点并加以支持的社会;他捍卫一个"开放的"而不是"封闭的"社会,在其中,人人有能力享有自由和繁荣的生活,而这种能力得到赞美和培养,在其中"应得"和"不应得"、"值得"和"不值得"之间的武断区分被摒弃,取而代之的是对世界主义和普遍主义的要求。归根结底,波普尔在《开放社会及其敌人》中对非理性主义的批判,其核心是它假定了"人和人之间的不平等"。不能否认的是,"人类与世界上所有别的东西一样,在许许多多方面都是并不平等的,"他说,"我们也不能否认,这种不平等是非常重要的,甚至在一些方面而言是非常需要的。但是这一切与我们是否应该平等待人,特别是在政治上,或者尽可能地平等地对待人——也就是说,拥有平等的权利、对平等待遇的平等要求——这样的问题是毫无关系的;与我们是否应该相应地建设政治制度等问题也是毫无关系的。'法律面前人人平等'不是一个事实,而是一个基

学术生涯

33

于道德决策的政治要求。"①因此,贯穿波普尔政治思想的悖论,以及在他讨论其政治思想时一再出现的重要问题,就是平等与自由之间的主要关系问题,以及他最初关于没有贫困的平等社会的进步观点在何种程度上可以与一个以个人自由(不受国家、他人的约束,不存在个人的无知)为前提的社会达成一致的问题。

1994 年 9 月 17 日波普尔去世时,许多人都认为他已经放弃了这项事业,但事实上,他对那些支撑他过去的平等主义价值观的执着依然十分明显。诚然,他抛弃了社会技术,认为其并非是解决政治问题的适当答案。他表达了对大众民主的担忧;他与冷战时期的自由主义者联合起来,致力于在世界舞台上倡导自由主义原则,他的政治思想在苏联的过激行为和威胁自由的非自由主义团体的壮大下,越来越清晰。但尽管如此,他对个人自由、对人类通过努力可以增长知识的认识,以及他对想当然的知识和权威的怀疑,都是坚定不移的。波普尔后期的政治观点,一些就像在他早期的作品中阐发的观点一样,我们能看到他对种族和民族主义的保守主义的憎恨,对特权的排斥,对所有人的能力的真诚信任——相信假以机会和凭借恰当的资源,人人都有能力摆脱阻碍他们生活的无知、暴政和财富、权力的不平等。正是这种信仰——相信全人类的启蒙、理性和平等地位——与当代的政治和哲学息息相关,并与 21 世纪的许多政治理论产生了共鸣。

① Popper,1945/2006:259.

波普尔的思想

在漫长的学术生涯中,波普尔的写作题材广泛,著述颇丰,涉及了众多领域的多种论题。然而,他的主要兴趣,以及驱使他在音乐、历史、逻辑、数学、科学、社会科学和政治学等不同领域进行写作的共同动力,是"宇宙学问题,即了解世界——包括作为世界一部分的我们自己、我们的知识——的问题"①。

波普尔认为这是哲学的核心问题。在关于这一点的论辩中,他认为自己深谙理性主义哲学家的悠久而崇高的传统,对这些哲学家来说,追求知识(关于世界的知识,更重要的是关于知识本身的知识)至关重要。从"柏拉图到笛卡儿、莱布尼茨、康德、迪昂②和庞加莱③;从培根、霍布斯、洛克到休谟、密尔、罗素。启发知识的理论的是一种希望,希望我们不仅能更多地了解知识,同时还促进知识的进步",特别是科学知识。这个希望也是

---

① Popper,1935/2007a;xix.

② 皮埃尔·迪昂(Pierre Duhem,1861—1916),法国物理科学家、科学史家与科学哲学家。译者注。

③ 昂利·庞加莱(Jules Henri Poincaré,1854—1912),法国最伟大的数学家之一,理论科学家和科学哲学家。译者注。

波普尔所怀有的。由于怀有这个希望,他反对维也纳学派的逻辑实证主义者和 J. L. 奥斯汀、吉尔伯特·赖尔这样的"日常语言"哲学家,这二人都基于个人认识认为哲学从根本上是对语言的研究。他写道:"有哲学家认为哲学特有的方法是对日常语言的分析,这些哲学家中的大多数,似乎已经丧失了可敬的曾启迪理性主义传统的乐观。他们的态度似乎已是一种放弃,如果还称不上是绝望的话。"①

波普尔的哲学应该被解读为劝说人们反对这种放弃,并推翻他视为其导因的有缺陷的哲学学说的一种努力。我们在第一章已经提到了其中的一部分(反对心理主义、逻辑实证主义、维特根斯坦的语言哲学,以及认为哲学应被理解为寻求意义而不是解决世界具体问题的观点),我们在后面的章节中将对此作更多的讨论。波普尔的目的是建立一种认识论,一个能够解释世间知识的地位和发展的理论,它可以应用于所有寻求知识的人类研究领域。它并不像逻辑实证主义者认为的那样,把"科学"从"形而上学"中区分开来,以便将后者视为垃圾,而是把科学与伪科学区分开来(也就是把科学理论与那些自称科学而其实并非科学的理论划分开来)。他的结论是激进和深远的,不仅影响了他在科学、逻辑和数学方面的著述,还影响了其政治学和社会科学方面的作品内容。在此,我们不可能全面评述波普尔的科学哲学思想,因为本书主要关注他的政治哲学。因此,我首先将充实上一章所述的一些观点,特别是他的认识论中对他的政治哲学影响最为重要的部分,然后再讨论他如何将这些观点应用于社会研究(《历史决定论的贫困》),然后应用于政治学说中

（《开放社会及其敌人》）。接着，我将在第三章讨论他的政治观点在《开放社会及其敌人》出版后几年间发生的一些转变。

波普尔的认识论

波普尔认为，"认识论的核心问题一直是……知识增长的问题。而知识增长的问题，可以通过研究科学知识的增长而得到最好的研究。"[1]那么，科学知识是如何增长的？以什么方式增长？科学发现是如何实现的？

根据传统观点，科学是一个归纳过程，科学家首先对关于世界的观察进行整理、分类，以便从这些观察中推断出总体的自然规律。这些自然规律反过来可以用来解释世界（通过检验关于世界的特定主张），并预测未来事件。因此，科学首先是观察（如铅、水或氢等元素或化学物质，或如车轮、螺旋桨或原子等物理对象）某种自然属性或行为。可见，科学首先是通过科学实验观察特定的、可孤立的属性或行为，然后从这些实验中得到结果（即观察结果），之后用这样的结果来推断普遍规律。因此，科学家的一项重要工作就是要建立进行观察和检验的适当环境，以免导致意外或错误的结果。因此，科学理论是从观察到的关于世界的事实中推断出来的，而这些事实是通过在受控条件下进行反复实验和实证检验的过程中收集到的。由此产生的理论具有预测性、可检验性；通过孤立并观察特定对象的特定行为（例如，重力对坠落的苹果的影响），可以验证（或证明）关于世界的

---

① Popper，1935/2007a；xix.

主张（如"苹果不会朝天上飞"）是否正确，并可以预测未来事件（例如，"如果我放开手上抓着的苹果，它就会掉下去"）。理论可以通过恰当观察的事实得到证实或证明，科学进步正是由这种理论的增加所驱动，而且也是以这种理论的增加来衡量的。理论用这种方式可以解释的现象越多，适用性越广泛，我们就认为这个理论越重要。

关于科学方法的这个观点——作为从特定的、可观察的事实来建立一般自然规律的归纳过程——具有悠久而纯正的历史和血统，被大多数科学家普遍认同，也被认为在历史上的许多最伟大科学家，包括伽利略、哥白尼、开普勒和艾萨克·牛顿的著作中，得到了例证。例如，牛顿对微不足道的东西——如落下的苹果——的观察，使他建立了万有引力的一般理论，这进一步使他极其成功地精确解释了行星的运动，并预测其未来的运行轨迹。牛顿理论对于许多人的开创性意义，主要在于它来源于对特定事件或特定事物属性的观察，这个理论结果却可以应用于所有的物理对象。通过对特定对象的特定观察，牛顿得以推导出普遍的、可广泛适用的自然规律，因而有助于形成有关认识宇宙基本结构的总体的、广泛的规则体系。在他之前和之后的科学家已经使用归纳法来寻求关于世界和广阔的宇宙的真理，他们希望其观察能够使他们推断出同样普遍的、可广泛适用的规律，既能解释现象，又能预测事件。

波普尔认为，对科学的这种传统理解从根本上是有缺陷的。他的理由是多方面的。首先，他认为归纳法根本依赖于一个哲学和逻辑的不可能性，即"理论的正确性可以从特定的观察与陈述的正确性中合乎逻辑地推断出来"①。波普尔论述道,恰恰相反,"无论重复观察多少次,也没有规则能够保证从正确的观察中推断出的普遍规律是正确的"②。他还援引了休谟在《人类理解研究》(*Enquiry into Human Understanding*)中对归纳法的批评。在书中,休谟指出,没有任何有效的论证可以让我们确定"那些我们没有经历过的情况会与我们已经经历过的情况相似"。因此,休谟写道,"即使观察到事物频繁或经常出现巧合,我们也没有理由对任何超出我们经历之外的事物进行任何推断",因此,我们不应该"形成任何超越我们过去曾经历过的情况的判断结论"③。换言之,过去发生过某件事,即使曾经发生过上百次、上千次乃至上百万次,也并不意味着它会在未来以同样的方式发生;多次观察到某一特定事件在特定情况下发生,并不能无可争议地证明它总会以我们预期的方式再次发生,或者它根本就不会发生。我们不能通过观察过去来预测未来,无论我们有多么确信我们对过去作出了正确的观察,并且辨认出了过去的规律或趋势。

这个观点使波普尔得出了一个激进的结论,即长期以来我们认为科学家应该致力于从世界上的特定事件或事实中推断出可普遍适用的自然规律,这种观点是错误的、无用的。此外,他总结说,归纳法的问题意味着我们所确立的任何理论都永远不可能在科学上被证明——它们只能被证伪。"所有天鹅都是白色的"这个陈述,不能通过观察到任何数量的白天鹅来得到证明,但是只要观察到一只非白色的天鹅,就可以确定地得到证

---

① Popper,1963/2007b:251.

② Popper,1963/2007b:71.

③ Popper,1963/2007b:55—56.

伪。"堡垒坚不可摧",无论企图攻破其防御的努力失败多少次,这个说法都无法得到证明,但只要成功一次就可以确然地驳倒它。阿兹特克人相信如果不祭拜太阳神,早晨太阳就不会升起,祭拜成功的次数再多也不能证明这个理论,但如果未做祭拜而太阳仍然升起,这一事实便确定地驳倒了这个理论。事实无法证明一个理论为真,但可以证明其为假。而一旦被证明为假,这个理论就具有了对知识的切实贡献:我们可以说什么是不正确的,这比我们说什么是正确的要确定得多。因此,被驳倒的陈述是有价值的。它们并非无用(如传统观点所认为的那样);对波普尔来说,驳倒了一个理论代表了科学知识的真正发展,值得庆贺和重视。因为发现某一个理论不可能正确,我们就会离发现正确或可能正确的理论更近了一步。相反,无用的理论是那些不能被证伪的理论。由于在科学领域里不可能提供无可辩驳的证明或确定的真理(因为归纳法存在的问题),那些被设计为看似无可辩驳的真理却不可证伪的理论实际上是不科学的,也是无益的。例如,思考这两个陈述:

（a）我们祭了神,明天就会下雨。

（b）我们祭了神,将来就会下雨。

（a)有可能是真理(因此是科学的),(b)是不科学的,这是因为(a)可以被驳倒,而(b)不能。也就是说,我们目前可能不具备必要的知识来驳倒它,但由于它的结构框架,有一天我们有可能会驳倒它。陈述(a)是严谨的,而(b)是不严谨的。(a)的严谨性意味着它可以被检验(通过等到明天看是否下雨),而(b)的非严谨性意味着它不能被检验,我们可以好几代人等着下雨,然而,由于我们无法无限期地等下去,因此我们永远不会知道将来是否会下雨。所以,(b)不能增加我们对世界的认识,而(a)可以

（尽管它仍然可能为假）。波普尔认为，预测（在科学及其他领域）是重要的，也是可能的，但必须是严谨的，从而是可证伪的，而不是概述性的、不可证伪的。预测也应当是短期的。推理可以是预测性的，但必然是有限的、易谬的。任何个人或团体都不能通过推理来预测特定行为或反应的各种长期后果；因此，预测一定是尝试性的、短期的，而不是根本性的、长期的。科学不能也不应该致力于建立可证明世界上特定事物的理论（即证实某个陈述或主张的正确性的理论），相反，科学应该致力于消除目前已经存在的可证伪理论中的错误。而且，理论无法被证明是正确的这一事实，意味着所有现存的理论——无论多么理由充分、令人信服或广泛适用——都必须被视为具有固有的推测性和假定性。因为没有任何一个假设可以被证实，它永远只能是一个假设（除非它被证明是错误的，在这种情况下它就被摒弃）。

其次，与此相关地，波普尔对科学始于观察这一观点在哲学和历史上的准确性提出了质疑。波普尔认为，恰恰相反，科学是从提出关于特定问题的理论开始的。这代表着对科学的传统归纳法理解的反转。归纳法论者认为科学从观察（或事实）走向理论（或一般规律）。但波普尔认为，科学实际上始于我们确定问题，提出关于问题的理论，这些理论可能反过来被其他理论或观察所证伪。这与第一章提出的观点相关，即对波普尔来说，知识的增长源自我们与真正问题的对抗，而非源自如语言陈述的含义。他认为，科学不是一个归纳过程，而是一个演绎过程。科学家发现世界上的某些问题，提出理论来解决这些问题，然后致力于证伪这些理论。如果可以证伪，那么这些理论就被摒弃（任何经得起检验的残留成分除外）；如果不可证伪，那么这个理论继续存在，而科学们继续根据目前已知的情况试图对其进行反驳。这样的理论不能被视为正确的,但可以被假定为正确的,或可能为正确的。也就是说,事实不能用来证明理论,也不能被认为是一般自然规律的来源,相反,事实可被用来推断一个特定的理论,根据目前所知的关于世界的知识,是否正确。因此,科学并非始于观察,而是始于提出关于问题的理论。

再次重申,这个观点对于我们理解科学具有彻底而深远的意义。科学具有(而且应该具有)超脱于世界的不带感情的、冷静客观的特征,并被理解为一个在受控环境中进行观察、实验和对结果整理分类的过程。这已经成为一个公认的真理。波普尔认为,这带有以培根和笛卡儿为代表的理性主义传统的特殊烙印。培根和笛卡儿认为,为了了解世界,我们必须首先"清除我们头脑中(可能影响我们发现的)所有的猜想、推测或偏见",仅凭我们的理性来揭示真理。[1] 我们在第一章中看到,这也是逻辑实证主义者的观点。然而,波普尔则认为,科学的发现不是空洞地将理性应用于世界而产生的,而恰恰是从培根、笛卡儿和逻辑实证主义者劝说我们置于一旁的那些猜想、推测和偏见中产生的。"科学的开始……既非来自于收集观察结果,也非来自于发明实验,"波普尔论述道,"而是始于对神话的批判性讨论。"[2] 人们倾向于通过试图解释世界和自己的生活而为其施加秩序,特别是试图用可以依赖并可以用来解释目前事件、预测未来事件的规律或趋势来解释世界。儿童是这样的(如波普尔 1927 年在教育学院的论文中所写),成年人也是如此;它显而易见地存在于我们希望建立起包罗万象的自然规律的愿望中,也存在于

---

① Popper,1963/2007b:19.
② Popper,1963/2007b:66.

卡尔·波普尔

我们对为我们的生活建立秩序和语境的其他神话和故事中,如民族神话、宗教、文化、历史等。这些神话和传统非常重要,因为它们设定了进行科学研究的初始框架。"观察总是有选择性的。"波普尔论述道,"它需要一个选定的对象、一个明确的任务、一个兴趣、一个观点、一个问题。"[1]科学家的工作不是收集有关世界的随机观察结果,而是通过试图证伪那些已经存在的具推测性的解决方案(或理论)来解决问题。科学和其他领域一样,在其中"我们无法知道,我们只能猜测。我们的猜测是以我们对于可以发现的法则、规律的非科学的、形而上学的(尽管在生物学上是可解释的)那些信仰为指导"[2]。科学家们不能只看(或听,或感觉),他们需要知道他们在寻找什么,以及如何去有效地寻找。同样,他们不能仅仅去创造,他们需要获知关于能够达到目标(某个需要解决的问题)的一些背景情况。波普尔写道:"再多的科学也不能告诉科学家制造一把犁、一架飞机或一颗原子弹是正确的事。目标必须由他自己选取,或是交付给他;而他作为科学家只是构建实现这些目标的手段。"[3]因此,理论"主导实验工作,从最初的规划到实验室的最后阶段"[4]。

此外,波普尔认为,科学发现始于观察而非提出理论(常常源自神话和形而上学的观念)的观点对于宇宙学历史上的一些最重要的发展而言并不适用。"因为这是个事实,"波普尔写道,"纯粹的形而上学观点……一直以来对宇宙学都极其重要。从泰勒斯到爱因斯坦,从古代原子论到笛卡儿关于物质的思考,从

---

① Popper,1963/2007b:61.

② Popper,1935/2007a:275.

③ Popper,1963/2007b:483.

④ Popper,1935/2007a:90.

吉尔伯特、牛顿、莱布尼茨和博斯科维奇关于力的推测到法拉第和爱因斯坦对于力场的思索,形而上学的观点都为他们指明了方向。"①例如,"哥白尼把太阳而不是地球置于宇宙中心的想法并不是新的观察结果,而是来源于半宗教性的柏拉图哲学和新柏拉图主义哲学的观点(关于自然秩序中太阳的主导地位),是对众所周知的旧事实全新解读的结果。"因此,他说,哥白尼的天文学革命不是"从观察开始,而是从一个宗教的或神话的观点开始"②。同样,开普勒称行星围绕太阳以椭圆形轨道运行,其速度在整个运行过程中都在变化,这个观点也并非来自观察,而是因为他想要证明行星按圆形轨道并以匀速运行的先已存在的理论。爱因斯坦的量子理论具有令人难以置信的推测性和抽象性。波普尔认为,这完全不能称之基于特定的观察。因此,他认为科学主要源于感官经验(或观察)的积累,这与形而上学的观点理论化是相抵触的——除了维也纳学派的逻辑实证主义者之外,还有许多科学家都持这种看法——如果这样的看法是正确的,那么,这些理论以及无数其他的理论,都不能被理解为真正的"科学"理论。故而,逻辑实证主义者采取的立场其反讽之处就在于,他们认为科学优于哲学(并试图通过归纳的科学方法来划分有效和无效的哲学探究),结果他们对科学的定义(因此对哲学的理解)"使得科学显然无法对我们认识世界作出任何贡献",也无法涵盖历史上许多最重要的科学发现。③

因此,科学不是形而上学理论化的敌人,因为形而上学和既定的信念往往为科学家应该提出什么问题,应该如何提出这些

① Popper,1935/2007a:xxiii.
② Popper,1963/2007b:253—254.
③ Popper,1935/2007a:xii.

问题提供指导，从而为科学发现提供了出发点。但科学确实代表了我们凭以知道哪些形而上学的立场——或者某个特定立场的哪些方面——值得支持的一种手段。他提出，我们所有的形而上学猜想，"一旦提出，不会被教条地给予支持。我们的研究方法不是要捍卫它们，以表明它们是多么的正确。相反，我们试图推翻它们。我们使用我们的逻辑、数学和技术军械库里的所有武器，试图证明我们的预期是错误的——以求取而代之地提出新的未被证明也无法证明的预期，新的被培根戏称作'轻率且不成熟的偏见'"①。许多形而上学的理论可能包含错误的主张，但是这些主张可以通过批判性的讨论或实证检验被揭示、被驳斥。科学（按波普尔的理解）提供了有助于形而上学立场的重要工具（通过消除那些可能被证明错误的方面），但是科学不应该被认为是这些立场的敌人，或是一般而言形而上学的敌人。

波普尔提出通过将知识增长的概念重建为一种对理论进行检验和批判性讨论的非归纳性过程，以解决归纳法的问题，如此一来，他就为维也纳学派的逻辑实证主义者提出的关于划界的原命题提供了一个更有说服力的答案。请记住，他们的主张（波普尔对此极为赞同）是，哲学将得益于科学的严密性，因此科学的方法应该被应用于哲学。对于逻辑实证主义者来说，这意味着要弄清楚哲学学科的哪些方面与科学学科特有的方法（以传统的归纳法来理解）兼容并蓄或者可以被纳入其中。因此，科学的方法为科学与形而上学、科学与非科学之间的划界，因而也为有效和无效的哲学问题的划界，提供了坚实的基础。波普尔对此表示反对，他颠覆了归纳法，主张科学知识的增长与其他领域

---

① Popper,1935/2007a:278—279.

的知识增长进程一样，而且事实上是依赖于其他研究领域的。科学发展如同其他领域的知识发展一样，是不可预测的，往往是复杂、散乱和不确定的；它的发展并不总是遵循一个既定的模式，即便有既定模式，我们也不见得能事先预测这种模式；而且它源自一个反复试错的过程，一个在群体中进行理性和批判性讨论的过程。因此科学与其他领域一样，其知识的增长是一个公开过程。例如，知识的增长不仅仅是单个的科学家私底下孤立研究的结果；它产生于对这些单个科学家提出的理论进行的公开讨论和批评当中。因此，所有知识（包括但不限于科学知识）都是由跨越多门学科的许多个人对问题进行持续的批判性讨论而产生的。

这就是波普尔否定科学具特有方法的本意：人类的所有研究领域的知识，都产生于个体与个体之间相互探讨解决问题的可能方法，以及对已经存在的理论进行证伪的过程。因此，波普尔对于把知识探索划分为个别的学科领域，各自遵循自己的方法、惯例及习惯做法的倾向——这在现代学术界极为常见，在逻辑实证主义者的观点中也有所暗示——深感怀疑。他认为，想要创造这种学科细分的愿望，武断地分裂了本应在所有学科中广泛统一的认识论发现过程。"认为有诸如物理科学、生物学或考古学这样的东西，并认为这些'研究'或'学科'可以根据它们的研究主题予以区分，这在我看来是人们认为理论必须从其主题的定义出发的那个时代的遗毒。"他写道，"然而研究主题……并没有……构成区分学科的基础。"将对知识的一般追求细分为各个学科领域，实际上只不过是为了行政管理上的便利。所有这些"分类和区分都只是一种相对不重要的表面文章。我们不是某个研究主题的研究者，而是解决问题的研究者。我们研究的问题可能跨越任何研究主题或学科的边界"。① 虽然对学科间的某些区分有时是有益的,但这些学科的研究者们应该明白,他们都参与了同一个发现过程,使用的方法大体相同。诸如"什么是哲学?"或"什么是经济学?"这样的问题是多余的、自以为是的,只是维特根斯坦派对寻求词语意义的愿望,或是亚里士多德派对理解现象"本质"的需求的衍生物。哲学家、科学家和经济学家不应该试图将自己的方法与其他学科的方法加以区分,以此来确定自己学科的"本质",相反,他们应该直面问题,对现有的一切观点和理论采取批判的态度,通过理性、批判性的讨论过程来提出理论并对其证伪——这个讨论不限于某一个学科关注的一系列问题,而是涵盖所有学科和研究领域。例如,科学发现可能而且已经从宗教理论或数学中涌现出来,而政治改革可能(而且已经)从一般认为是经济学家、心理学家或社会学家独占的禁区中涌现出来。重要的是,那些从事这些领域的人并不是想要将自己的研究与外界隔离,而是以开放的态度热情地与这些理论(及其提议者)进行批判性的互动。波普尔称之为"批判理性主义",即来自古希腊人的传统,"对理论进行自由讨论,目的是发现其弱点以便对其进行改进";来自各学科的人员应该在解决世界的问题上互相交流,在这些讨论中,他们应该采取"一种愿意听取批评意见并从经验中学习"的态度。② 因此,批判理性主义在根本上就是"一种承认'我可能错,你可能对,通过努力,我们可以更接近真理'的态度"③。

通过这些论述,波普尔认为,他不仅提供了对物理科学的更

① Popper,1963/2007b:88.

② Popper,1963/2007b:67.

③ Popper,1945/2006b:249.

合乎逻辑的定义,而且提供了一个普遍的认识论理论,不仅可以解释科学领域,还可以解释所有领域和所有学科内的知识增长。波普尔的演绎方法表明,致力于为我们了解世界作出贡献的科学家和哲学家,应该认识到他们是在从事一项共同的工作,而不是由不同的方法论和主题所定义的不同工作。科学家和哲学家的职责是(或应该是)面对问题、提出问题的解决方案,并与其他人就现有的理论以及他们自己提出的理论的有效性或一致性进行批判性的对话。这样做就确保了科学的客观性。"认为科学的客观性依赖于科学家个人的精神或心理态度,依赖于他受到的教育、他关心的事物和科学的超然,这种天真的看法,自然会产生怀疑科学家永远无法客观的观点。"但科学的客观性并不依赖于科学家个人的心理;相反,正是"科学及其体系的公共性对科学家个人实施了一种思想训练,维持了科学的客观性和批判地讨论新思想的传统"①。各门学科和各个领域的成员间的公开辩论能引发知识的增长,这个认识确保了参与者之间的坦诚和信息披露的充分。因此,波普尔的认识论并没有试图划定一个独特的科学方法,因为这样的东西并不存在;相反,它提供了一个标准,用以判断某个特定的理论或主张是否应该被视为能够帮助我们了解世界(不论主题的任何领域)。

将这些不同的观点结合起来,我们可以看出,为什么波普尔关于科学(以及一般而言知识的增长)的观点曾经以至现在都如此具有争议。波普尔提出,关于科学的传统观点(即科学是从特定的观察推断出关于世界的一般规律或假说,并能证明有关事实的陈述是否正确的一个归纳过程)应该被取代,科学应该被理

---

① Popper,1957/2005:144.

解为一个演绎过程,在这个过程中提出解决问题的理论方案,然后通过对事实或其他理论的批判性讨论来进行证伪。因此,不可证伪的理论是不科学的。没有任何理论能够得到确定的证实。但可以被确定地证伪。因此,科学家通过公开讨论、辩论和实证检验来寻求的不是对科学理论的证实,而应是证伪。一些理论很容易被证伪,另一些则不然。然而,正是反复不断地对现有理论进行证伪,并以其他理论将其取代的努力,才推动了科学发现的进程,增进了我们对世界的总体认识。从这个观点来看,科学变成了一个猜想和反驳的试错过程。个人提出关于世界的特定问题的理论(通常是大胆的理论),同时邀请其他人来证伪这些理论。科学发现要求对问题及其假设性解决方案采取批判性态度,科学发现出自于个人群体内的批判性对话:

科学的进步并不是因为越来越多的感性经验随着时间的不断积累,也不是因为我们的感官利用得越来越好。无论我们多么努力地收集和分类,未经解释的感性经验中都不能提炼出科学。大胆的想法、未经证明的预感、推测性的思想,是我们解释自然的唯一方法:……我们了解自然的唯一手段。[1]

科学发现不是清楚明了的;恰恰相反,科学史"就像所有人类思想的历史一样,是不可靠的幻想、痼疾和错误的历史"[2]。我们应该致力于通过对现有的理论、观点、传统和叙述进行批判性对话。根据我们自己的发现以及其他人相似的想法和发现来对它们进行检验,从而消除错误。而不是试图仅仅通过应用理性来寻求对普遍真理的概括与证明。把科学理解为关于世界的

波普尔的思想

---

[1] Popper,1935/2007a:280.
[2] Popper,1963/2007b:293.

特定真理的积累,"不仅妨害了我们对问题认识的大胆性,也有损于我们对问题的检验的严谨性和完整性。关于科学的错误观点(或'传统'观点)渴望其自身的正确性,这恰恰令其露出原形;因为科学家之所以成为科学家,并不是因为他拥有知识或无可辩驳的真理,而是由于他坚持不懈、不顾一切地对真理的批判性追问"。[1] 因此,波普尔的总体结论是,我们应该"放弃探究知识的终极来源,承认所有的知识都是人类的一部分;它与我们的错误、我们的偏见、我们的梦想、我们的希望混杂在一起;我们所能做的就是尽可能地摸索真理,尽管它遥不可及"[2]。

从科学到社会科学

人们经常认为,波普尔建立了一种"科学哲学",然后把这种哲学应用于社会科学。但我们已经看到,波普尔的目标其实有些不同。他不仅是为了建立一种科学哲学,也是为了提供一个认识论的理论,可以解释我们关于世界的知识可能的发展过程并为其作出贡献,也可以说,是为了建立关于"一般人类思想的发展,特别是科学思想的发展"[3]的理论。因此,波普尔并没有试图将他的"科学哲学"应用于社会和政治;相反,他试图为收集信息、了解世界的过程提供一个一般性的解释,这个解释既适用于科学,同时也适用于社会科学或政治学。

因此,广义而言,波普尔认为,社会科学领域的知识增长应

卡尔·波普尔

① Popper,1935/2007a:281.
② Popper,1963/2007b:39.
③ Popper,1963/2007b:421.

该被理解为以与物理科学大致相同的方式——按照相同的逻辑——在发展。社会科学的探究应该从确定社会和政治的问题开始,通过猜想和反驳的试错过程,消除目前存在的理论和实践中的错误,消除其他人提出的假设性解决方案中的错误,并设法解决这些问题。社会理论的任务不是对未来的历史进程进行可归纳的、长期性的预言,而是——如同在物理科学领域——用可能会受到他人批评和检验的方案解决具体问题,并弄清那些已经在运用(并体现在社会和政治体制以及社会实践中)的解决方案是否正确。社会科学领域和物理科学领域一样,其知识的增长源于对社会和政治问题及其假设性的解决方案采取批判性的("批判理性主义的")态度,并且批判性地与其他人讨论现有的理论和观点。

因此,波普尔提出,物理科学和社会科学都以"方法统一"为特征。也就是说,他认为"所有的理论科学或归纳科学都使用相同的方法,无论是自然科学还是社会科学",这个相同的方法是由对现有观点、理论和实践采取批判理性主义态度的个人组成的群体,对现有问题的可证伪假说进行猜想和反驳的试错过程。[1] 关于社会——关于社会问题——的理论因此需要以同样的方式进行证伪,与通常被视为物理科学领域的问题的理论一样。正如波普尔认为可证伪性是物理科学领域划分科学与非科学理论的合理标准,他认为对社会科学理论,以及其他领域的理论也是如此。通过这些论证,波普尔认为,他能够揭示许多自称是科学(因而自称增加了人类的知识)其实并非科学的理论的弱点(或至少是非科学性的特点)。这样的理论有阿德勒的"个人

---

[1]　Popper,1957/2005:120.

51

心理学"理论、弗洛伊德的精神分析理论等。波普尔认为,这些理论的问题正是它们不可证伪,它们无法被驳倒。他认为,打动了如弗洛伊德的信徒和阿德莱的追随者的正是他们的理论的解释力,事实上,"它们似乎能够解释它们涉及的领域内发生的一切"。研究这些理论似乎

在你眼前揭示出一个崭新的真理,而那些尚未接触这些理论的人却看不到。一旦你的眼界被打开,你就会看到确认的事例无处不在:世界充满了对这些理论的证实。发生的每一件事都在证实它。因此它的真理性似乎清楚明了。不相信的人显然都是不愿看到明显真理的人;他们拒绝看到真理,要么是因为它违反他们的阶级利益,要么是因为他们的心理压抑仍然"未经解析",亟待治疗。①

因此,我们看到这些理论犯了以观察或体验进行验证作为划分科学理论与非科学理论的界限(在物理科学领域以及社会科学和心理学领域)的错误,荒谬地从事实(归纳地)推断出理论;换言之,事实往往可以证明理论家愿意证明的任何东西,因此它什么都证明不了。波普尔认为,像哥白尼、开普勒和伽利略等科学家的理论之所以成为重要的科学理论,是因为他们的理论可以被证伪。即便是牛顿的万有引力和力学理论也是可证伪的,爱因斯坦就曾证明了这一点。但就算是爱因斯坦,也不能证伪弗洛伊德的精神分析理论、阿德勒的"个人心理学",因为无论是诉诸事实还是相反的理论都无法削弱他们的理论。任何一个弗洛伊德精神分析的病人,如果觉得自己的行为不能用这种或那种被压抑的冲动的某种组合来解释,就会被认为不过是"拒绝

---

① Popper,1963/2007b:45.

接受现实",需要进一步治疗。

同时,详细理解波普尔对历史主义的批判非常重要,因为这是他关于社会科学的适当行为和政治实践的思想基础。

波普尔把历史主义描述为广义而言"认为历史受特定的历史或进化规律约束的学说,发现这些规律使我们能够预言人类的命运"[1]。因此,它体现了这样一种观点:"对政治的真正科学或哲学的态度,对社会生活总体上更深层次的理解,必须建立在对人类历史的思索和诠释之上"[2]。他说,这是一种"社会科学的研究方法,假设历史预言是他们的主要目标,并假设这个目标可以通过发现历史发展的'节奏'或'韵律'、'规律'或'趋势'而实现"[3]。故而,历史主义就是通过把社会和政治现象理解为历史力量的产物,理解为具有起源性质的事物——这种事物被认为是朝着自我定义的终点或目标发展,并以其现有的存在形式作为历史事件的高潮——来理解社会和政治的一种方法。因此,对社会和政治体制、规范和惯例的研究,不能从带来这些体制、规范和惯例的历史力量和历史条件中抽象地进行。从这个观点来看,对政治和社会的研究,差不多就是对历史的研究。

波普尔认为,这个观点在人类历史、政治思想史和当时所谓的社会政治话语中非常流行,有害无益。他认为,历史主义的一些最古老、最明显的例子,是那些确定"选民"的宗教,选民的角色是成为"按(上帝)意志选定的工具",如果他们正确地承担了这个角色,就"将会承继整个世界"。[4] 在这样的学说中,历史发

① Popper,1945/2006a:4.
② Popper,1945/2006a:3.
③ Popper,1957/2005:3.
④ Popper,1945/2006a:4.

展的规律是由上帝的意志确定的,选民的任务就是要尽其所能来加速实现圣谕中必将实现的预言。因此,波普尔认为,宗教和世俗形式的历史主义具有大体的相同特征:它们是集体主义的,因为它们按群体而非按个人的口吻来发言(例如,它们称"人民""民族""种族"或"阶级"),它们所预言的目标总是遥不可及。因为尽管我们可能清楚地了解我们奋力实现的目标,但"我们必须要走很长一段路才能到达。道路不仅漫长,而且曲折,上坡下坎,左转右拐。因此,有可能把每一个可以想象得到的历史事件都囊括于诠释的体系之内"①。和弗洛伊德学派的精神分析学家、阿德勒学派的心理学家的主张一样,预言选民命运的宗教教义是不可证伪的,因而不能对人类知识增长作出贡献。

波普尔认为,社会科学和政治科学的历史中充斥着历史主义思想家。如柏拉图、黑格尔、卢梭、密尔和孔德等具有哲学和政治结论的思想家,虽各执己见,却都接受了历史主义的方法。例如,对于黑格尔来说,"选民"就是"民族",历史发展的规律描述了民族(被视为精神的化身)走向自由或自我实现的辩证过程。黑格尔及其他历史主义思想家的共同观点就是,人类社会是历史发展的客观总体规律的产物,这一事实决定了社会科学的合理行为和政治学的合理特征。它也使那些能够了解历史规律的人得以预测人类的未来。对于历史主义者来说,社会科学的要务就是揭示那些在任一时期决定社会性质和内容(因此也就是我们彼此间的社会关系、我们的社会态度以及管理和规范我们生活的隐含的社会规范)的历史发展规律。政治学的要务——以及国家等政治制度的正确角色和责任——首先是为实

---

① Popper,1945/2006a;5.

现历史发展规律所确定的这些目标或目的设定适当的条件。波普尔从与历史主义思想的交战中建立起自己的社会科学方法。因此,在本节的剩余部分,我将讨论历史主义方法对社会研究的含义(以及波普尔对其的批判),然后在下一节继续讨论其政治含义。

我已经提到,对于波普尔来说,历史主义的根本特征是主张社会科学家的适当角色是寻求那些决定社会性质和内容的历史规律,因此,历史主义主张社会学差不多就是理论史的研究。所以,历史主义体现了对以下主张的根本否定:自然科学和物理科学的方法可以毫无问题地应用于社会科学。历史主义者认为,不能期望物理科学的方法产生关于社会和政治生活的洞见,主要有四个原因。

首先,历史主义者反对以下观点:我们有可能以自然科学家认为在物理科学中可以使用的方式推断出支配社会和政治生活的可普遍化的、不会改变的规律。历史主义者主张,物理科学家的总体目标是推导出支配宇宙结构和物理元素行为的一般规律,这些规律并非源于任何特定的历史时期,因此被认为是永恒的。(物理科学告诉我们,)"物理定律或称'自然法则'随时随地都是有效的;因为物理世界遵循一个无论空间、时间都恒定不变的物理科学统一系统。然而,社会学规律或'社会生活法则'在不同地方不同时期都是不同的。"① 尽管历史主义者也许会承认,在社会生活的特征中能够辨认出一些微不足道的规律,这些规律可能会超越某一个特定历史时期,但同时他们认为,我们不可能识别出更具有实质性的(因而是有用的)规律,能够独立于

——————————

① Popper,1957/2005:4.

它们所产生的历史时期。"根据历史主义的观点，忽视这种局限性、试图概括出一种统一的社会规律，这暗含的假设是我们所讨论的规律是永恒不变的。"[①]这样的理论否认"社会在发展，或者会发生巨大的变化；社会发展如果存在，就会影响社会生活的基本规律"[②]。因此，历史主义者主张，我们不应该采用"方法论上的幼稚"观点，即把物理科学的方法简单地引入政治学和社会学的研究中，而应该认真看待社会关系的历史根源。例如像卡尔·曼海姆（Karl Mannheim）和哈贝马斯、阿多诺、霍克海默等批判理论家，都宣称社会研究在根本上应该是一个分析任一特定时代所特有的特定社会关系（及其出现）的过程，而不是推导出在任何时代都永远是真理的社会生活普遍规律。同样，黑格尔和他近期的支持者的唯心主义——受到逻辑实证主义者及波普尔的强烈反对——表现了他们拒绝"真理"可以通过科学被发现这一观点，声称真理本身是一个历史现象，只能通过与产生真理的那些历史规律彼此互动得到揭示。他们及其他历史主义者主张，要了解社会，在对社会关系的研究上，我们必须将社会关系视为一种历史现象——由历史力量产生，由历史环境塑造，作为历史的产物本身来得到理解，而不是从其起源抽象出便于理解的东西。重要的是，我们应该认真看待文化的重要性，重视人类塑造他们未来社会的能力。历史主义认为，寻求永恒的社会规律，没有为行动主义——社会的个人成员通过自觉的意志或意外事件，塑造自己的未来和社会的未来的可能性——留下任何空间。创新和创造力只存在于支配所有时代的社会生活的总体

---

① Popper,1957/2005:5.
② Popper,1957/2005:5—6.

规律的结构之内,并由其定义。决定社会和政治生活特征及社会变化进程的正是这些规律,而非人类自身。

这听起来可能令人困惑,因为我们已经提出,历史主义的特性是其捍卫者在寻求总体的历史规律。因此,我们重申,在波普尔看来,历史主义的目标不是要发现任何一个特定历史时期的规律,然后断言这些规律一定适用于所有的历史时期;相反,其目标是发现那些决定了由一个历史时期向另一个历史时期过渡的更普遍的规律。这一点十分重要。也就是说,历史主义寻求历史发展的规律。例如,一位社会科学家可能会关注当代资本主义社会,确定其内部适用的某些规律(如对某种稀缺资源的需求增加会提高该资源的市场价值)。这个规律在资本主义社会中成立,但可能并不适用于经济体制不同的社会(在历史上或世界上其他地方):如封建社会或计划经济体制。因此,提出如上面所说的那种超越历史的普遍规律是不可能的,因为这些规律只会在特定社会的特定时期适用。我们说适用于所有历史时期的经济学规律,这是没有意义的;事实上,我们只能说资本主义时期的经济学规律或封建时期的经济学规律等。因此,历史主义者寻求的不是从一个特定时期的具体观察中推断出可概括的、超越历史的社会行为规律,而是推断出决定一个历史时期如何、何时、为何会变成另一个历史时期的更深层次的规律。例如,黑格尔的辩证历史观不仅描绘了已经存在的各个历史时期,还提供了预测未来历史发展的手段,以及历史自身必然走向的结局。而且,波普尔认为,我们可以在柏拉图、孔德、密尔、卢梭和所有那些有过社会科学著述的历史主义者的著作中找到类似的主张。他认为所有这些主张的共同点,就是认为社会学的目的是推导出历史上的一般规律或"一致性",从而可以解释先后存在的历史时期的发展,因此也能解释每一历史时期所特有的每一系列社会关系的起源。

历史主义者对社会研究采用自然科学方法所作的第二个批评与第一个批评紧密联系,即在物理科学中获得可靠知识的主要手段在社会和政治背景下则是完全不适当的。物理科学家通过观察物理元素的行为来推断一般规律。他们引入"人为的控制,人为的隔离,从而(确保)相似条件的再现,并随之产生特定的效应"①。他们认为,以这种方式观察社会和政治现象,可以从这些在所有时期都存在的观察结果中推导出一般规律,这种观点是荒谬的。这是因为在物理科学中起作用的推理结构在社会和政治背景下不起作用。在物理科学中,观察特定行为,并由此推断在相同的条件下,相同的元素或过程将以相同的方式表现或发生,这是有可能的。因此,物理科学家的一个重要目标是对测试特定行为和假设所需的特定条件进行规定,然后将其隔离出来。也就是说,科学家进行的实验旨在为具体问题提供具体的答案,从而为一般规律提供基础。然而,历史主义者认为,研究社会时不存在这种推理关系。波普尔以曼海姆的《人与社会》(*Man and Society*)为例说明了历史主义的这个论点,但在他后来与哈贝马斯和阿多诺在 20 世纪 60 年代的"实证主义辩论"的口水战中,我们可以清楚地看到,他同样认为这是批判理论家所持的一个观点。这种观点认为,将物理元素分离出来是可能的,但是以同样方式把社会和政治现象分离出来则是不可能的,所以"社会实验"总是会产生不确定的结果。此外,他还主张,像曼海姆、阿多诺和哈贝马斯这样的历史主义者认为的那

---

① Popper,1957/2005:7.

样,任何社会实验都必定是彻底的、全面的。社会的组成部分是不能分解开来进行孤立考察的,因此,社会实验不应该追求这样的做法。社会科学的主题(即人)太过复杂、太过多变,无法符合物理科学对客观性、控制性和对单个主体进行客观隔离的要求。因此,观察和实验尽管对于物理科学的知识收集是完全有效的、可以理解的,却不能为社会科学家提供他们需要的明确的、客观的知识,以便推断出适合所有时期、所有人的普遍性规律。另外,如我们前面所说,历史主义认为,"在相似的情况下,将发生相似的事件",这个推论只在特定历史时期才真正适用。文化会产生变化,观念会发展;因此,每一个新的历史时期都很可能代表着一个全新的关系、观念和假设的体系,这一类体系是前所未有的。因此,在过去绝没有可以观察到的、超越历史的"相似的情况",可以用以理解现在或未来。用波普尔的话来说:

> 在一个由物理科学描述的世界里,没有什么发生的事是真正的、本质上的新东西。我们可以发明一个新的发动机,但是我们总是可以把它解析为旧元素的重新组合。物理科学中的新事物仅仅是新的安排或组合。与此直接相对立的是(对于历史主义者来说),社会新事物是本质上的新事物……因为在社会生活中,新安排中的同样的旧因素永远不是真正的旧因素……(历史主义者)认为这对于考虑历史上的新阶段或新时期的发展具有重要意义,每一阶段与另一阶段都有着本质上的差异。[1]

对于历史主义者来说,在社会生活的研究中,没有哪个时刻比一个崭新的历史时期出现的那一刻更为重要。历史主义者认为,物理科学的方法不能理解这样一种变化,甚至无法把这种变

---

①   Popper,1957/2005:9.

化以可以理解的方式呈现。

历史主义的第三个相关特征是它的整体观。历史主义者声称,物理科学的方法是原子论的方法。它们研究特殊情况下的特别元素。它们也是非历史的,因为它们不考察研究对象的历史特征,而只考察它在某种条件下的行为。他们主张,这种方法完全适用于物理科学。虽然探索太阳系的历史可能很有趣,但若是为了了解太阳系的现状,就没有必要这样做。这是因为太阳系的现状"独立于太阳系的历史。太阳系的结构及其未来的运动和发展,完全由太阳系里现有的星群来决定……这个结构的历史尽管可能很有趣,却对我们了解其行为、机制或未来发展没有什么作用"[1]。然而,社会群体则完全不同。历史主义者认为,社会群体永远不应该被理解为单纯的个人集合。社会群体不仅仅是其全体成员的总和,也不仅仅是在任何时刻其成员间存在的个人关系的总和。对于曼海姆这样的历史主义者来说,理解这一点至关重要:"所有社会群体都有自己的传统、自己的制度、自己的仪式。历史主义者声称,如果我们希望能理解和解释群体的现状,如果我们想要理解和解释它的未来发展,我们就必须研究这个群体的历史、传统和制度。"[2]因此,我们再次注意到历史主义的观点:要了解社会,我们就必须了解群体的历史。这就是为什么对于历史主义者来说,社会学只不过是理论史的一种形式——要了解任一特定历史时期的社会生活,就有必要从整体上审视社会群体的总体特征及其历史渊源。我们不应该仅仅考察任一时刻构成这个群体的个人,而应该把整个群体的

---

[1] Popper,1957/2005:16.

[2] Popper,1957/2005:16.

内部活动和性质作为研究主题。

第四，波普尔声称，纵观历史，从柏拉图到孔德、卢梭和哈贝马斯，这些历史主义者都一致主张，社会科学家应该采用一种方法论的本质主义——而不是方法论的唯名主义——的方式来了解社会。在前一节我们提到过波普尔对本质主义的反对，他声称，寻求特定学科的"本质"并使它们相互割裂，这样做是愚蠢的。然而，这些术语在当前的语境下需要进一步的解释。波普尔把方法论的本质主义理解为亚里士多德所创立的一种科学方法，它声称，为了解释某个东西，人们必须"渗入其本质"。波普尔认为，"方法论的本质主义者倾向于用'什么是物质？''什么是力量？'或'什么是正义？'（或者如我们之前讨论学科时所说的'什么是哲学？'或'什么是科学？'）这样的术语来表达科学问题。他们认为，对这些问题做有见解的回答，揭示这些术语的真实或基本含义，从而揭示它们所表示的本质的真实性质，这即使称不上是科学研究的主要任务，至少也是其必要前提"[1]。另一方面，方法论的唯名主义者则并不寻求这样的根本答案。相反，他们根据事物在一定条件下如何行为来设计他们的问题。从我们之前的讨论来看，很显然，历史主义者将方法论的唯名主义归咎于物理科学，而且他们理由充分。物理科学确实有着方法论唯名主义的强烈趋势。例如，物理科学并不企图定义光或引力的"本质"，而是观察这些事物在特定条件下的行为。历史主义者认为，这对于社会研究而言是不够的。为了理解社会生活，我们必须理解它的内在活动机制、结构、历史和起源。因此，我们必须做的不仅仅是观察其成员的行为，还必须深入其内部，以超越

① Popper,1957/2005:25.

对其表面行为的简单描述。我们必须寻求其本质。我们需要掌握群体文化内容，以及该文化在历史进程中的发展方式。

那么，综合考虑历史主义的这四个特征，为社会科学提供了一个普遍的方法论，这与波普尔所捍卫的方法论完全相反。这个方法论是本质主义的、整体论的，因为社会科学家应该设法理解整个社会群体的基本性质，而不是社会个体成员之间发生的特殊关系或相互作用。这瓦解了社会研究与社会史研究之间的区别；研究社会只不过是研究社会史而已。此外，尽管历史主义者反对自然主义的自负——后者认为有可能通过在特定历史时期观察到的行为来建立普遍的社会规律，但他们仍然坚持波普尔所认为的归纳法的最糟糕的方面，声称有可能揭示历史发展的总体规律，从而可以预言社会历史的长远未来和人类的命运。因此，波普尔在历史主义中同时辨认出了反自然主义和亲自然主义的学说，历史主义者反对方法论上的唯名主义、原子论、非历史主义，以及他们在物理科学的方法中所看到的观察和实验的首要地位，却至关重要地保留了自然科学方法中适合他们目的的其他方面，主要是社会科学可以并且应该推断出能够预测长远未来事件的一般社会（即历史）规律的观点。

然而，波普尔指出——许多读者应该已经注意到了，所有的历史主义者对科学方法的批评，实际上都是对波普尔试图削弱传统归纳法科学观的批评。这些批评代表了对社会理论中我们所谓的"科学至上主义"的批判。因此，对于波普尔来说，他们的基本立场（即在社会科学中使用物理科学的研究方法是不恰当的）的前提是他们对科学以及在社会研究中采用科学方法意味着什么有着根本上的误解。在波普尔看来，历史主义者的问题并不是他们认为归纳法模型不适用于社会研究（事实上，波普尔同意这个观点），而是他们从这一点上得出了错误的教训，并提出了一个错误的替代选项。要记住，他们的主张是，归纳法确实适用于物理和自然现象的研究，但不适用于社会现象的研究。因此，与逻辑实证主义者和其他人一样，历史主义者的任务是根据不同学科的不同主题和各自适用的方法，以波普尔反感的方式来划分各学科之间的界限。历史主义者无条件地接受物理科学中归纳法的至高地位；他们主张，自然科学家和社会科学家应该各行其是。波普尔当然不同意这个观点。他主张归纳法模型不是研究社会的适当方法，仅仅是因为他认为归纳法模型不是研究任何东西的适当方法。因此，他同意历史主义者的观点，即社会科学家应该抛弃归纳法模型，不是为了以历史主义取而代之，而是为了用更合乎逻辑的科学概念和科学方法来取代它。

波普尔捍卫的不是历史主义和科学主义，而是围绕他的批判理性主义概念建立的社会科学观，即牢牢扎根于他更广泛的认识论思想，强调思想的冲突、推理的易谬性，以及在严格的检验、批判和辩论的基础上建立的社会和政治生活的渐进式改革。它特有的原理与历史主义相反，如下：

（1）社会科学的主要目的是在认识论不确定的情况下，通过提出关于社会问题的理论，并将这些理论和其他理论应用于严格的反驳和检验过程，来确定社会问题并试图加以解决。社会科学家的任务不是对社会的未来历史发展作出长期的普遍预言，也不是通过诉诸不可证伪的社会和历史规律来证明社会和政治改革的合理性，亦不是像黑格尔等人一样去揭示"历史的终结"。因为没有任何历史发展规律可以从特定的观察推断得出，所以社会科学家的预言无法超出已经存在的知识总和所支持的预言。他们必须将他们的预言和理论建立在可用信息的基础上,因为这就是全部所有。人类的行为往往会导致意想不到的结果。出于善意的社会改革可能将产生预期之外的后果。政治活动可能会导致不可预见的事件和出乎意料的结论。因此,"理论社会科学的主要任务"不是预言人类发展的未来,而是"追踪有意识的人类行为产生的意外的社会影响"[①]。社会生活"不仅是对立群体(如阶级或国家)间的力量的较量,它是在一个或多或少有弹性或脆弱的制度和传统框架内的行动,它制造出……框架内许多不曾预见的反应,其中一些甚至可能是无法预见的"[②]。因此,社会科学中的预言与物理科学中的预言一样,只应该是短期的、有限的、可证伪的;历史主义者所沉迷的那种预言都不具有这样的特点,因此是不科学的,不能构成对知识的贡献。

（2）社会探究的适当对象并不是如黑格尔主义者和其他历史主义者所主张的那样,是历史规律或社会群体,而是可观察到的社会制度和安排,以及人类个体的行为和互动。因此,社会科学应该是"方法论的个人主义",而不是"方法论的集体主义"。社会应该被理解为个体的集合,个体在这个体系中的行动应该被认为是重要的。历史主义使个人服从于社会,它不关心个人行动者的具体行为,而是关心在任一时刻支配社会所有成员行动的一般社会规律。历史主义者远非强调个人按照他们的集体意志——他们公开承认的意图——去塑造社会的能力,而是提出了这样一个社会观,即个人的行为和思想被历史所扼杀,被他们无法控制、无力逃离的历史力量所决定。因此,历史主义者和

① Popper,1963/2007b:460.
② Popper,1945/2006b:105.

那些认为有可能在人类社会研究中推断出普遍规律的归纳法优越论者一样,陷入了同一个陷阱。

(3) 社会科学具有一个重要的实用功能,即通过单个社会科学家的努力——他们对社会问题和社会科学话语中普遍接受的理论采取了适当的批判理性主义态度,与他人就这些主题进行了批判性的讨论和辩论——可以为立法者提供以人性化、公正、符合个人自由的方式进行社会改革所需要的理论。社会科学为社会改革提供了指导。由于上文第(1)点提到的所有原因,改革必定是短期的、渐进的、零星的,而不是长期的、彻底的、理想化的。社会科学家不应该试图通过诉诸某个总体计划——来源于被揭示出来的关于社会和政治制度的真实本质或目的的知识——来一次性解决社会的所有问题。而是应该确认具体问题,并致力于通过一个猜想和反驳的过程来解决问题。通过这样一个过程,随着理论被提出、辩论、检验,并有可能在不断试错的过程中被否定,问题可以按零星的方式得到确认、考察、解决。因此,社会科学家的主要任务是确定现有社会和政治制度的目的,评估它们是否成功地实现了它们的目的,如果没有,则提出新的、大胆的替代安排。

(4) 社会科学应该是"方法论的唯名主义",而不是"方法论的本质主义"。社会科学家的任务不是追踪特定社会关系的历史渊源,也不是掌握特定社会的本质,而是找到真正的社会问题,研究如何解决这些问题。根据波普尔的更广泛的认识论,现有社会制度(以及对其进行辩护和解释的理论)的目的、合法性和有效性不可避免地具有推测性;政府或其他社会机构的角色可能会随着我们对世界和社会个体成员的理解的广泛变化而改变,因此,任何制度或安排都不可能永远合理。同样,没有一套

65

特别的社会制度可以合理地宣称自己属于某个预期的全人类的未来目标,支持特定安排和制度的论证(以及这些安排和制度本身)必须保持其推测性,并可能被经验或理论挑战而证伪。因此,社会科学的目的不是建立关于社会和政治的本质的宏大理论,不是寻求社会关系的起源,也不是寻求关于社会及其发展的本质的确定无疑的、无可辩驳的真理,而是根据所有与问题有关的知识(来源于所有不同"学科")总和检验那些提议的社会和政治理论,消除其中的错误。

概括而言,我们可以看到,波普尔对社会科学的观点来源于他关于认识论的更广泛的见解,即科学、社会科学和其他领域的知识以相同的方式、按照相同的逻辑发展。波普尔认同历史主义者的观点,即归纳法模型不适合社会研究,但从根本上不同意他们提出的替代方案。他认为历史主义者在寻求一种社会探究的新形式,主要关心的是通过确定历史规律(决定社会关系的性质和适当结构以及个人在其中的行动)、考察整个社会的文化,来预言人类的未来,是为了能够按照固定的计划或蓝图来构建社会。而波普尔则认为,历史主义的方法和归纳法都应该被他自己提出的方法——强调试错法、猜想和反驳、以消除社会及其问题的现有理论中的错误为指导进行零星的社会改革——所代替。波普尔认为在社会科学中,就像在物理科学中一样,其推动思想是我们可以从错误中学习。通过发现问题,提出解决方案,与那些和我们一样愿意倾听理性论证的人批判性地辩论这些问题,我们就可以找出现有理论中的不合逻辑和错误之处,也可以找出现有实践和制度中的问题;这样一来,我们也可以找到最好的办法,并通过零星的社会改革过程来发现和解决社会问题。

卡尔·波普尔

从社会科学到政治学

　　波普尔关于社会和政治制度的适当角色和责任的观点,代表了历史主义立场的反转,即对它所基于的所有规范、认识论和方法论基础的否定。请记住,历史主义者的目标是研究社会以揭示决定其性质和形态的历史发展规律。完成了这项任务之后,历史主义者就可以根据这些根本的历史规律来推断出社会的未来发展。一旦获得了足够的社会知识——关于其文化、深层的历史、主观交流和假想构成的复杂网络(这两者相结合创造了社会整体)的知识——历史主义者就有可能弄清社会是如何走到现在这一步,以及将要走向哪里。因此,发展的历史规律不仅为历史主义者提供了解过去的钥匙,还提供了预言未来所必需的工具。历史主义者通过诉诸过去的实例和事件,了解人类的本质以及人类所处的特定社会和历史背景,就认为可以相对确定地预言政治提议和决策的后果。此外,确定是什么带来了新的社会和历史时期——也就是说需要什么样的社会、政治、经济和法律条件来实现社会从一个时期向另一个时期的转移——历史主义者就觉得能够使用这些知识为社会和政治改革提供正当的理由。一旦了解到社会是按照客观的历史规律在发展,而且历史需要一定的条件才能使社会进入下一个阶段,那么,显然,社会、经济和政治变革就应该设计为能创造条件有助于迎接新时代,或保护社会不受这种变化的影响。因此,社会改革被历史主义者视为一种工具,利用它可以使社会为新时代的诞生做好准备,或使社会免于进入更糟糕的新状态。

那么，重要的是，波普尔认为，历史主义政治学从根本上是乌托邦式的和精英主义的。称其为乌托邦是因为历史主义社会科学不仅仅是了解和解释历史规律的被动过程，它既主动又有目的，它体现了一种探索的愿望，不仅想要发现社会在过去是什么样的，还要发现它正走向何处，更重要的是，它应该前进的方向以及如何到达那里。因此，历史主义要求，"在采取任何实际行动之前，我们必须确定我们的最终政治目标，即理想国家。只有当这个最终目标确定了下来——至少有了雏形，只有当我们拥有了像我们的目标社会的蓝图这样的东西，只有这个时候，我们才能考虑实现这个目标的最佳方法和手段，才能考虑去制定一个理性行动的计划"[①]。社会工程，或旨在解决社会和政治问题的社会改革过程，因此是一个整体的、集体主义的事业，其目标正是全面的社会重整，以便于产生或保护一个符合历史规律的理想化的政治形式。社会工程的乌托邦形式要求我们在进行社会改革之前知道我们努力的目标。要实施一项政策或一系列改革，却不知道为什么要这样做，也不知道想要实现什么样的结果，这是不理性的做法。因此我们要弄清楚我们想要的是什么样的社会和政治，然后再从事那些有助于产生这样的社会和政治的活动（由历史发展规律所决定）。

因此，乌托邦社会工程"建议对社会进行整体重建"，旨在为我们的社会和政治安排带来彻底和长远的变化，以符合我们关于全人类应该如何生活及社会应该是什么样的一个遥远的理想化的概念。然而，波普尔认为，这样的观点被证明是不合逻辑的。因为我们无法以历史主义者相信可以的方式，确切地预测

① Popper，1945/2006a：167.

我们的行动或决策的后果。这也是因为推理是易错的,我们可能认为我们可以为实现某个未来社会提供一个成功的计划,我们可以预见在这个过程中一切潜在的问题,但是我们不能。我们在上一节第(1)点看到,我们的决策的实际和长期后果"由于我们的经验有限而难以计算"。历史主义者"声称为整个社会作出理性的计划",但是"我们没有任何事实性的知识,而这些知识是实现如此雄心勃勃的声明所必需的。由于我们在这类规划方面的实践经验不足,而对事实的认识必须以经验为基础,因此我们无法掌握这些知识。在目前,大规模工程所必需的社会学知识根本就不存在"①。波普尔认为,我们可以(而且应该)预先规划一个社会应该如何,然后按照这个计划来实施社会改革,这种想法是错误的。"只有少数社会制度是有意识地设计的,而绝大多数是作为人类行为的无意的结果而'产生'的……(而且)我们有意识地成功设计的少数制度中的大部分……都并未按照计划得以实施……这是因为刻意的创造产生了意想不到的社会影响"②。因此,如我们在上一节所讲,了解社会,以便对其未来进行合理的规划和预测,这不应该被视为社会科学的重要任务;相反,鉴于这一过程最终注定要失败,社会科学的任务应该是"研究社会事物的不易处理性、回弹性或脆弱性,以及对我们企图对其进行塑造所产生的影响的抵制"③。我们之所以无法确切地预言我们决策的后果,或者我们应该以什么样的长期社会和政治条件为目标,正是因为我们不可能从目前的情况或事件中推断出这些东西。我们之所以不能根据过去来计划未来,我们之

① Popper,1945/2006a:171.

② Popper,1945/2006b:103.

③ Popper,1945/2006b:104.

所以不能通过诉诸一个理想化的未来(通过适当地把握历史发展规律可以实现)来证明社会和政治改革的合理性,是因为这样的途径要求采用归纳法,而这正是波普尔认为错误和不合逻辑的方法:它要求过多的推理。鉴于归纳法存在的问题,以及理性无法为我们的行动和举措的未来长期后果提供绝对确定的认识,波普尔认为,我们最好的做法就是承认乌托邦思想不能提供历史主义者所要求的蓝图或确定性,而采用他的零星的社会工程观点来代替,零星的社会工程不要求对历史规律进行归纳推理,而是来源于我们对于世界的经验——尽管是短暂的、有限的——并符合他关于知识发展的更广泛的认识论观点。

我们将在本章稍后和下一章详细讨论零星社会工程。在此之前,讨论一下波普尔对历史主义政治学的第二点批评——精英主义的——十分重要。波普尔认为,历史主义的政治学研究方法是精英主义的,因为它预先设定权力应该掌握在那些能够看到和了解发展规律的人的手中,因此也就是能够预知人类未来、社会和政治决策的必然结果以及如何最好地建立理想国家的人的手中。波普尔认为,这就是对集中计划的辩护,对权力统一的辩护,那些掌握了必需的知识以实现社会和政治改革来创造新的历史时期的人们手中才握有权力。他说,这个论点在历史上已经被独裁者和暴君所利用,他们无视人们表达出来的意愿,压迫人们,残酷对待人们,并声称这么做是为了人们自己的利益,是为了追求一个只有暴君才能看到或了解的目标。在这个主张中我们可以看到前面提起的观点,即历史主义体现了"选民"的概念。波普尔认为,历史主义的所有形式都具有这样的特征,即关于历史(以及如何确保历史以正确的方式发展)的知识并不属于每个人,而仅仅属于少数人。由于政治权力应该只属于那些拥有这种知识的人，所以历史主义就代表了支持权力集中在少数人手里的论点，并为这些少数人做任何他们想做的事提供了正当的理由，这些人始终声称那些只有他们才能了解的目标证明了他们行为的合理性，即使其他人拒绝同意，他们的观点和想法也是正确的。

此外，波普尔认为，作为历史主义政治学内核的精英主义和乌托邦思想协力扼杀了自由表达、自由思想和对当权者的批评。他说，其原因是，这种属于历史主义政治学的长期的、大规模的、深入的社会改革，会"给很多人在相当长的时期内带来很大的不便。因此，乌托邦的工程师将不得不对众多的抱怨听而不闻；事实上，打压不合理的反对意见将是他的一部分任务……但是在这样做的同时，他必然也会压制合理的批评"①。那些能够获得历史所蕴含的特殊信息的人，不仅能够确定应该做什么、不应该做什么，而且还有权决定什么是合理的批评、什么是不合理的批评。蒙昧的大多数人得不到这种特殊信息，就几乎没有理由批评统治者的行为，或就社会和政治制度的适当目的进行有意义的辩论，或判断其统治者的合法性或非法性。他们根本不具备必要的知识作出这些判断，或就国家应该做些什么或者应该实现什么样的目标进行有意义的辩论。

因此，对于波普尔来说，历史主义在认识论上是错误的，在规范上是令人反感的。它以错误的认识论假设——推断历史发展规律是有可能的——为前提；说它在规范上令人反感，是因为它诉诸这些历史规律，目的是为知晓（仅有他们知晓）秘密信息的领导者对一般大众的压迫进行辩护。而且，由于执政的精英

---

① Popper, 1945/2006a:169.

分子所致力的任何目标都必定是长期的,因此在目前统治者或独裁者有生之年是不可能实现的,所以独裁者的继任者是被任命的,而不是被选举出来的,这一点至关重要。举行自由公正的选举,允许公众决定谁来统治他们,很可能导致选举出来的统治者没有也无法拥有必要的知识来进行管理,从而建立理想国家。因此,民主选举被否决,代之以一个允许统治精英任命其继任者,从而使他们不可动摇的统治地位万代长存的制度。

波普尔因此认为,历史主义为极权主义提供了哲学上的理由,因为它将不受限制的终极权力交到了统治精英的手中,他们无需为了任何原因向任何人证明自己的合法性。这使得民主政治成了不可能,因为它剥夺了公众形成自己的政治判断所需的必要资源,剥夺了他们选举或者撤销统治者所必需的民主制度或机制。它夺走了公众批评统治者的能力。而且,更重要的是它使个人的利益服从于整个社会的利益。所有这些东西都在纳粹主义、法西斯主义中得到了现代的表达,因此他认为历史主义为世界历史上一些最邪恶、最压迫的政权提供了规范和哲学的基础。这些当然是强有力的主张。但是,使得它们更加有力,并使得《开放社会及其敌人》如此具有爆炸性和争议性的,却是他在主张了历史主义中存在现代极权主义的种子之后,进而主张历史主义的种子存在于一些历史上最受尊敬、最有名望的人物的著作之中。波普尔把现代极权主义的兴起归咎于一批来自各个领域的思想家,他们到当时为止一直被公认是西方社会和政治思想发展中最重要、最高尚的声音。那么他是如何得出这样的结论呢?

虽然波普尔辨认出密尔、孔德和卢梭的历史主义倾向,他却用《开放社会及其敌人》的大部分篇幅通过柏拉图、黑格尔等人的著作来追溯历史主义——以及现代极权主义——的发展。他认为,极权主义最早的化身存在于古希腊哲学,特别是赫西奥德(Hesiod)的思想中,赫西奥德"利用了历史发展的一般趋势或倾向的观点"[①]。他认为,这种倾向是一种物质上和道德上的堕落。他在另一位古希腊哲学家赫拉克利特(Heraclitus)的著作中也辨认出了这一点,赫拉克利特声称世界不是静止的(这是当时的主流观点),而是以不断变化为特征。重要的是,赫拉克利特的历史变化观包含了一个重要的观点,即世界不仅处于一种持续变化的状态,而且这种变化是根据某个"不可阻挡、不可避免的命运法则"发生的,这个观点后来成为所有历史主义思想的特征。[②]

在波普尔看来,这个观点被柏拉图进行了最为充分和明确的表达。波普尔认为,柏拉图的世界观融合了赫西奥德和赫拉克利特的思想元素,因为他认为世界具有变化的特征,而且这种变化带来了道德和物质上的堕落。柏拉图认为,社会不是静止的。社会在变化,在变化中走向衰败和堕落。因此,他认为公正国家的主要任务是阻止一切变化,从而保护政体免于堕落腐化。波普尔对柏拉图关于正义以及公正、合法的领导者应该具有的品质的观点进行了大篇幅的慷慨激昂的解构,他认为柏拉图的政治观旨在不惜一切代价停止历史发展,维护安定和团结。波普尔宣称,理解这一点的关键是柏拉图的形式理论。柏拉图认为,所有现有的世界现象都有一个理想形式,这个理想形式在现实世界中是无法真正或完全实现的。任何现存的物理对象,都

---

① Popper,1945/2006a:7.
② Popper,1945/2006a:10.

只是这些事物的形式的有缺陷的物质体现,而这些形式在某个理想化的过去是存在的。因此,任何现存的国家都只是存在于理想化的、纯朴的、过去的国家形式的一个不完美的副本。所以,在柏拉图看来,一切事物的历史发展,只不过是它们远离理想和完美形式(存在于过去)而走向一个更腐败、有缺陷的形式的一个持续过程。

波普尔继续写道,对于柏拉图来说,公正国家的根本特征是团结与和平。国家形式是统一和谐的,不受既得利益或冲突的影响。统治政权的形式可以保证所有成员的这种团结。因此,公正国家是一个尽可能统一和谐,尽可能不受内部冲突的影响,并由这样的政治领袖来进行统治的国家:他们具备必要的力量和知识,能确保社会和政治条件尽可能与其形式相同——完美、统一、不变。柏拉图很清楚,任何社会可能遭受的最糟糕的命运就是它允许任何不团结的产生。在他关于国家历史的概述中充分地证明了这一点,在其中他宣称(波普尔认为这种举动是所有历史主义者的特征)他已经确认了一系列不同的社会和政治时期,柏拉图认为这些时期是由于在本来和谐的国家引入了不和谐的倾向和不团结的事件而产生的。柏拉图认为,最公正的国家是君主制国家,在其中政治权力由"最睿智、最像神的人"所掌控。① 然而,如果不精心保护,这样的国家势必会由于个人野心和贪图权力而堕落为荣誉政治——由那些追求名望的贵族来统治。当一些社会成员变得嫉妒有权者,他们就试图通过获取经济和社会资源来获得权力和荣誉,统治能力就变得与才智无关,而与财富相关。直到一段时间后,荣誉政治崩溃变为寡头政治,

---

① Popper,1945/2006a;40.

即富人通过一项法律,使得"拥有财产达不到规定数额的任何人都不能从事公职"①。寡头政治反过来又加剧了贫富之间的冲突和敌意,最终导致两个阶级之间的内战爆发。穷人在数量上超过富人,他们推翻了富有的压迫者,平等地分配权力,进入了民主时期。然而,这个民主统治的时期是短暂的,一旦一个"知道如何利用民主国家内的贫富阶级敌对,并成功建立起一个自己的卫队或私人军队的受欢迎的领袖"出现,这个民主统治时期就会被暴政所取代。"那些刚开始为他欢呼,视他为自由卫士的人们,很快就被奴役;接着他们必须为他而战,在'一场又一场他必定会挑起的战争中……因为他必须让人们感到他们需要一个将军'。"②国家的表现从最公正到最卑鄙的这个历史过程中的每一个新阶段,都是由于其成员破坏政府稳定的倾向、动机和情绪而产生的。贪婪、既得利益、情绪、激情,这些东西使国家动荡摇摆,因此,要实现公正,就需要对这些加以防范。故而,柏拉图认为,国家应该清除那些会激化这些具有破坏性的激情和倾向的东西。所以,政治统治者的任务就是尽可能地通过平息内部不同意见的纷争,建立严格的劳动分工,将权力集中在统治精英手中——这些精英经过严格的教导和培训,以能够进行有效的统治(不关心他们的个人发展或志向)——来消除社会变革和不团结的可能性。

波普尔认为,柏拉图主张公正国家应该防止不和谐,这使他能够以"阻止变化"为理由来为粗暴侵犯个人自由进行辩护,他把公正国家描绘成具有道德义务侵入人们生活的方方面面,以

① Popper,1945/2006a:42.
② Popper,1945/2006a:44.

便消除潜在的不团结和不稳定的根源。这也使他能够为将所有政治权力集中在那些能够看到形式的王国（因此也就能看到国家形式）的人的手中进行辩护。因为柏拉图认为不是每个人都有能力知道理想国家应该是什么样的。他特别论述道，只有能够看到和理解国家形式的哲学家精英阶层才应该拥有政治权力。此外，理解理想国家的本质所必需的那些品质可以经由社会和政治生活而得到塑造，但若是要灌输给那些生来就没有的人则是不可能的。因此，统治能力是与生俱来的，生来就具有能洞察国家形式的智慧和眼光的人应该掌握权力；那些不是生来就具有这种见识的人则不应该掌握权力。

　　对于波普尔来说，柏拉图的国家形式代表了典型的封闭社会，代表了对一个真正公正的（即开放的）社会得以建立的所有原则和理念基础的摧毁。它的特点是统治精英——被定义为一个种族——他们行使政治权力的能力是由出身决定的。它代表着为了保持群体的稳定而对个人的自由思想和主张进行广泛和深刻的压制，通过将国家内部所有人生活的方方面面进行政治化，以及彻底的、在政治上强制实行劳动分工来消除公私之间的差别。柏拉图认为，当人们被限制在出生时就被赋予的角色里，被劝阻为了任何理由去超越自己角色限定的范围进行思考，被剥夺参与管理自己的国家或自己生活的权利，唯恐他们会造成不和谐、不团结或变化，这样的国家运转得最好。人们应该做他们天生就该做的事：天生有修鞋技能的人应该修鞋，天生有造船技能的人应该造船，天生有统治才能的人应该统治国家。民主是一种腐败、低质的政治形式，其中一个原因就是它把权力交给那些不具有能适当行使权力（即追求只有某些人才能看到的形式的王国中的目标）的技能或知识的人的手中。因此，波普尔在柏拉图身上看到了这样的主张,即为了社会整体的利益,个人不要试图改善自己,或试图超越他们在社会中被规定的角色范围,或学习新的东西,以免他们开始提问题、质疑权威、不满足于服从他们的监管人——优等种族,这是至关重要的。

波普尔认为,在这一切中,柏拉图表现出了他是自由和个人的敌人,因此也是建立在自由主义原则基础上的开放社会的敌人。柏拉图否认所有个人凭借其基本的人性,在某种意义上都是平等的,同等地具有理性思考和理性行动的能力。他否认人们应该按照他们自己考虑过并认为值得的目标和价值观——而不是按照被自己的出身(或者更确切地说,被那些能够确定人们有哪些技能、没有哪些技能的少数当权者)强加给他们的目标——来自由生活。他否认存在任何应该被视为超出国家的能力范围之外的人类生活领域,我们的目标、我们的理想、我们的思想本身都必须为了更大的利益而受到控制。他否认个人可以通过自由讨论和民主辩论来形成对道德或政治问题的恰当的共同回应;相反,这种问题的答案存在于理想化的过去,由那些有能力去揭示、去发现的人揭示和发现,然后传达给那些愚昧无知、毫无头绪的人。他否认政治领袖获得权力应该征得人们的同意,因此,他否认领袖必须以他们向其负责的人们认为适当的、清楚明了的方式来证明他们行为的合理性;相反,他们从一个只有他们才知晓的理想的社会愿景获取权力。他还否认自由主义的主要观点,即国家应该尽可能地支持所有个人按自己的方式过自己的生活的愿望,国家管理的方式必须符合并保护所有个人追求自己自由选择的目标的能力,不给予强制或约束;相反,他认为国家应该始终保持警惕,防备个人产生自己的思想、追求自己的目标、质疑统治者,或做任何事情扰乱由上至下强加给他们的秩序与和谐。

从这个观点来看,柏拉图关于理想国家的概念,就是极权主义——一个少数人在军队的协助下对大多数人实施完全控制的国家,并且通过诉诸一个只有他们才能看见,因此只有他们才能实现的神话般的、对全人类有益的未来,为他们压迫民众、虐待民众寻找正当理由。按此理解,柏拉图的理想王国确实与斯大林的苏联共产主义国家有着深刻的相似之处:拆散家庭,否定私有财产(因为它可能引发冲突),以维护社会和谐为名压制艺术,为压制异见对个人私生活实施政治化,反对民主或自治的观念,以共同稳定为名剥夺个人自由,特选出来的精英恒久不变、无所不在、专制独裁地行使权力——这些精英的合法性并非来自民主,而是来自一个只有这些精英才能看到或理解的乌托邦目标。在波普尔看来,柏拉图的理想王国所表现出的不过是一个在种族上优越的少数群体(被灌输、洗脑,被清除了所有的个性,为了让他们不关心个人地位地进行统治)对在种族上劣等的民众(被剥夺了教育或资源,无法挑战或质疑现状)进行统治的制度。

波普尔明确地将柏拉图的公正概念与现代极权主义联系起来。他认为,柏拉图著作中呈现的理想国家的观点,代表了苏联共产主义、意大利法西斯主义和德国纳粹主义等现代极权主义直接的哲学先驱。我们确实可以看到它具有历史主义的所有印记(就其政治学和社会学而言)。柏拉图的社会学是集体主义的、整体性的,因为他认为社会应该被视为不仅仅是个体的集合,而是一个有机的整体;他的方法是本质主义的,因为他认为在最后确定应该如何构建社会之前,掌握社会的本质是至关重要的;他的公正观点的前提条件是历史是按照由可辨认的社会和政治条件所引发的不连续的时期或时代来发展的。

这些是柏拉图与历史上许多历史主义学者所共有的观点，但最为明显的是黑格尔的唯心主义著作。然而，尽管波普尔认为柏拉图的历史主义是悲观的——因为它把历史发展描述为从社会和谐（因而公正）走向不和谐（不公正）的过程，波普尔却把黑格尔的历史主义描述为乐观的。黑格尔认为，历史按照固定的发展规律在一系列时期或时代中发展，但是与柏拉图不同，黑格尔认为社会发展的每一个阶段都代表了人类社会和政治关系的演变过程中积极的一步。黑格尔和柏拉图、亚里士多德一样，采取了一种方法论的本质主义方法来了解社会和国家；也就是说，黑格尔和柏拉图、亚里士多德都认为掌握国家的本质，弄清国家在过去是如何发展起来的，而未来将如何发展，是至关重要的。和亚里士多德一样，黑格尔也认为自然现象是向着一个最终原因或终极目的发展的。波普尔认为，黑格尔对历史发展的看法比柏拉图更为乐观，是因为他理解国家的理想形式存在于世界上的国家的每一个历史化身的本质中，而不是存在于某个理想化的过去。因此，在黑格尔看来，历史的不断发展进一步揭示了每一个连续的历史时期所隐藏的或潜在的本质（因此也揭示了国家的理想形式），因而使人类更接近于将其实现；它并没有如柏拉图所认为的使人类远离它。因此黑格尔的历史主义是乐观的，因为隐藏在一切现象（包括国家）内的本质是"自我运动的；它们是自我发展的，或者用更时髦的术语来说，是'正在显现的''自我创造的'。它们朝着亚里士多德式的'目的因'自我推进，或者如黑格尔所说，走向一个'本身就是自我了解和自我实现的原因'"①。因此，黑格尔持有与赫拉克利特和柏拉图相同

①　Popper,1945/2006b:40.

的观点,即世界处于不断变化的状态,但与他们不同的是,黑格尔认为这是一件好事;黑格尔认为不断变化的世界代表了一个"'自然发生的'或'创造性进化'的状态;它的每一个阶段都包含了前面的那些阶段,它们都是它的起源;每个阶段都取代了以前的所有阶段,一步步接近完美。因此,发展的总体规律就是进步的总体规律"①;在这个过程中通过思想的辩证冲突系统地揭示了万物的本质。

尽管黑格尔的历史主义具有乐观的力量,但波普尔认为黑格尔的哲学不过是让"现代极权主义迅速发展的肥料"②。他认为其原因在于,我们在黑格尔的思想中发现了后来被全世界的极权主义独裁者利用来把权力集中在一个无所不能的国家手中的所有论证和哲学假想。在波普尔清楚地视为故意显得愚钝、充斥着术语的文章背后,黑格尔的历史理论只不过是一个关于民族主义兴起的故事,是国家走向极权主义的历程。他认为,黑格尔与柏拉图一样,把国家看作是一个有机体,而且黑格尔"追随了卢梭,卢梭为国家提供了一个'普遍意志',而黑格尔为其提供了一个有意识的思想实质,即'理性'或'精神'。这种精神……同时也是形成国家的集体主义的民族精神。"③因此,要了解国家,我们就必须了解它的本质或精神,要做到这一点,我们就必须了解它的历史。"民族的精神决定了它的历史命运;每一个希望'出现并存在'的民族必须通过登上'历史舞台',即通过与其他民族作战,来宣称其个性或灵魂;战争的目标就是统治

卡尔·波普尔

---

① Popper,1945/2006b:40.

② Popper,1945/2006b:63.

③ Popper,1945/2006b:41.

世界。"①

因此,波普尔在黑格尔的思想中辨认出了这样的观点,即历史是按照总体发展规律发展的,历史的根本推动者——其"选民"——就是民族。历史就是民族从粗野、无法律的乌合之众发展成为一个在国家之下的积极的、军事化的统一整体。因此,历史就是走向单一民族国家的进程,其理想就是成为无所不能的国家。这个理想通过意志和想象的辩证式跳跃,缓慢但确定无疑地在每一个依次出现的历史时代的本质内体现,直到最终被完全揭示出来,这时历史发展就终止了。因此,在黑格尔的思想中,我们看到了这样的主张:"民族国家是……地球上的绝对权力",而且,就像在柏拉图的著作中一样,我们可以看到封闭社会战胜了开放社会之后的狂喜。

波普尔认为,根据其核心假设,像海克尔这样的黑格尔门徒相对而言比较容易使用黑格尔主义为基于种族的特别可憎的民族主义形式辩护。黑格尔把民族国家提升为自由的最纯粹表现形式,他主张"国家是……人们生活中所有具体元素的基础和中心,是艺术、法律、道德、宗教和科学的基础和中心",在这些观点中,波普尔看到了对极权主义国家的辩护,极权主义国家的"力量必须以其全部的功能渗透和控制人们的整个生活"②。因此,黑格尔的哲学以其本质主义、整体主义、集体主义的思想,以及个人的自由和利益服从于整体利益、服从于无法阻挡的历史步伐,体现了历史主义所有最恶劣的极端思想。黑格尔对人的热情和意志、对流血和战争极为重视,在波普尔看来,黑格尔是在

---

① Popper,1945/2006b:41.

② Popper,1945/2006b:68,引用黑格尔的论述。

世界上释放出民族主义和部落主义的毁灭性能量的第一人，为此后的暴君和独裁者提供了他们所需要的哲学来源，以便为他们诉诸部落政治的腐败堕落的做法进行辩护，以便他们回避以自由、平等、理性和个性为特征的开放社会，他应该对此负责。

在波普尔关于马克思的论述中我们也看到了类似的问题。尽管波普尔对马克思的敬重远远高于对黑格尔（或者说似乎也高于对柏拉图的敬重），柏拉图和黑格尔坚信政治学由历史发展规律驱动并塑造，他们却仍然认为历史进程可以被人为干预所改变或引导。例如，柏拉图确认了导致国家走向不公正的原因，然后概述了国家成员可以阻止这个过程的所有不同方式。同样，黑格尔的辩证法也认为国家走向不公正是受到了国家成员的推动——他们的思想、激情、冲突——因此，对他来说，历史是人类思想以及塑造了这些思想的民族传统的发展的故事。然而，对于马克思来说，人类几乎无法影响历史的发展。马克思对黑格尔唯心主义的颠覆，将历史发展规律从人类手中完全夺走，并把它们放入更广泛的、非个人化的经济力量之中。他赞成社会和历史的决定论：

> 如果要有社会科学，以及相应地要有历史预言，那么历史的主要进程就必须是预先设定的，善意和理性都没有权力改变它。留给我们的合理干预方式，就仅有通过历史预言，确定即将到来的发展道路，并消除道路上的障碍。[①]

正如马克思自己在《资本论》（*Das Kapital*）中所说，当"社会发现了决定自己运动方向的自然规律后……即使到那个时候，它既不能超越它的演变的自然阶段，也不能把这些阶段从世

①　Popper，1945/2006b：94.

界上一笔勾销。但是它可以做的很多；它可以缩短和减轻它的阵痛"[1]。

因此，在马克思看来，社会科学家和社会工程师的任务是明确的。社会科学家应该致力于确定资本主义瓦解并被共产主义所取代的确切的社会和经济条件，而社会工程师应该致力于改革社会，以加速这种瓦解。如我们前面所示，这要求社会科学家和社会工程师采取一种集体主义和整体主义的方法来了解社会，这种方法的主要目标是把社会（和政治制度）根据经济"基础"的发展而演变的各种方式拼合到一起。马克思亲自提供了这个过程的一个详细草图，最为人所知的是在他的《政治经济学批判序言》(*Preface to a Contribution to the Critique of Political Economy*)中。尽管自由主义者认为个人意识塑造和决定了社会、政治和经济安排的特征，众所周知的是，马克思却认为恰恰相反，是一个人所处的社会、政治和（最重要的是）经济条件塑造和决定了他的意识（他指的是一个人的观念、偏好和价值观，对世界的理解，对自己在世界中所处的位置的理解）。因此，在马克思看来，人的意识与我们所处的特定的社会和历史环境紧密联系，并由其决定。这就是为什么我们会接受资本主义，尽管它对我们的生活和人性都有着毁灭性的后果。我们通过我们所处的社会关系网络，来理解世界，理解我们的想法、我们的抱负和承诺，这些反过来又由经济力量所决定。因此，资本主义制度本身就决定了关于世界我们知道什么、不知道什么，因而扼杀了对它的批评；资本主义剥夺了我们的人性，使我们脱离了那些使我们成其为人的东西，使我们的生产劳动力商品化，鼓励我

① Popper,1945/2006b;94.

们把自己看作是彼此竞争的孤立个体——每一个都有自己的利益、偏好和"权利"——而不是共有的社区里相互合作的成员。通过这样的方式,资本主义就使得我们无法获得与环境之间必需的关键距离,以便对环境进行有意义的反思或批评。因此,马克思主义社会工程师的任务就是帮助鼓励这种环境,使人们能够渐渐认识到资本主义制度残酷对待他们、破坏他们人性的多种多样的方式。资本主义的持续发展(用黑格尔的话来说)将揭示其本质内的各种矛盾,它的缺陷将在身处其中的人看来更为明显。当这些矛盾变得如此明显以至于难以维持,如此不公正以至于不合情理,人们就会起来试图改变这个制度,从而开创一个共产主义的新历史时期。那么,对马克思来说,政治和社会行为就起着一定的作用,但却是非常有限的作用,仅限于建立条件使得工人阶级可以全面理解其受压迫的程度,并力图有所行动。

因此,对于波普尔来说,马克思主张"决定人的社会存在的不是人的意识——相反,决定人的意识的是人的社会存在",这代表了对心理主义的一个重要批判(波普尔对此极为称赞),而且还支持了"一种社会理论"①,以及人类(和政治学)面对自己无力控制的、势不可挡的历史力量时的无能为力。它鼓励我们去认为我们的观点和想法并不是我们自己的,不仅我们的行为还有我们的思想都是由别人或者由历史本身决定的。它不仅否认个人自由行动或者根据自己的世界观改变他们所生活的社会和政治世界的能力,它还提出人们可能拥有的最深刻、最个人的想法(例如,他们的自我意识、爱、恐惧、希望、志向)是由历史,特别是历史发展规律所决定的。个人不可能把自己的意志施加于

① Popper,1963/2007b;eg.165.

社会,从而带来变化,因为他们的意志的内容正是由他们试图改变的社会、政治和经济关系决定的。他们所能做的只能是等到他们所处的经济条件发展到一定的程度,使得资本主义制度固有的内在矛盾被揭示出来;只有这个时候,当时机成熟,人类才能像新的占主导地位的经济条件所要求的那样,起来迎接新的社会和政治制度。那么,"一种社会理论"所暗示的就是,人们不能形成自己真实的意见,而是受到强大的个人和群体的设计的摆布。波普尔认为,这个观点使得个人在历史进程中不受关注,并且它使得马克思否认或忽视个人所表现出来的偏好。任何一个不同意马克思的哲学观的人都可以被轻易指责为有"错误意识"。事实上,他们不同意马克思的观点这个事实被视为证明了,而不是削弱了马克思的观点,而且仅仅被视为证明了资本主义制度有能力愚弄人们,让人们误以为一切都很好。通过这些论述,就可以相当简单地证明政治行动的合理性,即只要人们能从资本主义意识形态的禁锢中摆脱出来,这就是他们愿意要的东西,而不是他们实际声称想要的东西。

波普尔对马克思哲学的认识在此我们无法全部提及。我们只需要说他认为马克思比其他人走得更远,马克思的核心主张:(a)通过揭示历史发展的总体规律来预言社会的未来发展是可能的和恰当的;(b)为了了解个人,我们必须首先了解个人所在的社会整体(阶级、社会、民族、文化等),因此社会科学应该是方法论的集体主义;(c)为了了解社会(以及其中的个人),我们需要掌握社会整体的基本性质或结构(即由持续发展的经济力量所决定的),因此,我们需要采取一种方法论的本质主义的方法;(d)根据社会和政治改革是否有助于实现人类注定的命运(人们对此可能表示支持,也可能不会)来证明社会和政治改革是否合理,这是可能的和恰当的;(e)在约束个人、扼杀个人对自己身处的世界形成自己判断的能力、决定个人的所有思想和行动的客观的总体发展规律面前,个人是无能为力的。

开 放 社 会

波普尔认为,历史主义的社会和政治思想产生了一个彻底可憎、堕落、压迫的国家的理论,代表着对封闭社会的辩护。他还认为,它源于一个千疮百孔的方法论和错误的认识论。因此,他认为,我们需要反对历史主义核心的规范和认识论思想,代之以一种以他更广泛的认识论思想为前提并与之相容的政治学形式。一旦我们承认没有任何群体或个人(无论是科学家、社会科学家还是政治领袖)可以声称自己知道真理,我们就必须承认,没有任何个人、制度或社会实践可以被认为是永远正确的、无可置疑的。没有永远正确的真理,那么就应该任由个人自己去弄清楚政治制度应该担任什么样的角色,应该实施什么样的公共政策,政治学的目的是什么。正如科学不应该被理解为对伟大真理或实证的追求,而是通过消除现有理论中存在的错误来解决问题,政治学也不应该被理解为对伟大真理或理想的追求,而是通过消除社会和政治制度所造成的,或体现在社会和政治制度中的错误,来消除困扰社会的社会问题。因此,波普尔赞成他所谓的"消极功利主义",即社会科学和政治学的要务不是增加人们的快乐或幸福,而是使损害和痛苦减到最小,其方法是辨别这种损害的来源,并以零星的方式对其进行改革。这对于设计社会和政治制度以及公共政策都是适用的。

根据波普尔对消极功利主义的承诺和对乌托邦主义的否定,社会和政治制度不应该设计为使个人统治者或精英有能力追求某种理想的利益,而应该设计为防止他们"造成太多损害"[①]的制度。也就是说,开放社会的法律框架,应被视为一套"保护性制度",而非一套使统治者在任何时候都能行使其意志的规则。因此,国家干预个人的社会和经济生活有时是必要的,但是这些干预只能由旨在保护个人(和他们的自由)的制度来执行,而且这些制度由于知识、经验和批评的累积,以零星的方式逐渐发展,在这种情况下,这些干预才是合理的。如果它们只是某个统治者意志的产物,那么就是不合理的。因此,波普尔的消极功利主义及批判理性主义所支持的制度设计原则,其核心理念就是支持零星社会工程,反对剧变。改革可以是具体而持久的,但是改革必须源于对这些问题的认识:在过去是什么起到了作用,什么没有起到作用,是什么导致了我们走到了现在。我们实现长期目标的方式(以及这些目标本身)必须要根据可能存在的所有反面的论点来经受批评,甚至可能是否定。那么制度的重点就是要通过支持重要的个人自由,培养人们可以在其中参与进行民主对话的环境,来对领导者的权力进行必要的控制,并消除激进的(因此也是不负责任的)的剧变的可能性。除了保护公民个人的自由,保护社会免遭不负责任的变化之外,波普尔认为他的方法还有另一个好处,即法律框架"可以被个人公民所了解和理解"。事实上,他觉得,这个制度"应该被设计得非常容易理解。它的功能是可以预测的。它将一种确定性和安全感带入社会生活……与此相反,个人干预的方式必定在社会生活中引

① Popper,1945/2006b:142.

波普尔的思想

入一种不断增长的不可预测性,会产生社会生活不合理、不安全的感觉"①。

在政治学方面,波普尔的消极功利主义代表了对任何诉诸长远未来利益为自身辩护的理论的反对,反过来强调了对具体社会问题的零星式的确认和解决。他认为,迄今为止,我们所确认的"可以通过社会合作予以纠正或减轻"的最明显的社会弊病包括"贫穷、失业及类似形式的社会不安定、疾病和痛苦、刑罚暴行、奴役和其他形式的农奴制、宗教和种族形式的歧视、缺乏教育机会、严格的阶级差异以及战争"②。开放社会的制度其责任正是以批判理性主义的精神,以符合波普尔关于认识论、知识增长、反激进主义、经验重要性的更广泛的主张的方式,来解决这些问题。

因此,政策和制度都不应该按照仅有少数选民能看到的标准来衡量,而应该根据更为程序化的短期标准,如特定的制度或政策是否起到应有的作用,或者目前正在着手解决的社会问题是否正确,并且是否在以最有效的方式得到解决来衡量。波普尔认为,政治学的要务不是制定不可持续的蓝图或理想社会的梦想,而是要确认当前社会面临的社会、政治和经济问题,寻求有效、合理和渐进的解决方案。他再次重申,社会工程应该是零星式的而不是乌托邦式的,应该基于关于政治优先次序、制度应该实现的目标,以及这些制度本身是否可以改革或被取代的公开辩论。乌托邦的社会工程师让我们相信社会实验的唯一有价值的形式就是大规模的社会实验,而零星式的社会工程师与其

①　Popper,1945/2006b:143.
②　Popper,1963/2007b:497—498.

不同,他们承认小规模、短期的实验和建议的价值:

引入一种新型的人身保险、新型的税收、新的刑罚改革,都
是社会实验,对整个社会都产生了影响,但没有对整个社会改
型……我们能从中学到最多的一种实验,就是一次只改变一种
社会制度。因为只有用这种方式,我们才能学会如何把制度纳
入其他制度的框架,如何调整它们,使它们能够按照我们的意图
起到作用。而且只有用这种方式,我们才能犯错误,从错误中吸
取教训,而不会造成必然危及未来改革意愿的严重后果。[①]

乌托邦主义反对科学方法和知识增长(因而也就是反对确
定和解决社会和政治问题),因为它和它所基于的科学的归纳法
模型一样,鼓励我们面对理论失败的证明时仍然坚持理论,而不
是接受它们的失败,从错误中学习,并提出新的——可证伪
的——理论来取而代之。

因此,波普尔的政治学概念非常重视个人自由,并致力于保
护个人不受任意的干涉和压迫。最重要的是,它致力于使个人
摆脱已确立的不容置疑的真理的暴政,并致力于向所有人提供
必要的政治、经济和知识资源,以保护他们免遭密尔(在托克维
尔之后)所谓的多数人的暴政。个人自由不能服从于社会整体
的利益,也不能为了实现社会团结、稳定或民族团结而牺牲。历
史主义核心所固有的集体主义和本质主义应该被摒弃,代之以
方法论的个人主义和唯名主义。个人不应该再认为自己的利
益、理想和抱负,在社会的总体需要或历史的宏大而不可逾越的
力量面前是不重要的。社会和政治学家也不该再企图把握国家
和社会的本质,以便弄清楚它们应该如何被构建以及应该实施

波普尔的思想

---

① Popper,1945/2006a:172.

哪些政策。个人应该被给予摆脱部落主义和民族主义（"群体政治"）的束缚所需的资源，这些主义鼓励人们把自己看作不过是某个更广泛的、被神话了的社会整体的成员，这个社会整体拥有自己的命运，胜过了人们自身的命运。个人应该被给予所需的资源，培养他们与他人进行政治辩论的能力；他们应该能够就社会和政治制度的正当目的形成自己的观点；他们应该能够表达这些观点，并且能够以影响民主制度的方式按照这些观点行事。特定制度或个人的权威从来就不是固定的，就像为它们提供合理性的论辩和哲学立场也从来不是固定的一样；相反，人们可以通过持续的民主对话进程来对它们进行辩论和质疑——就像在科学或任何其他领域一样——对话的双方是平等的，人们对现有的社会和政治理论、提议、社会实践和制度采取一种批判理性主义的方法。正如关于物理科学中的现有理论的公开辩论在所涉及的各方之间建立一种客观性的形式，关于社会科学和政治问题的公开辩论也建立了类似的客观性或公正性：关于政治的公开辩论去除了建立在不诚实、欺诈或操纵之上的论点，迫使当权者以公众能够理解和认可的方式证明自己行为的合理性。

因此，波普尔的政治观正是源于对个人自由和民主的重视，源于这一重要观点，即社会问题可以通过以猜想和反驳的试错过程为框架的辩论过程，来得到确认、初步理解和解决。在这个过程中，没有人可以声称自己知道最终真理，所有现有的理论都是可证伪的，因而是可以辩论的。没有绝对正确的真理，就不存在所有人的终极利益，可以用来为特定的制度、实践或特定的人提供其合法性，或者可以始终为制度设定其应该解决的问题。我们所能做的就是尽可能严谨、尽可能创新地着手处理每一个政治问题，这意味着要根据我们所了解的关于世界的所有事实的总和,检验我们现有的社会和政治理论,目的是为了对其进行证伪。

波普尔摒弃了民族主义,捍卫了乐观的国际主义——起源于人类理性和自由相统一的愿景的世界主义政治学。柏拉图认为,"意见是每个人都有的,但理性只有上帝和极少数人才具有"①。黑格尔把理性的重要性放在激情和意志之后,因此,他寻求一种民族归属的政治学。波普尔是一个理性的易谬论主义者,他劝导人们别去相信理性的反思可以提供一定的知识的天真看法,他反对一些启蒙思想家存在的一种盲目信仰,即相信理性能够提供社会和政治蓝图。然而,尽管如此,他仍然与历史上的自由主义者和理性主义者共同主张这样一个启蒙主义观点:所有个人都具有理性的能力,无论他们生活在哪里,属于哪一个群体,正是这种共同的推理能力使我们能够体恤他人,理解他人的痛苦,理性"在想象的支持下,使我们能够理解那些远在他乡、我们永远不会见到的人,和我们一样……通过运用思想和想象,我们可以随时准备帮助所有需要我们帮助的人"②。任何民族或国家都不能诉诸历史、群体的利益、传统的价值观等来统治或压迫他们的民众,任何政治领袖都不能以国家主权的概念为借口,来为自己妨害民众的个人自由进行辩护。

因此,波普尔对自由、理性的立场和对批判理性主义的立场是密切相关的,并对国内和国际政治学产生了影响。在国际上,我们已经说过,它支持世界主义的自由主义形式,建基于全人类的道德平等,以及对如何最好地解决社会、政治和经济问题的国

① Popper,1945/2006a:252.
② Popper,1945/2006b:265.

际对话的需求。在国内，它要求对社会和政治制度进行改革，使其能够保护个人自由，保护社会个体成员共同商议——通过进行理性讨论——如何最好地解决社会和政治问题所需的协商性环境。如柏拉图所说，理性不是一种"'能力'，可以由不同的人在差异迥然的各个程度上拥有和发展。诚然，智识的天分可能在这方面有所不同，可能对理性产生影响；但并非一定会产生影响。聪明的人可能非常不讲道理；他们可能会坚持自己的偏见，可能不希望从别人那里听到任何有价值的东西"。然而，波普尔认为：

> 我们的理性不但要依靠别人，而且我们在理性上也不可能超越别人，从而让我们可以要求获取权威；我们认为权威主义和理性主义是不可调和的，因为包括批评在内的论证和听取批评的艺术是理性的基础。因此，我们认为理性主义与所有那些现代的柏拉图式的梦想都截然相反，在这些美丽新世界的梦想中，理性的增长被某种优越的理性所控制或"计划"。理性像科学一样，是通过相互批评的方式来增长的；"计划"其增长的唯一可能的方式是建立那些保护这种批评自由——也就是思想自由——的制度。①

由此，我们发现了这个主张（前面也提过），即人类理性体现在鼓励和保护理性的制度中，人类理性也只能在这种制度下才能繁荣发展，这种制度以公开为特征。

因此，波普尔相信进步的可能性，但这种进步却与历史主义者所捍卫的那种进步完全不同。例如，他在《历史决定论的贫困》一书中概述的科学进步的观点认为，人类知识的发展与特定

① Popper, 1945/2006b: 253.

的制度——演讲和写作等制度以及实验室、大学和研究机构等体系——相联系并依赖于它们,在这些制度与体系中,科学家们可以就现有理论进行公开辩论。因此,为了实现科学进步,存在着恰当的社会制度是非常重要的,他指的是那些保护和鼓励自由辩论的制度。这些主张与波普尔关于制度在推动政治或社会进步中的角色的更广泛的主张息息相关,如果我们重视进步、知识发展、自由以及社会制度通过纠正困扰社会、破坏人类基本平等的问题而改善社会的能力——我们正该如此——那么我们就必须建立和保护这样的社会制度,它使我们能够为政治学的恰当目的相互辩论,形成我们自己关于政治学的判断,批评别人的判断,同时在别人的批评面前捍卫我们自己的观点,并在必要时否定我们自己的理论,接受更新的、更有说服力的理论。他认为,只有"制度化的方法才能使我们根据讨论和经验作出调整"。

只有它,才使得我们可以把试错法运用到我们的政治行动中。它是长期的;但永久性的法律框架可以慢慢改变,以便为不可预见和不希望得到的后果、为框架的其他部分改变等留出余地。只有它,才使得我们可以在为了某个目标而进行干预的时候,通过经验和分析,弄清楚我们实际上在做些什么。统治者或公务员的自主决定在这些理性方法之外。它们是短期的决定,是暂时的,每天都在变化,或者至少每年都在变化。一般说来……它们甚至不能被公开讨论,因为缺乏必要的信息,也因为决策所基于的原则是模糊的。[1]

政策如果不能起到应有的作用,就应该被放弃,被能够起到

---

[1] Popper,1945/2006b:143.

作用的政策所取代。制度如果不能胜任所要求的任务,就应该进行改革,以便更好地应对面临的社会和政治挑战。政治家如果不能有效执政,就应该被撤职,被更适合担任公职的人所取代。所有这些决定——包括前面与制度、政策和政治家的恰当角色有关的问题——在一个开放的社会中,都由自由平等的公民通过保护个人自由的制度,相互进行理性的民主辩论来决定。因此,历史主义者为本质主义、整体主义、乌托邦社会工程、极权主义以及个人服从于社会和客观历史发展规律进行辩护,而波普尔则捍卫唯名主义、个人主义、零星的社会工程、民主以及每一个人自身的重要性,个人不是为了实现某种理想状态而被使用和操纵的纯粹的工具,个人本身即是目的。

卡尔·波普尔

波普尔哲学的反响和影响

　　波普尔对认识论、科学方法和政治哲学的许多干预，在那个时代是独创的、新颖的、激进的。他对这些领域的影响非常重大，研究自然科学的哲学就不可能不涉及波普尔的思想，若是不熟悉波普尔在这个领域的观点，想要掌握这一领域的许多研究的意义，可以说是不可能的。波普尔的研究以自己的方式解决了认识论和科学中的一些最基本的问题，可谓鼓舞人心，影响了科学哲学史上一些最著名的科学哲学家。例如，约瑟夫·阿加西(Joseph Agassi)，波普尔的学生、伦敦经济学院的研究助理。约翰·沃特金斯(John Watkins)，他对科学哲学作出的重大贡献，明显运用了波普尔的观点，针对怀疑论为科学发现的可能性进行辩护。[①] 伊姆雷·拉卡托斯(Imre Lakatos)致力于将波普尔的进化认识论与托马斯·库恩(Thomas Kuhn)关于科学是一种革命行为的概念联系起来。[②] 对于一代科学哲学家来说，波普尔的著作提供了当代人进行归纳、演绎、真理和知识辩论的

---

① Agassi,1993;Watkins,1984.
② Lakatos,1976,1978a,and 1978b.

背景。当然,这并不是说他们都同意他的观点。例如,保罗·费耶拉本德(Paul Feyerabend)最初折服于波普尔的方法,后来却反对波普尔的证伪主义理论,认为其限制性太强,反而主张以一种科学的无政府主义来代替全面的、包罗万象的方法论。[1] 包括希拉里·普特南(Hilary Putnam)在内的一些思想家批评波普尔关于证伪的论述,理由是他没有充分注意到任何理论可能对反驳"免疫"的程度;这个批评导致波普尔将逼真性的概念——现有理论应该被替换为更接近真理的理论——在他的理论中更进一步凸显。[2] 奥曼·蒯因(W. V. O. Quine)和皮埃尔·迪昂都提出,理论的证伪是非常复杂的,原因在于单独的假设不能孤立出来进行检验,因为每个理论都是更广泛的理论网络不可分割的一部分,每个理论都与另外的理论相互依赖。[3] 托马斯·库恩 1962 年出版的《科学革命的结构》(*The Structure of Scientific Revolutions*)提供了对科学发现的另一种描述,即一个革命发展的过程(或"范式转变"),他认为这更好地描述了科学家们实际的工作方式。对于库恩这本极有影响的著作,波普尔的回应是指出(在《框架的神话》中)库恩关于科学范式的不可通约性的主张,来源于遏制了知识增长、为道德和社会相对主义辩护的那些错谬的假设。[4]

《历史决定论的贫困》,尤其是《开放社会及其敌人》也得到来自各个政治领域的思想家的广泛赞誉。例如,伯特兰·罗素和哈罗德·拉斯基等社会主义者热情地捍卫《开放社会及其敌

---

[1] Feyerabend,1975/1993.

[2] Putnam,1974.

[3] Duhem,1954;Quine,1960.

[4] Popper,1994a.

人》，因为它对自由放任经济学的批判和对非马克思主义的社会民主形式的辩护。同时，像哈耶克、路德维希·冯·米塞斯（Ludwig von Mises）、米尔顿·弗里德曼（Milton Friedman）这样的政治右翼哲学家和经济学家，也欣赏波普尔的著述，并用它们来支持他们对社会和经济计划的批判，以及他们对自由市场和政治渐进主义的辩护。他在社会科学方面的著述对卡尔·门格尔（Carl Menger）[①]、冯·米塞斯[②]、卡尔·波兰尼[③]等经济学家关于历史、本质主义和国家在经济学研究中的角色而进行的辩论起到了重大作用，但并非出于任何特定的意识形态立场。

波普尔对 20 世纪自由主义、保守主义、自由至上主义、社会主义和社会民主主义思想发展的影响，可以并且已经被许多哲学家和历史学家所汲取（如麦基[④]、米勒[⑤]、席尔摩[⑥]）。他的政治思想已经被这么多不同的思想家所采纳和捍卫，这证明了其独创性和持久的吸引力，同时也提出了一个超越了波普尔，进入了更普遍的政治思想方法论的难题。波普尔是保守主义者吗？他是一个自由主义者吗？他是一个社会民主主义者吗？这些问题由于在一般意义上主义的不确定性，尤其是保守主义和自由主义的不确定性（我们将在下一章节讨论）而变得复杂化。但之所以复杂化，也是由于波普尔不愿意定义他的许多基本立场，以及他作为学者和辩论家的双重角色所固有的紧张关系。波普尔在

---

① Menger，1871/1981.

② Mises，1949.

③ Polanyi，1944/2001.

④ Magee，1973.

⑤ Miller，1994.

⑥ Shearmur，1996.

《开放社会及其敌人》中的语言和腔调激怒了许多敌人,也导致许多潜在的盟友把他的著作视为没有学者风度的作品而予以摒弃。波普尔当然不是一个对蠢人有耐心的人。我们应该记得,在《开放社会及其敌人》中波普尔指责柏拉图(可能是西方文明史上最德高望重的人物)憎恨自由、为一己私欲故意歪曲苏格拉底的哲学、提倡有目的地屠杀种族劣等的社会成员、提出"哲学之王"的统治,如此种种,为柏拉图自己掌握权力提供理由。他称费希特为"骗子"和"废话大王",将亚里士多德(可能是西方文明史上第二位德高望重的人物)形容为"没什么独创性思想的人"(尽管他确实"发明了逻辑",波普尔认为应该为此感谢他)。他用各种词汇描述黑格尔的哲学,"言过其实且歇斯底里""难以理解""尤其缺乏独创性"。事实上,"说到黑格尔,"他声称,"我甚至不觉得他有什么才华……黑格尔写的东西中没有什么是在他之前的人没说过的。"①此外,在好几个地方,波普尔赞许地引用了叔本华对黑格尔的描述,称他是一个"愚蠢无知、平淡无趣、令人恶心、不学无术的江湖骗子,厚颜无耻到极点,胡拼乱凑一些疯狂无稽、迷乱不堪的胡言乱语"②。显然,对波普来说,黑格尔不过是一个"小丑",普鲁士的腓特烈·威廉一世的一个无可救药的辩护士,他故意采用令人费解的写作风格,以便使他的读者产生错觉,误以为他的作品中有独到见解。

因此,1945 年《开放社会及其敌人》出版后,可想而知,许多人奋起捍卫柏拉图、亚里士多德和黑格尔等,声称波普尔对他们的著作及其意义的解读犯了巨大而严重的错误。研究柏拉图的

①　Popper,1945/2006b:35.
②　Popper,1945/2006b:36.

学者们尤其感到愤愤不平。尽管出现了一些批评柏拉图厌恶民主的作品（如菲特①、克罗斯曼②、温斯皮尔③），但古典学者和历史学家普遍认为，柏拉图代表了一种人性和理性的声音。波普尔的恶毒攻击确实令人震惊，不仅是他说话的内容，还有他说话的方式。大多数古典主义者发表辩论性的评论予以回应，而其中两人——约翰·威德（John Wild）和罗纳德·莱文森（Ronald Levinson）——甚至写了专题论文长度的文章为柏拉图辩护，反对波普尔的批评。④ 问题似乎不仅仅是波普尔误读了柏拉图和亚里士多德，而是他对他们不够尊重。例如，约翰·普拉梅纳茨（John Plamenatz）认为波普尔对亚里士多德的论述表现出的态度如同"一个刻薄的人有时对他认为不如自己有知识的人所采取的态度；通常在这种情况下，我们更看清了轻视别人的人，而不是他所轻视的对象"⑤。古典主义者的主要感觉是（现在仍然是）波普尔尖刻的、往往是辩论式的文章忽略了柏拉图思想中的许多细微差别和难懂之处，使得波普尔对柏拉图的解释变得复杂化。例如，他们指出，对《理想国》进行更仔细、更包容的阅读就可以看出，柏拉图所说的优生学并不像波普尔认为的那样是直截了当的"法西斯主义"，古代雅典并不像波普尔所说的那样是明显进步或开放的，波普尔对雅典帝国主义的理想化是不现实的，是基于其不准确的认识。也没有什么证据支持波普尔的主张，说苏格拉底致力于波普尔所定义的批判理性主义、个人主

---

① Fite，1934．

② Crossman，1959．

③ Winspear，1940．

④ Levinson，1953；Wild，1953．

⑤ Plamenatz，1953/1967：267．

义和平等主义,许多人反对将柏拉图称作波普尔所暗示的那种历史主义者,称柏拉图的形式理论诉诸哲学理想而不是历史理想。

波普尔对马克思的批判同样被批评为过于狭隘、过于简单化。例如,他没有讨论 1932 年在德国出版的马克思的《1844 年经济学和哲学手稿》(*Economic and Philosophical Manuscripts of 1844*)——该书被很多人认为是马克思最重要的著作之一,也没有讨论到 1939 年才在德国出版的《政治经济学批判大纲》(*Grundrisse*)。此外,波普尔没有提及其他重要的马克思主义者的著作,如葛兰西(Gramsci)和索列尔(Sorel)(他们反对必然变革的观念),尽管"在 20 世纪 20 年代初,卢卡奇(Lukacs)经常光顾波普尔居住的陋所……波普尔却似乎并不熟悉《历史和阶级意识》(*History and Class Consciousness*,1923)及围绕它的争议。他知道罗莎·卢森堡(Rosa Luxemburg),也见证了维也纳的议会运动,但在《开放社会及其敌人》中却没有提到这些。他忽视了奥地利马克思主义者阿德勒(Adler)、鲍尔(Bauer)、希尔费丁(Hilferding)和伦纳(Renner)。他的书中可以看到与鲍尔的政治文章相似的论见,但仅此而已"[1]。尽管波普尔自称对马克思极为尊重,但他在对其观点进行辩论时,却似乎不愿意善意地考虑到其思想的各种复杂性,也没有考虑到他的思想被其追随者以各种方式加以解释、提炼和重述的情况。他没有把马克思主义作为一种动态的、不断演变的学说——它激发了许多聪慧和坚定的人,它也是学术界内外一个很有争议的话题——予以呈现,而是抨击马克思是一个历史主义的假先知,他似乎对他

---

①   Hacohen,2000;440—441.

的结论引起的更广泛的论战或其结论的应用不感兴趣。因此，他对马克思的批评似乎是相当抽象的、干涩的，脱离了包含马克思思想的丰富思想传统。

许多批评家也对波普尔批评的内容有所质疑。例如，他们认为，波普尔错误地将某个观点——政治在经济变化面前无能为力——归于马克思。[①] 除了别的意见之外，他们还提出，他误解了马克思和黑格尔之间的关系，低估了个人和阶级在资本主义的崩塌中的重要性。然而，波普尔至少试图对马克思作出一个合乎逻辑的批判，与他对马克思的意图和动机总体上的承认相称。这些意图和动机是：缓解贫困、理解资本主义经济和社会的特征，以便超越其主要弊端。然而，波普尔对黑格尔的激烈谴责（在《开放社会及其敌人》的 900 页中他只用了 80 页）似乎既源自分析的严密性，也源自他的义愤。他对黑格尔的批评完全不如他对柏拉图和马克思的批判那么彻底，尽管他声称黑格尔代表了"所有现代历史主义的根源"[②]，因此也代表了现代政治实践和研究所面临的主要威胁的根源。当时和之后的黑格尔学者没兴趣研究波普尔的观点，也没有把他的观点当成一回事。批评家们很快指出，波普尔并没有直接讨论黑格尔的著述，而是几乎完全依赖于一本编集——雅各布·鲁文贝格（J. Loewenberg）编辑的《黑格尔选集》（*Hegel Selections*）——作为他的资料来源，而这本书是为学生编写的，没有包含一篇完整的著作。同样，为了建立黑格尔与纳粹主义的联系，波普尔在很大程度上利用了奥勒尔·科尔奈（Aurel Kolnai）的著作，大量援引

---

① Cornforth，1968.

② Popper，1945/2006b：30.

了他的《反西方战争》(*The War Against the West*)中的内容。但是，科尔奈的许多主张在当时(现在仍然)极具争议。然而，波普尔只是简单地把它们当成是真理，常常断章取义地加以引用。似乎很少或没有证据表明波普尔检查过这些主张的可靠性，或者就其可行性提出自己的独立结论。① 此外，批评家提出，为了建立从黑格尔到纳粹主义的一条几乎清晰的发展路线，波普尔似乎混淆和简化了胡塞尔(Husserl)、舍勒(Scheler)、海德格尔(Heidegger)、雅斯佩斯(Jaspers)等不同思想家之间的思想关系——夸大了他们之间的联系，弱化其分歧，不合逻辑地把不相干的主题和观点牵扯到一起。再者，他反复为叔本华(Schopenhauer)、J. F. 弗里斯(J. F. Fries)等思想家反对纳粹主义原型黑格尔的著作进行辩护，似乎浑然不觉弗里斯和叔本华曾经表达过反犹主义的观点。② 沃尔特·考夫曼(Walter Kauffman)、查尔斯·泰勒(Charles Taylor)等黑格尔哲学的捍卫者以及许多其他人一起，提出波普尔深刻地误解了黑格尔的形而上学，将黑格尔对国家的辩护曲解为捍卫种族纯洁的政策。③

更普遍而言，波普尔被指责未能说明和定义他的主要目标——极权主义。正如他似乎没兴趣讨论关于黑格尔、柏拉图或马克思的更广泛的文献一样，他似乎也没什么兴趣讨论关于极权主义的更广泛的著作，或者在最宽泛的术语之外去详细定义极权主义。这一点很重要，因为波普尔对极权主义的理解与许多现代著述者截然不同。当时存在的大多数极权主义理论都

① Popper,1945/2006b:354.
② Kauffman,1959.
③ Taylor,1958.

强调其独特的现代性,特别是它与现代工业和技术的联系(如阿伦特[1]、布热津斯基[2])。然而,波普尔却提出极权主义早在柏拉图和赫拉克利特等早期思想家的文章中就已经以某种形式存在。波普尔提出这些主张时,似乎觉得没有必要提及不断增多的关于极权主义国家的性质、起源和特征的各种文献(如阿隆[3])。相反,波普尔任由他的极权主义——以及开放社会的主要敌人——的概念模糊不清。同样,尽管在《历史决定论的贫困》中,波普尔花费了大量时间从最有利的角度来重建历史主义的论点(为了"建立一个真正值得攻击的立场"[4]),但令人吃惊的是,几乎所有这些旨在证实他关于"历史主义者思考些什么"的断言所参考的文献都源于同一本书——卡尔·曼海姆的《人与社会》。波普尔显然认为曼海姆的社会和政治科学的方法是错误的,然而,我们不清楚波普尔对曼海姆的解读有多么准确或公正,也不清楚曼海姆的观点如何可以轻易地被看作是历史上其他历史主义者的模板,从柏拉图、赫拉克利特到黑格尔、马克思、密尔和孔德。批评家们再次提出,我们在《历史决定论的贫困》中(如在《开放社会及其敌人》中)看到,波普尔不愿意讨论某些思想家的某些论点,而是倾向于把许多不同观点的思想家混在一起,以图一网打尽。

布莱恩·麦基(Bryan Magee)等为波普尔辩护的人试图通过强调《历史决定论的贫困》与《开放社会及其敌人》背后的意图以及写作背景,来还击对波普尔的研究方法缺乏学者风范的普

① Arendt,1951/2004.
② Brzezinski,1956.
③ Aron,1957.
④ Popper,1957/2005:3.

遍指控。我们还记得，波普尔将《开放社会及其敌人》称作"战斗书"。他离开了在法西斯主义的阴影下被战争撕得四分五裂的欧洲，流亡新西兰，在这个时期快速完成了这本书。支持者们声称，如果说他的语气在有些地方有点太过尖刻，或者说他对历史上某些德高望重的思想家的处理不公平或有失偏颇，这是因为他受到了一种道德决心的驱使，想要消除诞生了当时对世界产生威胁的那些罪恶的思想根源。波普尔在新西兰写《开放社会及其敌人》的时候，还笼罩在担心日本人不过数月就会抵达的恐惧之中。欧洲受到纳粹统治的威胁。他根本没有时间阅读黑格尔和马克思的全部著作，或者对柏拉图的当代学者、当代马克思主义者或黑格尔主义者提出的哲学、历史或语言上的复杂性进行长时间的辩论；世界需要对开放社会的捍卫，而且时间紧迫。人们或许可以承认，这样的努力有其重要性。然而，这种做法和波普尔关于知识增长和学术辩论的适当操守的更广泛的观点似乎不大协调。麦基提出，波普尔并非意在恶意中伤，他的方法总是先构建针对其对手理论的最有力、最正面的论述，然后再摧毁其核心要点。① 按照这样的思路，波普尔可以说是通过在自己的著作中批判理性主义的规范来实践他所宣扬的东西。他当然声称这是他在《历史决定论的贫困》一书以及在自然科学哲学的著作中的意图。然而，对于波普尔是否在《开放社会及其敌人》中也使用了这个方法，仍然存在着深刻的分歧。他对柏拉图和马克思的处理，尽管有时相当尊重，却是恶毒的、无情的，而且许多人都觉得是基于对这一领域文献的片面、故意的粗略理解。对于他在企图摧毁黑格尔的整个哲学体系之前，是否试图展示

---

① Magee，1973.

了黑格尔最好的一面,几乎没有什么不同意见:他显然没有兴趣这样做,而且他对黑格尔及其哲学也没有什么好话。若干年后,波普尔提到他对黑格尔的论述时说:"我不可能也不希望花无限的时间去深入研究一个我所憎恶的哲学家的历史。"[①]无论对黑格尔有什么看法,这个说法显然违反了波普尔自己关于知识辩论的必要操守的主张,并且提出了一个有趣的问题,即波普尔关于黑格尔(也许还有马克思和柏拉图)的观点是否可以——用波普尔自己的话来说——称作是对知识的有意义的贡献。

波普尔、伯克,以及推理的易谬性

尽管如此,波普尔关于社会和政治思想的著作给整个政治领域的思想家都带来了影响。波普尔坚决不愿意被贴上任何特定意识形态拥护者的标签,这意味着支持者和批评者都可以引述他的著作来捍卫或批评各种各样的哲学和政治立场,包括自由主义、古典自由主义、社会民主主义和社会主义。波普尔唯恐被认为自己在支持某种意识形态,尽管他本来对传统的观念(若是理解得当)有一定的同情。恰恰是波普尔思想中的这种反意识形态主义,让许多人将他归入了保守主义阵营。保守主义带有各种各样的历史伪装,往往——至少在一定程度上——以反对意识形态为特征。它的捍卫者经常把它看作是一种理解社会和政治权威的方法,而不是一套具有规范性内容的原则。总的来说,保守主义者把自己定义为实用主义者,更关心通过诉诸现

---

① Popper,1945/2006b:446.

有传统、制度和价值观所包含的累积的智慧，而不是诉诸定义某个特定的和理想的未来的原则，来确认和应对社会问题。

可以这么说，我们已经看到从某些角度我们可以称波普尔为保守主义者。然而，保守主义在其历史进程中已经发生了变化，如果要掌握波普尔与保守主义的联系，理解这些变化是相当重要的。在20世纪70年代末和80年代初之前，保守主义在传统上一直与埃德蒙·伯克（Edmund Burke）等思想家的著作有关联。从根本上讲，它是一个关于权威和政治改革的理论。众所周知，伯克公开抨击法国革命和它所依据的启蒙运动原则，称其为拙劣的滑稽模仿，声称启蒙运动仅仅代表了关于人类平等、理性、自由的重要性的一系列含糊的错误，革命只不过是对正当权威和传统的暴力攻击。[①] 他认为，法国的事件并没有像其捍卫者所说的那样预示着自由、平等、博爱的新时代的到来，而是代表了一次与政治领袖和制度的合法权威性所依据的传统的灾难性的决裂，代表了对能够指导制度该如何构建、应承担什么角色以及谁最适合掌握权力的累积知识和经验的摒弃。伯克为政治渐进主义辩护，反对政治激进主义。法国革命体现了这样一种启蒙思想，即有可能通过应用理性来推翻权力和特权的传统等级制度。因此，他认为，革命者对于理性影响剧变的力量过于乐观。他们沉迷于一种冲动的、不负责任的观念，即只需要理性，就可以从零开始建立公正、有效的社会和政治秩序，就可能扫除一切之前的事物，建立起全新的政治制度，仿佛旧的政治制度从未存在过。而伯克则相反，他是一个理性的易谬主义者。他认为，理性的力量是有限的，理性无法确定地预测决策的后

① Burke, 1790/1986.

果,仅凭理性不能为有效的政治制度提供基础。因此理性需要传统来提供信息,我们只能通过搞清楚在过去是什么起到了作用,并依赖于这些知识,才能明白我们的政治制度应该是什么样的、应该做些什么。

伯克还批评了启蒙思想家普遍持有的一种观点,即行使权力的权利与理性相关。因此,所有具有理性的生命都应该被认为有能力负责任地、公正地行使权力。伯克是一个精英主义者,他认为人类天生就不平等。他不同意革命捍卫者关于所有个人都应该行使政治权力的观点,也反对理性(与传统分离)可以可靠地事先确定政治权力应该由谁掌握的观点。仅凭理性反思产生的原则太抽象,太不确定,无法对关于应该做什么、由谁来做的复杂问题提供足够的答案。伯克还认为,这些问题通过诉诸传统可以得到更具体的解决;历史表明有些人适合执政,有些人不适合执政。伯克因此认为权力应该集中在少数人手中——贵族,历史已经显示他们被赋予了有效行使权力的必要品质——而不是不加选择地向普通大众发放。这是保守的实用主义的一个很好的例子。其观点是,政治不应该受到教条的意识形态原则的制约,而是应该足够灵活地处理现实世界中发生的每一种真实的情况;没有人——即使是世界上最伟大的哲学家——可以坐在舒适的扶手椅上解决谁应该执政、谁不应该的问题;相反,这些问题需通过搞清楚在任何一个特定的社会中谁已经显示出最有能力去有效地、负责任地行使权力以及谁没有,去得到最好的回答。伯克的政治观点因而具有三个重要的含义。首先,社会以阶级分化和等级制度为特征,而不是自由主义、启蒙主义想象中的由平等的人联合起来的社会。其次,代议政制的精英制度下,当选的政治家根据自己的良知(超群的)和观点,而不是根据选出他们的选民的观点来执政。第三,社会和政治变革的概念必然是渐进式的,即社会和政治制度随着时间,根据我们关于世界的知识和我们尝试新事物、运用有效措施并放弃无用措施的经验的增长,而逐步发展。

因此,我们可以看到伯克在很多方面影响了波普尔,在很多方面没有影响到。当然,波普尔对于政治统治应该由一个历史上的精英阶层来掌握——或者说有些人就是适合执政,有些人不适合执政,这可以证明精英阶层执政的合理性——的观点并无兴趣。他对阶级的观念也没有兴趣。我们还记得,在波普尔看来,历史主义的主要罪状之一就是,它对个人的兴趣仅限于他们是群体的成员:马克思对人的兴趣就不如他对阶级的兴趣;黑格尔对个人没有兴趣,而是对民族感兴趣;柏拉图的共和国的观点以彻底的、不动摇的阶级制度(基于种族)为特征。我们已经看到,波普尔认同法律面前人人平等和个人自由等启蒙主义价值观。他还和启蒙运动思想家们一样,认为阶级、民族、种族等群体是随心所欲的人类建构,不能引起道德上的共鸣,我们真正应该投身的共同团体是全世界所有人的共同体。因此,他反对像伯克这样的保守主义者提出的主张,即为了证明变革的合理性,我们必须弄清楚是什么最符合"民族""社区"或"群体"的最佳利益。波普尔认为,这种主张是封闭社会的特征,源于看待历史命运的、过时的、有害的思想,表现出个人利益有意地服从于他们所属的群体或机构的利益。波普尔认为,如果要证明社会和政治改革的合理性,那么就需要由那些承担其后果的个人来证明,并且要证明给他们自己看。而且,由于任何变革的最终后果都不能事先预测,所以任何变革都必须谨慎、负责,并以我们目前所掌握的最佳证据为基础。如果事实证明某个特定的行动是错误的,那么它就必须是可以撤销或者可以改变的。再次重申,变革以及证明其合理性的理由,都必须被视为是可证伪的。

波普尔相信个人有能力通过发现问题、寻求解决办法来改善他们的社会和政治生活。但是,和伯克一样,他不如许多启蒙思想家那么乐观,认为理性的力量能够为从零开始构建新的复杂的政治制度提供所有必要的信息。因此,他像伯克一样,认为社会改革应该以世界目前拥有的所有累积的知识为基础,新的制度应该产生于已经存在的制度之中。在科学领域,为了实现思想持续的剧变和转换,激进的批评是适当的,然而在性命攸关的政治领域,就需要走得更慢,以零星的方式逐步实施和尝试变化。因此,波普尔赞成伯克对法国革命的反对,并与伯克一样,反对所有制度都应被理解为有意识的人类意志的产物,认为这是傲慢自大的偏见。与之相反,他与伯克(以及后来的哈耶克)同样提出,许多社会制度不是"被创造"出来的,而是"作为人类行为的无意的结果"产生出来的。[①] 但是与伯克不同的是,波普尔并不认为这些制度的天然性使它们合理化或合法化。他并没有像伯克和其他人那样捍卫贵族统治的合法性;事实上,他的政治哲学对任何这样的理论都是正面的挑战。对于波普尔来说,政治合法性可以通过检验现有制度能否实现公众要求其实现的目标,能否确保允许这种检验和公众认可发生的必要的社会和政治条件,从而得到保证。对波普尔来说,特定的制度或个人由于有历史先例,或者因为它们一直这样存在,就应该被认定为合法的,这不仅令人憎恶,而且是错误的、不公正的。对伯克来说,

波普尔哲学的反响和影响

---

① Popper,1957/2005:59.

传统为现有的社会和政治条件，包括现有的权力结构、权力来源、不平等以及法律等，提供了存在的理由。然而，对于波普尔来说，传统代表了关于世界的（有争议性的）知识的有用积累，理性可以运用它来为零星的社会改革提供指导。

尽管他们在平等、阶级、精英主义和权力的恰当来源等方面具有诸多分歧，但波普尔和伯克仍然共同反对彻底变革，反对他们认为其他思想家所持有的盲目的信仰——相信人类理性有能力预测事件和决策的后果。伯克关于理性的易谬主义导致他反对启蒙运动树立独立政治生活观念的目标，这种观念是与历史无关的，脱离了之前的一切的。波普尔支持伯克的观点，同时指出仅凭历史就能为政治安排提供另一个理由来源是错误的。两位思想家都承认理性的局限性，尽管他们从中得出了不同的结论：伯克用它来证明诉诸历史传统的合理性，而波普尔则用它来支持他对批判和批判理性主义的认识论立场。两位思想家都更加关心如何概述出社会可以适当变革的方式，而不是提出一个全面的政治生活愿景。波普尔和伯克都不是单纯意义上的保守主义者，认为变化本身就是坏事。特别在波普尔看来，变化并不是坏事；毕竟，波普尔对柏拉图的主要批评就是，柏拉图致力于压制人类的创造性和自由，目的是为了"阻止一切变化"。对于波普尔来说，如果不能改变效率低下或不符合目标的社会或政治制度，或者不能改革不公正的社会和政治规范，就可能带来灾难。波普尔（及伯克）认为关键是要确定证明改变的合理性的恰当理由，并弄清楚哪一类改变会被视为是负责任的改变。虽然他同伯克一样反对乌托邦主义所支持的那一类变化，但是他拥护个人在对现有和可能的实践进行正确的理性分析的基础上，实施零星的改革。波普尔详细论述了我们不应该追求哪一类制度和政策（即历史主义制度和政策），但刻意模糊了我们应该采取哪一类政策和制度，正是因为对这样的事情进行预测必定会陷入乌托邦的意识形态化。鉴于我们无法确知采取特定政策或制度（甚至是我们最喜欢的）的后果，我们就应该避免在一开始过于详细地进行规定，而应该确保一定的条件，让我们能够弄清楚哪些制度和政策在任何时候都能够最好地满足社会个体成员已经确认的需求。

激进的政治学、激进的哲学

在第二次世界大战后的几年里，保守主义已经开始具有更广泛的含义，许多与伯克的古典保守主义毫不相干的作家被贴上了保守主义者的标签。这个重新贴标签的过程主要是受到其批评者的推动。例如，关于波普尔是否是保守主义者的争论在很大程度上是由他的批评者——主要来自于左派——所推动的，他们把他对个人主义和广义的市场导向的经济的立场解读为代表了当权派的观点，表现了他不愿挑战自由资本主义的意识形态主导地位。尽管在许多方面，《开放社会及其敌人》代表了二战以来统治欧洲的社会民主主义共识的强大声明，然而波普尔还是被其批评者与其他"冷战自由主义者"放在了一起，如在 20 世纪 50 年代面对共产主义而捍卫自由个人主义和自由市场的以赛亚·伯林和雷蒙·阿隆（Raymon Aron）。尤其是伯林，他也和波普尔一样，对极权主义渐渐渗入的威胁感到担忧，并与波普尔一样确定了相同的民主的敌人；他的就职演讲（也是他最著名的文章）《自由的两个概念》（*Two Concepts of*

Liberty）将极权主义的哲学根源追溯到黑格尔和卢梭这些曾经为自由的"正面"论述辩护的思想家。他的其他一些文章，包括《历史必然性》(*Historical Inevitability*)，则具有波普尔思想的所有印记。

在 20 世纪 60 年代和 70 年代，波普尔被许多左派的人认为是无可救药地过时了，因为他仍然致力于个人主义的政治学——而不是拥护社会运动和公开抗议的激进的政治学，和批判、理性反思的启蒙哲学。他为自由主义、渐进主义以及激进规划无用论继续辩护，这在当时学术圈内外众多学者正转向一种以激进的社会变革为前提的更为"进步的"集体主义政治学的时局下，使他被归入了保守主义的阵营。批评者提出，例如，困扰英美社会的许多弊病，在当时盛行的理念中过于重要和根深蒂固，无法以零星的方式加以尝试性地解决。例如，美国的民权运动和妇女权利运动都体现了迅速解决根本问题，绕过一般认为是问题本身根源的常规渠道采取直接行动的政治意愿。波普尔的"制度方法"以及凭借零星社会工程的政治渐进主义似乎是反动的，似乎使他站到了那些为重要权利和平等而斗争的人的对立面。他主张负责任的变革是尝试性的、渐进的，隐含的前提是人们不应该为了影响变化带来的利益而脱离传统的民主辩论，应该与现有的制度合作而不是对立，这似乎暗示民权及其他事业的活动家公然反对现状是犯了错误，他们应该通过那些已经证明有效的渠道来更合理地提出他们的担忧。同样，他宣称所有的知识主张都必定是推测性的，这在很多人看来是向现有的社会和政治不公正低头。他们承认，尽管某些主张的确定性可能值得怀疑，但我们真的就不能确知，比如说，男女应该平等？或者，黑人不应该被剥夺白人所拥有的权利？或者，同性恋者不

卡尔·波普尔

应该因为害怕被排斥或虐待而被迫隐瞒自己的性取向？

　　当时的政治学以激进主义为特征，其核心是这样一种观念，即尽管传统的自由民主政治制度和机制的所有主张都是支持人人平等，却把主流多数派的声音（因此也是利益）置于少数群体之上。也就是说，在平权待遇、自由、个性以及所有个人都能充分和有意义地参与政治进程的自由标语背后，传统的自由民主政治仅把密尔所谓的"多数人的暴政"奉若神明。许多人认为，还需要为同性恋者、黑人、移民和其他那些利益被多数派有组织地践踏的人们做更多的工作。他们的答案是一种身份认同、社会运动和公开抗议的新政治学；认识到如果边缘化群体的成员一起发出同一个声音，这个声音就会比他们单独发言要响亮得多。因此，这个答案就是反对传统的个人主义，反对传统的自由主义关注的所有那些将个人区分开来的东西，代之以强调那些将人们团结一致的东西；反对传统的对现有社会和政治制度的服从，代之以激进的反正统、反文化。新的行动主义取代了源于个性和理性的抽象启蒙主义政治观，强调的是共同的身份、社区，以及认为人们可以由自由主义原则和批判理性主义的立场之外的东西团结在一起，如共同的文化、种族、民族或性别。自由主义者传统上认为这种区分是有害的、不相关的，是有待被超越的东西。波普尔同意这种看法。但是新的行动主义提出，它们可以成为伟大的社会和政治统一和力量的源泉，而且在多数派自由民主国家的背景下，可以成为实现仅凭个人主义永远无法实现的社会变革的一种手段。

　　因此，许多批评家提出，尽管波普尔在《开放社会及其敌人》中对平等和政治地位平等的人之间进行公开辩论的重要性夸大其辞，但他对个人主义政治的顽强坚持、对社会团体重要性的反对(认为是封闭社会的部落政治的复辟)只不过表现了对问题本身的描述:一种自以为打碎了分裂人们的障碍而洋洋自得,实际上是将实权放在多数派手中的排外主义和精英主义的政治制度。波普尔以之为基础的民主审议的愿景只是进一步将这个问题恶化。他的理论以他更广泛的认识论主张为前提,即知识是在猜想与反驳、批判、试错的动态过程中产生的。因此,许多人怀疑这样一个政治愿景如何能够指望产生政治上必需的那种一致和共识。波普尔设想的似乎是一个在理性主义批判传统的基础上缓慢演变的社会,不过其特点是不断地辩论、反驳、猜想、提出大胆的政治举措以及随后对其证伪。但批评者指出,民主不仅仅是谈话。民主要有效地行使职能,就必须能够在公民、立法者和政治家之间达成合理共识的基础上作出决定,采取行动。我们的担忧是——在卡尔·施密特(Carl Schmitt)等思想家的著述中可以看到这种忧虑的最激进的表现形式——民主辩论变得与政治决策脱离,尽管公民内部在讨论问题,但最重要的决策实际上是在幕后作出的。[1] 波普尔对审议式民主的理想化观念因此被许多社会主义者和同情集体主义与认同政治的进步人士视作既将边缘化群体排除在民主进程之外,又将民主辩论与政治决策过程分离。因此,这些人认为其理论事实上支持了精英统治,是保守主义的蓝图。

此外,波普尔坚定地致力于对个人自由和批判理性主义的"描述",这在左派中许多日益受到阿多诺、霍克海默、哈贝马斯、马尔库塞(Marcuse)等欧洲批判理论家和福柯(Foucault)等后结构主义者的影响的人看来是天真的和简单化的。波普尔的哲

---

① Schmitt,1923/1988;1927/2006.

学方法正好属于罗素和艾尔的分析传统;因此,他对马克思的批评是分析性的批评,他试图用自己的普遍主义——源于个人自由的自由主义的普遍主义——来取代马克思的普遍主义。后现代主义者、后结构主义者以及法兰克福学派的批判理论家虽然在其他方面有很大的不同,但是他们广泛联合起来,共同反对这样一个以现代性的元叙事为基础的事业,这些元叙事已经不再成立,并且其诉诸的那些观念、理想和价值观早已失去了意义。哈贝马斯等批判理论家指责波普尔只是一个实证主义者,他对马克思的批判,他的开放社会的设想——事实上,他的整个哲学方法——都被看作仅仅是资产阶级意识形态的一种表达,沉迷于自己对世界的片面理解,以至于无法捕获任何关于世界的重要东西;过于急功近利想要寻求"普遍"的原则,结果却根本不能普遍适用。[①] 在他的激进的批评者看来,波普尔的总体主张,即个人可以根据相同的过程和方法,以同样的方式在许多不同的人类经验领域中发现和解决问题,这个主张很天真,过于相信仅凭一个推理的概念就能够揭示自然世界、社会生活、政治、权力、自由等一切中所隐藏的、重要的错综复杂之处。因此,他们认为他的方法实际上限制了知识的增长;它完全忽视了这样一个事实:我们用以了解我们自己和世界的概念,我们用以相互交流和表达这些概念的语言是有问题的、模棱两可的、含混不清的,并且越来越不适合它们被使用的这个世界。

最为重要的是,对于批判理论家和后结构主义者来说,波普尔的论证并没有提到政治学最重要的东西:权力的性质和归属,以及自由民主国家权力运用的明确的和隐含的方式。波普尔同

---

① Habermas,1976.

意马克思的宣言——"决定人的社会存在的并不是人的意识,相反,是人的社会存在决定了人的意识"——削弱了心理主义的基础,但是他拒绝从这个宣言中得出和马克思主义者同样的结论。对于批判理论家和后结构主义者来说,马克思主张一个人的社会、政治和经济环境可以塑造其思想、兴趣和认识,这揭示了人的社会环境可以成为强迫的来源的各种重要方式。波普尔驳斥了这种主张,声称它是社会的"阴谋论",然后他以传统的自由主义的方式讨论了权力,即权力为国家所拥有,需要受到以尊重个人权利为基础的法律和政策的限制或约束。但批判理论家和后结构主义者认为,马克思的主张不能如此轻易被否定,一旦我们明白了一个人的兴趣和思想可能被社会本身所塑造(有时是微妙的,有时是隐性的,以我们可能会察觉或甚至察觉不到的方式),而不是由特定的人或制度所塑造,那么关于个人自由和权利的自由主义论点就根本不得要领。政治学的目的不应该仅仅是解决国家权力应该如何以及在多大程度上被限制,因此需要建立什么样的宪法和法律来保障个人不受其影响(如自由主义理论所言),而是揭示通过那些管理我们的日常行为的社会和政治规范来行使权力的多种方式,揭示谁有权力塑造和确定这些社会规范,并就如何打破这些占主导地位的和隐藏的权力结构提出建议。

这个重要的见解也是许多原本不属于后结构主义或批判理论阵营的思想家所持有的。尤其是女权主义者,一直在批评自由主义理论中暗含的那一类启蒙主义推理,这种推理在波普尔关于社会和知识增长的观点中也是显而易见的。包括最近的塞拉·本哈比(Seyla Benhabib)、南希·弗雷泽(Nancy Fraser)、南希·赫希曼(Nancy Hirschmann)和艾莉丝·马里昂·杨

(Iris Marion Young)在内的女权主义者都在他们的文章中引用了后结构主义的见解,以表明传统的自由主义权力观念(即权力体现在公共领域,并可以在公共领域进行规范)无法解释在私人领域特别是妇女受到控制和压迫的诸多方式,因此不能构成对父权制的平等主义回应的基础。[①] 许多女权主义者认为,妇女受压迫的主要根源不是国家,而是体现在自由主义者认为的管理个人关系的规范中隐含的权力结构,例如夫妻关系、母子关系,或是宗教或妇女所属其他群体的规范。我们已经看到,个人受社会和政治环境"控制",是因为他们的选择(以及他们选择的能力本身)在某种程度上由社会塑造并受到其阻碍,波普尔对这种观点是表示深切怀疑的。但是称这些主张是由那些使用狂妄言辞和冗长费解的句子(他也是这么做的)的人所散布的阴谋论是不够的。波普尔的理论对解决这个问题没有什么帮助,他只是说我们应该不论性别,认为所有人都平等,然后再讨论问题。他并没有提到更深层的主张,即许多女性感到无法作为自由和平等的个人参与公共审议或其他活动,是由波普尔哲学中虽未提到,但仍然有损于女性在生活中真正自主作出选择的自由的权力结构所造成的。波普尔对这个背景以及其他背景下他称之为权力阴谋论的理论的反对,在许多理论家看来,不过是进一步证明了他不愿意承认群体以及群体特有的规范的重要性。

面对这样一种对现代社会、自由主义以及我们理解概念和语言的方式进行得如此激进和彻底的批判,波普尔认为社会问题可以通过主张个人自由和公开对话得到解决,这样的信仰确实似乎是保守主义的。波普尔主张变革不能是彻底的,"社会实

---

① Benhabib,1992;Fraser,1997;Hirschmann,2003;Young,1990.

验"不应该在社会整体层面上进行;他认为我们应该采取一种方法论个人主义和唯名主义的方法来了解社会,而不是一个整体主义的、集体主义的和自然的方法,因为无论是理性还是历史都无法为人类的未来发展提供特定的指导。但是后结构主义者和批判理论家提出,一个理性的易谬主义者,对理解和解决社会和政治问题采取激进的方法,也是可能的。波普尔主张,社会科学家需要在理解社会的两种对立的方式中进行选择:一种是通过采取零星的社会改革方式,承认理性揭示关于长远未来的某些知识的能力的有限性(这种方式以批判的关键重要性和广义上的自由主义的个人自由的概念为前提);一种是致力于以整体主义的、集体主义的方式去理解社会,以历史规律能够决定人类未来发展为前提。然而,后现代主义者、后结构主义者和批判理论家似乎还提供了第三种方法,既认同历史主义者对整体主义和集体主义的立场,也认同波普尔对理性能够产生关于未来的某些认识的怀疑。批判理论和后结构主义的一个共同主题在当时是——现在也是——只有通过彻底解构任何社会和政治制度中所体现的语言和概念,我们才能理解在其中运用权力的方式以及运用权力要达到的目的。因此,为了揭示那些困扰个人生活、塑造他们的经历却往往不易察觉的不公正现象,我们应该寻求对这些事物以及社会整体的深层了解,而不是回避社会及其最阴险的问题。与波普尔相反,后现代主义者、后结构主义者和批判理论家以他们各自的方式,主张社会和政治科学必定是激进的;了解社会需要与其制度、历史以及构成它的人们进行全面的接触;解决它的问题需要根据我们的发现采取行动。它的问题并不一定会被零星的、尝试性的改革所改变,但一定会被具有深远的、可能是革命性意义的举措最终解决。

波普尔对这些批评的回应——尽管他没怎么回应——不是让步，而是进一步巩固他对个人主义和民主对话的立场。他在《开放社会及其敌人》之后的政治文章的特点是对自由主义民主胜过其他制度的优点给予坚持不懈的支持；他说，自由主义民主是"迄今为止人类历史上出现的最好的社会制度……迄今为止最好的——至少是我们在历史上所知的制度中最好的"[1]。对于那些指出他的开放社会设想过于抽象，不具有可以团结公民的实质性价值的批评，波普尔的回应是越发把批判理性主义定义为一种人们可以认同而不至于陷入部落主义的真正传统。[2]在他1965年的文章《框架的神话》中，波普尔抨击了作为后结构主义和批判理论核心的相对主义。在此之前几年，波普尔在为所谓的实证主义辩论所贡献的文章中，对法兰克福学派的理论家们冷嘲热讽。哈贝马斯指责波普尔只是一个实证主义者，"受他的方法论所限只会严守现状"[3]，对此波普尔指出——并非没有道理——他的整个学术生涯都致力于反驳维也纳学派的实证主义特征。他还把法兰克福学派的影响形容为"非理性主义的""摧毁智识"，并声称他无法"从知识分子或学者的角度来认真看待他们的方法论（不管这指的是什么）"[4]。他说，他们和黑格尔一样，陷入了一种自我放纵、不负责任的"不可理喻的狂热"。例如，哈贝马斯"不知道如何简单、清楚、谨慎地表达"观点，事实上，波普尔认为，哈贝马斯所说的大部分内容要么是琐碎的，要么是错误的。他觉得阿多诺"从来都无话可说"，其捍卫的哲学

---

① Popper,1963/2007b,496.

② Popper,1963/2007b.

③ Popper,1994a:68.

④ Popper,1994a:66.

观点仅仅是一种"故弄玄虚"。① 同样,他也认为霍克海默的文章"空洞""没有内容""无趣""只是马克思的历史主义含糊不清、人云亦云的一种形式"②。

在波普尔看来,指责其不可理喻并非是表面文章。我们还记得,波普尔认为,知识的增长取决于跨学科的批判性辩论;因此,他认为,任何致力于知识增长的人,其道德责任需尽力在作品中做到易于理解和清晰明了,以避免只有一小撮志同道合的知识分子才能理解。波普尔认为,批判理论家和后结构主义者故意把他们的理论搞得尽可能的复杂难懂,只不过是在满足自己的虚荣和自大,限制对知识的追求。波普尔主张,"所谓的法兰克福学派的批判理论的全部内容"是这样的:"让目前这一代人受苦并灭亡——因为我们所能做的就是揭露我们生活的世界的丑陋,痛骂我们的压迫者'资产阶级'"③。另一方面,波普尔赞成社会改良的可能性。他说,"我们现在可以做更多的事情来减轻苦难,最重要的是,来增加自由。我们不能等待历史女神或革命女神为人类事务带来更好的条件"④,就像批评理论家们所建议的那样。强调人类面对不可通约的语言和文化"框架"无法了解世界,有组织地削弱我们改变我们生活的世界的能力,这在波普尔看来是一种背叛、一个错误,属于他在家乡维也纳的咖啡馆里发现并反对的同一种傲慢自大的哲学精英主义传统。在阿多诺、霍克海默、马尔库塞等批判理论家看来——他们认为,看似简单的概念,其极有问题的本质恰恰是重点——波普尔的回应完全不着边际。

---

① Popper,1994a:78.
② Popper,1994a:79—80.
③ Popper,1994a:84.
④ Popper,1994a:80.

波普尔与新右派的兴起

到 20 世纪 70 年代末 80 年代初,公共话语和学术话语中保守主义的含义又进一步转向。波普尔声称,他写作《开放社会及其敌人》的主要目的之一就是把工会和社会主义者联合起来,共同主张极权主义已经取代资本主义成了世界面临的主要威胁。然而,到了 20 世纪 80 年代,波普尔的思想成了一个完全不同的政治议程的集结点。对于六七十年代的许多英美自由主义者和保守主义者来说,敌人不仅仅是在海外发展起来的极权主义或是国内的激进主义和反文化运动,还有已经渗透到欧美政治中的集体主义。集体主义的根源在于二战后不久建立起来的广泛的社会民主共识,其中许多要素在《开放社会及其敌人》中有所阐述。战后欧洲的重点是重建欧洲各国破碎的社会和经济。国家在财富再分配和福利提供方面比以前在自由主义制度下承担了更为主要的角色,政治家和广大社会成员普遍认为当时的政治要求加强统一和团结,超过了对个人主义和竞争的需要。

以这种共识为特征的许多观点一直存在,并在 1945 年至 20 世纪 70 年代后期得到了加强。例如,在英国,历届政府对于强调公共福利、国家干预经济、国家管理扩大到住房和公用事业所有权等领域的广泛的社会民主计划仍然表示欢迎。创造就业机会和重建工业的举措促成了劳工运动的加强,表现为工会的日益强大。因此,这样的观念越来越占主导地位:通过国家行为来促进社会统一,重视把人们凝聚在一起的东西(工人运动、阶级等),在某种意义上是政府的一项责任;国家有可能进行有计划的社会改革。对于致力于自由市场、个人主义和有限政治的自由主义者与致力于实用主义、传统、强烈的反社会主义(或者更确切地说,一种似乎与社会主义相左的深刻的反激进主义)的保守主义者而言,继续走向集体主义是一件值得担忧的事。因此,尽管存在许多差异,自由主义者和保守主义者开始越来越多地发现他们常常发表相同意见,反对他们所认为的集体主义和激进的(即意识形态的)社会工程的双重罪恶。担忧国家在从事不切实际的社会工程,担忧政治正在被工会等强大团体所控制,这在 20 世纪 70 年代后期达到了危机点。当时是一个社会、政治和经济相当动荡的时期,许多自由主义者和保守主义者都认为事态已经积重难返。国家被认为已经超出其界限,变得太过庞大笨拙,无法实现改革计划;摊子铺得太大,试图插手人们生活的太多方面,于是过多权力被下放给工会和其他部门利益集团。自由主义者和保守主义者因此团结在"新右派"的旗帜下,支持走另一条路:回归政治实用主义、有限政治、个人主义,把个人从一个事事都管、无处不在的国家的重压下解放出来。他们为此求助于波普尔长期的朋友兼同事弗里德里希·冯·哈耶克的经济和政治理论。

我们在第一章看到,哈耶克非常欣赏波普尔的著作,并且在《开放社会及其敌人》的出版和 1946 年波普尔在伦敦经济学院任职的过程中起到了积极作用。作为回报,波普尔称哈耶克"拯救了他的生命",并形容他是父亲般的存在,是他知识上的师长。哈耶克也是新右派背后的知识导师,被广泛认为是自由放任经济学在英美复苏的最重要人物。波普尔和哈耶克共有的不仅是友谊,他们还是同时代的人,共同关注个人自由、反对暴政,他们的思想发源于相同的激励哲学——"人不知道，也不可能知道所有东西，当他装作知道的时候，灾难就降临了"[1]。波普尔和哈耶克都反对法国大革命的那种激进变革，并且与伯克一起支持以一种特别的哲学理性主义来替代激进变革。两人都反对过于乐观的观点（以培根等思想家为代表），即认为理性——与传统和理论脱离——能够揭示出关于世界的确定的基本真理，因此，两人都赞同伯克的总体主张，认为有效的政治制度不可能仅凭理性来虚构。波普尔认为，"那些害怕权威和传统衰落的悲观主义者是聪明人。重大的宗教战争、法国和俄国革命的可怕经历，证明了他们的智慧和远见"[2]。

因此，波普尔、伯克、哈耶克与其他思想家如伯纳德·曼德维尔、亚当·斯密、大卫·休谟一样，采取了哈耶克所谓的"进化论理性主义"，而不是"建构主义的理性主义"。这是理性主义的一种形式，它承认智慧和传统积累在社会和政治改革的推理中的价值，而不是采取非历史的、抽象化的理论。[3] 建构主义的理性主义者，包括见解各异的思想家，如法国的笛卡儿、卢梭、孔多塞，英美的培根、霍布斯（Hobbes）及戈德温（Godwin）、佩恩（Paine）和杰斐逊（Jefferson）等法国革命的捍卫者，都强调人类能够"扫除现有的制度和实践，提议采取全新的、未经尝试的计划"，然而进化论理性主义者则建议应谨慎行事。[4] 哈耶克和波普尔认为，哲学的一个重要任务就是发现理性的局限，并在认识论不确定的情况下决定构建和改革社会的适当手段。那么，重

---

① Blundell，1999：12.
② Popper，1963/2007b：503.
③ Mandeville，1714；Smith，1789；Hume，1748.
④ Gamble，1996：32.

要的不是用传统主义来取代理性主义(即像奥克肖特等思想家所主张的,用对历史传统的照单全收来替代不加批判的理性的乐观主义),而是要构建一种理性主义的思想,注重传统中所体现的智慧,并承认这样的智慧无法确定或明确。哈耶克称之为进化论理性主义,波普尔称之为批判理性主义,许多人认为正是这个理论使得他们两人被归入了与伯克一样的保守主义阵营。这种方法尊奉波普尔的基本主张(在前一章讨论过),即知识往往从神话和传统开始,就像它从推理中开始一样,因此,它

允许……理性主义和传统主义之间的和解。批判理性主义者可以尊重传统,因为尽管他相信真理,但他并不相信自己必定拥有真理。他可以体会通向真理的每一步、每一点接近既是宝贵的,也是无价的。他可以看到我们的传统往往有助于激励这样的步伐,而且如果没有知识传统,个人几乎不可能向真理迈出哪怕是一步。因此,正是理性主义的批判方法——理性主义和怀疑主义之间的妥协,长期以来一直是英国中间道路的基础:尊重传统,同时认识到需要对其进行改革。[1]

哈耶克和波普尔一样认为,理性无法提供确定性,因此,不能精确地预测任何特定行动或决策的未来后果,这支持了一种不仅反对激进变革,也反对长期经济和社会计划,赞成通过试错法进行零星发展的政治规划。

尽管两位著述者之间——以及大体上与新右派之间——具有明显的相似性,然而,要准确地判断波普尔的著作对哈耶克的激进主义批判以及对社会、经济和政治规划究竟有多大影响,却十分困难。1982 年,哈耶克声称,"自从(波普尔的)《发现的逻

① Popper,1963/2007b:505.

辑》(*Logik der Fors. chung*)1934 年面世以来,我就一直完全追随他总体上的方法论哲学"①。他还认为,波普尔的用语会对左派分子起作用,尽管他们对哈耶克本人装聋作哑。新右派的另一位重要人物米尔顿·弗里德曼则建议将波普尔的证伪理论应用于经济学。哈耶克和波普尔一样,反对把对知识的追寻分解为专门学科的倾向;和波普尔一样,哈耶克批评保守主义者对知识追求的轻视(如果他们发现其中隐含了他们不喜欢的东西);和波普尔一样,哈耶克批评保守主义者支持制定经济政策的民族主义方式,而非国际主义的、世界主义的方式。哈耶克和波普尔都拒绝自己被归类为任何特定意识形态的支持者。两位思想家都不认为他们的职责是贩卖某个特定的意识形态立场,相反,他们都觉得他们的思想通过提出一系列关于知识和自由的描述性而非规范性的主张,超出了意识形态——超越了它们。哈耶克和波普尔都没有自称对知识提出"自由主义"的理解,相反,他们声称他们只是描述事实上知识在如何发展,对此我们可以作出什么评价,我们可以如何适当地利用它。之后,两位思想家汇合于自由主义(广义上的),认为它是最有能力在认识论不确定的情况下起作用的学说。

尽管如此,波普尔和哈耶克在自由主义的含义上却持有不同意见。特别是在国家干预社会和经济事务的适当程度上他们的看法不一致。毕竟波普尔的总体政治观是社会民主的。他对他所谓的"不受限制的资本主义"强烈不满,称之为"不人道""不公正"的。例如,在《开放社会及其敌人》中,波普尔明确表示,他的观点"与严格的不干预政策(通常称作自由放任政策,但并非

①　Weimer & Palermo,1982:323.

完全准确)无关。自由主义和国家干预并非相互对立的"。^① 波普尔强烈主张,无监管的自由市场和自由放任的经济学,由于未能保护经济弱者免受经济强者的欺凌,侵犯了个人自由,而不是保护个人自由。波普尔说,"即使国家保护其公民免受身体暴力的欺凌(原则上在不受限制的资本主义制度下确是如此),却可能由于未能保护他们免遭经济强权的滥用而无法实现我们的目标……不受限制的经济自由可能和不受限制的身体自由一样伤及自身,经济强权可能与身体暴力一样危险"^②。

因此,他主张,"(哈耶克和弗里德曼所倡导的那种)对不受限制的经济制度不干预的原则,必须被放弃。如果我们希望自由得到保护,那么我们就必须要求无限经济自由的政策被有计划的国家经济干预所取代。我们必须要求不受限制的资本主义让位于一种经济干预主义"^③。这样的一个计划完全符合他对乌托邦主义的反对,至少他是这么认为的。例如,我们可以"制定一个合理的保护经济弱者的政治纲领",而不至于陷入乌托邦主义。"我们可以制定法律来限制剥削。我们可以限制工作日……可以为工人(最好是全体公民)提供残疾、失业和养老保险。这样,我们就可以消除这种由于工人为了不挨饿而必须屈服的无助的经济地位而产生的剥削形式。"他接着写道,"不能允许经济权力主宰政治权力,如果有必要的话,经济权力必须被政治权力所抗衡和控制。"^④同样,他主张,这也是"国家的责任,要确保公民受到教育,使他们能够参与社会生活,利用一切机会发

---

① Popper,1945/2006a:117.
② Popper,1945/2006b:135.
③ Popper,1945/2006b:135—136.
④ Popper,1945/2006b:136—137.

展自己的兴趣和才智",不论他们是否有能力偿付。[1] "如果需要保护年轻人以免他们由于疏忽而无法捍卫自己的自由,那么在教育方面实施一定的国家监督……就是必要的,而且国家也应该确保所有的教育设施可以为所有人所用。"[2]

波普尔认为,干预"往往会增强国家的权力……这是非常危险的……(但)不成其为一个反对它的决定性的论点"[3]。干预必须伴随着民主制度的加强,应该总是以他的消极功利主义为指导,即追求与"具体的恶"交战,"而不是建立某种理想的善。国家干预应该仅限于保护个人自由所真正必需",即建立和改革社会和政治制度,使之鼓励公民自由辩论、能根据过去的经验和知识进行零星改革。哈耶克不同意这一观点,他认为认识论的不确定性会将社会、经济或政治计划的任何努力变为徒劳。

因此,波普尔的政治学不能被理解为是完全保守主义的,而是包含了影响保守主义并受其影响的要素。同样,显然可以看出,他的观点影响了自由主义思想家,但是也不能轻易被归入自由主义阵营。自由至上主义由于艾因·兰德(Ayn Rand)和罗伯特·诺齐克(Robert Nozick)等思想家,在美国一直特别具有影响力,他们主张减少国家的面积和范围,以便为所有人建立一个尽可能重要的私人选择的领域,不受威压强制,主张对个人主义、最低限度的国家及私人财产权的总体支持。[4] 然而在自由至上主义中实验和风险的主题同样强大;以及改革的主题,特别

① Popper,1945/2006a:139.
② Popper,1945/2006a:117—118.
③ Popper,1945/2006b:141.
④ Nozick,1974;Rand,1943.

是自由的个人有能力将自己的意志施加于社会,从而带来创新的做法,这些做法往往是与过去深刻而彻底的决裂。这些主题对波普尔和哈耶克而言都具有争议性,他们两人都对激进变革和冒险的社会改革持怀疑态度。的确,哈耶克对美国的自由至上主义持怀疑态度,正是出于以下原因:它似乎发源于理性的建构主义描述,而不是进化论的描述,因此陷入了与俄国和法国革命者相同的拔高理性地位(高于传统)的陷阱。[①] 波普尔也有这种担忧,而且他和哈耶克一样,也试图捍卫传统在政治和社会中的重要性,自由至上主义似乎与一种只有通过其个体成员的私利才能团结一致的社会观相结合。波普尔——也许是对他的激进批评者的部分回应——越发强调传统在团结个人中的作用。而且,区分波普尔的方法论(他的认识论)和这种认识论所产生的政治或实际后果是至关重要的。他的认识论是非常激进的,似乎与广义的自由至上主义观点相一致。人类知识在科学和政治领域的发展往往来自于人类个体对真理"鲁莽的"追求,他们总体上通过试图解释世界和自己的生活而对其施加秩序。各种观点在持续的批评和理性反思的过程中起起落落,就像市场经济中的公司一般。"科学,更具体来说是科学进步,"他论述道,"不是孤立努力的结果,而是思想自由竞争的结果。"[②]能够经受住严峻的智识竞争的理论将继续成为真理的候选者,不能经受竞争的则被抛弃。然而,这一动态过程的实际结果事实上就是政治渐进主义。社会应该作为现有的知识和传统背景下,在世界上各自打拼的人类个体所作出的许多零星的挑战和干预,而

卡尔·波普尔

---

① Gamble,1996.

② Popper,1957/2005:143.

慢慢地发展起来的结果。他认为，人们应该可以随意地犯错、冒险——事实上，知识的增长就依赖于这样的人。但他不认为国家应该以此为基础为社会改革辩护。社会和政治改革应该是尝试性的、渐进的、规避风险的，而不是激进的、冒险的。

关于意识形态的最终结论

具有讽刺意味的是，在《开放社会及其敌人》和波普尔后期的各种文章中阐述的政治观，代表着对1945年到20世纪70年代欧洲盛行的社会民主共识的有力辩护，却被那些自称是自由至上主义者、自由主义者和保守主义者的人用来摧毁了这个共识。尽管赞成有限的社会规划和国家干预经济的作用，但波普尔的认识论经哈耶克和弗里德曼过滤之后，却为新右派的兴起和政治集体主义的毁灭提供了哲学背景。他拥护财富再分配和公共福利，以保护经济弱者不受经济强者的欺凌，但他的观点却得到了世界领导人，包括撒切尔夫人（她称波普尔是她最喜欢的哲学家）和乔治·索罗斯（George Soros）这样的企业家的广泛赞誉，后者按照波普尔的原则投资全球市场，积累了个人财富。波普尔在一生中的大部分时间都是社会主义者；他一直敬重马克思，认同他对自由放任经济学的反对，但他却反对20世纪六七十年代的左翼政治，并为80年代左翼政治的毁灭铺平了道路。他与许多启蒙运动思想家一起，庆幸人类有改善世界的能力，但也同启蒙运动的批评家们一起，反对理性可以为激进变革辩护（在自由主义和社会主义革命分子的表达中能发现这种观点）。

波普尔的观点无法被轻易归入任何特定的意识形态阵营，所以我们不应该非要这么做。波普尔本人对这类标签没有兴趣，也没怎么参与关于他最该属于哪个阵营的辩论。他的反本质主义意味着他没有兴趣讨论"保守主义"或"自由至上主义"等术语的含义，他对于将知识追求分化为不同学科或方法论的反感，意味着他对划分观点的界限，从而形成不同的意识形态立场的行动并不关心。这是有一定原因的。批评者和支持者希望把波普尔这样的复杂思想家塞入固定的意识形态立场，这必然导致对他的观点的简化和歪曲；自称为保守主义者或自由主义者或自由至上主义者的人，可能都希望将波普尔归入自己的阵营，但是这样做的话，他们就必须得故意忘记他的理论中那些与他们的总体理论不一致却往往是关键的内容。波普尔对这种企图及其对知识增长所产生的压抑的后果持怀疑态度，这是恰如其分的。我们在思考波普尔在政治思想史上应有的位置时，或许也应该采取波普尔的方法，放弃对波普尔观点的意识形态"本质"的追寻（以及随之而来的想要给他贴上某个标签的愿望），而是讨论他的思想观点，并试图通过合理和严谨的思考及辩论来驳倒它们。

波普尔哲学的当代关联性

从许多方面来看,阅读波普尔的著作都像是透过一个窗口窥视另一个时代,一个自由民主受到极权主义威胁的时代,个人自由、平等、权利正被纳粹主义、斯大林主义和法西斯主义的原始集体主义政治所威胁;一个全世界人民在理性和进步的原则下对国际统一的追求,正受到民族主义和战争的强大力量所挑战的时代。作为一本哲学和政治学著作,《开放社会及其敌人》正是其时代的产物,由一股个人自由超越暴政的坚定信念所激发,充满了对科学、逻辑和理性的启蒙运动价值观的承诺,超越了波普尔视为神秘主义和排他主义的哲学唯心主义内涵。并且,它与《历史决定论的贫困》一起,代表了一个关于社会以及社会研究的声明,发源于一个特殊的历史时刻,但并非源自一个特定的政治意识形态。

然而,波普尔关于认识论、社会和政治学的主张不仅仅是历史的产物,它们还是对社会和政治思想具有持久意义的真正贡献。波普尔的政治哲学包含了关于政治能实现什么、不能实现什么,政治家、哲学家、社会科学家应该或不应该做什么的大胆而具有争议的观点。尽管如此,波普尔的著作在当代政治理论著作中往往被忽视，尤其是英美政治理论著作。一个学生没有学过波普尔却获得了政治学位，这是完全可能的，或许也是正常的。政治理论的本科课程很少用一周时间讲述波普尔，波普尔的政治学著作常常被更主流的哲学家所忽略，他们——如果说对波普尔有什么兴趣的话——关心的更多是他关于自然科学哲学的理论。也许一个可能的原因是，波普尔的政治学著作已经被政治事件淹没了。1938年，希特勒入侵他的祖国奥地利时，波普尔开始写作《开放社会及其敌人》。当时，法西斯主义不只是用来研究的有意思的哲学谜题——它还是世界政治的主导力量，共同致力于将权力集中在精英阶层的领导人手中，它声称比人民更了解人民自己的利益，并努力用这个认识作为其征服和暴政的理由。继纳粹在二战中战败及后来苏联在20世纪80年代末90年代初解体，这些威胁几乎从世界舞台上消失，使许多人或许觉得波普尔对激进哲学的剖析是多余的。

如果这确实是当代政治哲学家忽视波普尔的原因，那他们就错了。波普尔对政治中的极权主义和历史主义的批判，称其为多余是言过其实，他对封闭社会的反对继续对当代政治学有着重要的意义。因为尽管纳粹主义和法西斯主义确实销声匿迹了，全球政治却依然受到波普尔所抨击的许多弊病的诅咒。封闭社会的部落制特征仍然相当突出，表现为继续破坏世界上许多地区的种族和民族冲突，在许多国家中增多的宗教政治化和激进化，包括那些自由民主制度下的国家。全球化、移民增加、资本主义市场的扩大，以及国际货币基金组织、世界银行、欧盟、联合国等超国家机构的兴起造成民族国家的政治重要性下降。在许多社会和政治科学家、实践者和评论家中，关于民族和种族身份受到侵蚀的观点越来越流行，然而，许多人坚持文化、宗教或族裔身份，并为此而战，以其名义而杀戮的意愿却似乎从来没这么强烈。同样，非民主制的领导人和政权甘愿使用国家制度残酷对待本国公民，欺压暴虐，剥夺公民的基本自由，全都以某种更高的利益为名，给世界上数以万计的人们带来了长期的苦难。开放社会仍然有敌人。他们可能与波普尔所写的那些不同，但是波普尔对法西斯主义和极权主义的批判一样可以直截了当、合乎逻辑地适用于我们今天在身边可以看到的宗教狂热、权威主义、民族主义的更新、更明显的罪恶。

波普尔的政治哲学首先代表了对自由主义、民主和理性的辩护，对部族主义、权威主义和暴政的反对；它代表着坚定地捍卫世界上每一个人的权利，任何人都有权不生活在对统治者的恐惧中，有权参与决定他们的政治共同体的未来发展方向，有权过自己觉得值得的生活，自由自在，不受不公正的限制。因此，面对学术圈内外认为政治制度应该对源于宗教、种族、文化或民族身份的主张给予肯定或特别认可的观点，它代表着对世界性的个人主义的辩护。这些主张不仅在某些政治体制中，而且在政治哲学家中也越来越流行。国家（与公民）应该如何应对文化、种族和宗教多样性的问题，在近年来已经变得非常重要，特别是对美国和英国、荷兰等欧洲国家的决策者来说。少数群体应该在多大程度上吸收多数群体的价值观，自由国家应该如何在尊重少数群体的身份和鼓励所有个体的共同价值观——无论个人信仰和理想——之间取得平衡，这仍然是极其困难和有争议的问题，也是决策者、议会议员和实践者之间深刻分歧的根源。当代政治哲学在近年来也一样被政治理论家（包括自由主义阵营的内部和外部）的一股死灰复燃的倾向所主宰，强调自由主义民主政治中的特殊主义身份的重要性。某些自由主义理论家如威尔·金里卡①（Will Kymlicka）、约瑟夫·拉兹②（Joseph Raz），自由民族主义者如大卫·米勒③（David Miller）、耶尔·塔米尔④（Yael Tamir），社群主义者如迈克尔·桑德尔⑤（Michael Sandel）、阿拉斯代尔·麦金泰尔⑥（Alasdair MacIntyre），差异理论家如艾莉丝·马里昂·扬⑦、南希·弗雷泽⑧，以及其他许多理论家都主张自由民主政治中社区和群体在哲学、道德和规范上的重要性，并且以他们自己的方式，批评他们认为是传统自由政治思想核心的天真而抽象的个人主义。波普尔的社会和政治哲学代表了对这种理念的清晰持久的反驳，但这一点却几乎从未被提及或讨论。一些理论家提出，在不同群体中建立共同的政治是不可能的，因为这些群体中体现的许多价值观是彼此不可通约的，因此，不同群体没有共同基础可以相互沟通（如格雷⑨）。其他人则主张一种政治多元化的形式，承认不同群体有时有不相容的需求（如帕瑞克⑩）。波普尔与约翰·罗尔斯⑪和查尔斯·拉莫尔⑫（Charles Larmore）等当代政治自由主义者，以及艾莉丝·马里昂·扬⑬等差异理论家

① Kymlicka,1997.
② Raz,1986;1996.
③ Miller,1995.
④ Tamir,1993.
⑤ Sandel,1982.
⑥ MacIntyre,1986.
⑦ Young,1990.
⑧ Fraser,1997.
⑨ Gray,2000.
⑩ Parekh,2005.
⑪ Rawls,1993.
⑫ Larmore,2008.
⑬ Young,2000.

持有相同的观点，即不同社会的成员相互协商，找到解决政治问题的共同办法，这是可能的，也是必要的。然而，波普尔与其中许多人的分歧在于他提出，这类对话的各方必须把他们的宗教和文化信仰视作假设或猜想，而不是真正的主张，这样才是适合进行讨论和批评的主题。批评者提出，波普尔要求不同的文化和宗教群体的成员服从于他关于真理本质的观点，这样一种在不同的文化和宗教群体间寻求谈判和解的方法，其所造成的问题不亚于它解决的问题。这种方法实在是太过苛刻，因为它要求不同群体的成员以一种特殊的、有争议的方式来理解他们的价值观以及他们与之的关系。但是在这一点上，波普尔似乎和许多其著作被视为当代辩论焦点的自由主义者一样具有争议性，一样苛刻。例如，罗尔斯和拉莫尔试图建立一个审慎推理模型，避免要求人们对自己的信仰采取某种特定的形而上学立场，只要求对话的各方以特定的有争议的方式提出他们的主张，以便被持有截然不同的世界观的人们所接受。艾莉丝·马里昂·扬的差异理论落入了一个大体上与帕瑞克和格雷所捍卫的方法相似的陷阱，他们所有人都以某种方式，要求所有群体的成员"越过分歧进行对话"，并通过以特定的方式设计讨论的框架，根据决定行为规则的更广泛、更优先的原则来约束他们的商议，从而建立起共同的原则和制度。波普尔反对这样的"迷思"，即我们需要将个人理解为是互相排斥的"框架"内所固有的，框架定义了他们的身份，使得群体无法相互协商或达成协议。他的反对仍然极为有力、富有洞见，仍然在很大程度上被大多数政治理论家所忽视，其中很多理论家已经开始主张与波普尔近 50 年前捍卫的十分相似的审议式民主的概念。^① 波普尔的方法论个人主义——他认为政治分析的主要主体是个人，而不是个人所属的群体——以及他主张不同文化、宗教和民族的成员可以（而且必须）走到一起，彼此进行有意义的协商，以便确认并解决社会和政治问题，而排除他们之间的差异。这确实是具有争议性的，但这样的争议性和武断性与许多在文献中被视为典范的其他替代方法也差不多（见沃尔德伦相关论述^②）。

此外，正如波普尔的哲学削弱了以下这个观点，即认为在国内背景下的社会和政治改革可以通过诉诸普遍历史规律或凭借抽象推理（不依赖于更广泛的推测性知识和理论的系统）推导出来的理想化事态而被证明为合理，波普尔哲学同时也指出以相同的理由作为国际干预的基础——特别在民主化领域——是一种愚蠢的做法。它还特别削弱了这种观点——在英美等西方自由民主国家中占主导地位——认为在没有民主历史的社会中建立民主政体是可能的。认为非民主政体可以被扫除，并毫无问题地被替换为更民主、更进步的政治制度，这个观点已经被证明充满了危险，特别是在近期。例如，在伊拉克和阿富汗的战争可以说是对波普尔所说的那种推理（和政治激进主义）的局限性的一个恰当证明，正如自由民主社会的政治家和哲学家（受启蒙主义对理性力量的信念所驱使）不应该去凭空设想理想社会的愿景，并改革社会以实现这些愿景，他们也不应该以为自己的角色是要去设计一套理想的社会和政治制度，并将其强加于没有做好准备、对其不理解、没有参与制度制定的人们。这种激进主义

① Popper,1994.
② Waldron,2004.

是基于一种盲目的信念，相信理性能够对需要哪种制度、制度应该致力于什么目标、在制度建立的过程中可能遇到哪些陷阱等问题提供确定性。事实上，波普尔提出，不可能有这样的确定性，预见个人决策的所有可能变数和后果是根本不可靠的。因此，任何在非民主国家鼓励推行民主的努力必须是渐进的、零星的，是相关个人的真正对话的结果。

如果说波普尔的政治哲学往往由于其在历史上显得多余而被抛弃，那么它也同样频繁地因为其方法论上的含义而被否定。波普尔的思想既是为社会和国家的结构提供规范性或指导性的原则，同样也是（如果称不上更多是）为政治和社会生活研究建立适当的方法。他的思想是关于政治学和哲学的适当目的的主张，因此它们阐明了一个特殊的、有独创性的、有争议的政治和方法论的设想。这个设想不能轻易契合当代政治思想的许多主流方法。鉴于波普尔对证伪主义的认识论的立场和对归纳的证实主义的反对，也许我们可以说，讨论波普尔不是什么比讨论波普尔是什么要容易得多。

例如，波普尔不能被轻易描述为政治哲学的"剑桥学派"的成员，该学派的思想体现在昆汀·斯金纳（Quentin Skinner）和约翰·波科克（J. G. Pocock）等历史学家的著作中，他们认为政治哲学家的主要工作是通过将政治文本或话语置于特定的历史背景下来推导出其含义。波普尔认可斯金纳等历史学家的主张，即研究政治和哲学文本时，了解作者写作的历史背景从而搞清楚作者的意图，这是有一定重要意义的。也就是说，波普尔认为，通过重建文本或论述的写作或表述的历史环境和意图，推导出文本或论述的"情境逻辑",这在某些时候是很重要的。① 然而,他强烈反对他们更为激进的主张,即这样一个过程排除了关于政治或社会的更有意义的表述的可能性,或者说政治概念、文本或论述无法经受非历史的分析。波普尔认为,政治哲学不仅仅是研究特定理论家在特定历史时刻使用的语言,而且与维特根斯坦相反,他认为哲学的要务不只是推导语言或文本陈述的意义,而是要确定这些陈述的真理性或虚假性。因此,他认为,政治哲学的重点是确定社会和政治问题并加以解决。由此,他认为社会和政治科学的主要目标就是要确定关于社会和政治事务的主张是真还是伪,并弄清现有的社会和政治安排如何以及在何种程度上被视为或者变得合理。

波普尔也不是后现代主义者。他坚持认为使用理性和客观性的工具来揭示关于世界的方方面面的知识,从量子力学到社会和政治制度的适当设计,这是可能的。这个观点似乎与后现代主义者认为这样的努力注定要失败的看法相悖。尽管他与许多启蒙思想家背道而驰,他质疑理性揭示关于世界的某些真理的能力,但他却并非是与福柯或布迪厄(Bourdieu)相似的后结构主义者;尽管他是一个充满激情的批评家(对于科学、权威主义、极权主义、哲学诸多分支的其他理解),但他并非属于哈贝马斯、阿多诺、霍克海默等思想家传统的"批判理论家",所有原因我们都在第三章讨论过了。在波普尔看来,批判——理解为用相反的论证和证据来对假设进行检验——是通向真正的人类知识的基本途径,也是获得真正人类知识的唯一方式。波普尔憎恶他所认为的隐藏在后现代主义、后结构主义和批判理论背后

卡尔·波普尔

---

① Popper,1957/2005:136—141.

的道德相对主义,同时也反对它们中隐含的政治无能。他的最高目标是提供一个可以评估主张(关于世界的所有方面,包括道德)的真伪的机制,捍卫个人可以通过共同努力掌握自己的生活和未来的观点,反对"激进"思想家所普遍认为的人们事实上只能等待改变降临的主张。

波普尔不是剑桥学派历史学家、后现代主义者、后结构主义者或批判理论家,那么,他也许最接近于哲学实用主义者和英美传统领域的政治理论家。然而,他也不能被轻易地归入这两种传统之中。有无数理由说明波普尔为什么不能直接被标记为英美传统的成员。自从罗尔斯的《公正理论》在1971年出版以来,英美政治哲学就开始以寻求公正以及公正社会的恰当定义为主流。与剑桥学派的实践者不同,罗尔斯主义的政治哲学家倾向于在建立理论时不诉诸历史,最多只是沾一点边;相反,他们的目标是依靠分析传统来建立公正的社会和政治秩序得以构建的某些基本原则的合理性和规范性。换言之,英美规范政治哲学的主要目标是通过理性的商议过程,推导出一个实质性的公正的概念,用以指导社会和政治制度的设计,确定这些制度的角色和责任,并约束它们的行动。因此,制度、政策和决议由理性(通过可理性辩护的论证)决定是合理的,而不是由宗教、文化或民族传统中体现的特定价值观决定。结果,英美政治哲学家认为自己在从事启蒙主义事业,为政治安排——而不是偶然的、狭隘的成员资格或理想——在理性通用标准中的权威地位辩护。自由主义思想家如布莱恩·巴里[1](Brian Barry)、查尔斯·贝茨[2]

---

① Barry,1995.

② Beitz,1989.

(Charles Beitz)、托马斯·内格尔[1](Thomas Nagel)、托马斯·斯坎伦[2](Thomas Scanlon)和约翰·罗尔斯[3]早期作品中的契约主义,查尔斯·拉莫尔[4]和约翰·罗尔斯[5]后期作品中的政治自由主义,约瑟夫·拉兹[6]和史蒂芬·沃尔[7](Steven Wall)等思想家的综合自由主义,与埃米·古特曼(Amy Gutmann)和丹尼斯·汤普森[8](Dennis Thompson)、约书亚·科恩[9](Joshua Cohen)等理论家的审议式民主方法联合一致,提出政治制度的设计、改革的制定,都可以根据在多元化情形中积极寻求一致意见的个人行动者的理性商议所揭示的原则来实现,理性(不被特定的价值观或理论所污染)可以提供一个从零开始构建公正社会的蓝图。英美自由主义政治哲学因此从培根和笛卡儿等思想家的启蒙主义愿景中汲取灵感,这些思想家认为可以通过从脑海中去除所有的个性,用干净的眼睛观看世界而发现真理。

当然,波普尔同意政治权威应该由理性,而非由特殊性的身份或者价值观来证明其合理性,但他对培根或笛卡儿的理性愿景没有兴趣,而英美的规范设计似乎就建立在这种理性愿景之上,他认为这种愿景不负责任、傲慢自大、与知识的增长背道而驰。他并不赞同罗尔斯的观点,即认为政治哲学的目的应该是推导出可用于构建和管理社会和政治制度的公正原则。波普尔

① Nagel,1991.
② Scanlon,1999.
③ Rawls,1971.
④ Lamore,2008.
⑤ Rawls,1993.
⑥ Raz,1986;1996.
⑦ Wall,1998.
⑧ Gutmann & Thompson,1996.
⑨ Cohen,1989.

认为,这样的设计显示了许多启蒙思想家对理性力量的盲目乐观,认为它可以扫除历史,构建全面有效运行的社会和政治制度,就好像过去从未存在过。用波普尔的话来说,罗尔斯和他的许多追随者都不过是法国革命者的错误认识论的现代拥护者。因此,他们陷入了同样的困境:他们试图描绘一个有效的、公正的社会,却将不可避免地必定被那些冒充知识的东西的推测性所挫败,理性无法预见所有可能的变数,因此无法应对所有可能的挑战。罗尔斯的社会公正理论倾向苛刻而实际——例如,它们规定社会的利益和负担应如何重新分配,以及这些利益和负担是什么。波普尔关于抽象推理能够一劳永逸地彻底解决这些问题的可谬论,伴随着他对长期集中规划的怀疑论,对许多在英美传统领域工作的哲学家按他们现有的方式解决公正问题的愿望给予了极大的遏制,并提出他们应该以更谦逊的眼光来看待他们关于公正的主张,把它们看作假设和建议,而不是理性的可检验的真理。

同样,对于认为政治哲学的核心目标是定义"公正"等术语的含义的观点,波普尔也没什么兴趣。因此,他应该已经考虑到了许多英美哲学家中存在的倾向,他们总是依据本质的定义来设计问题(如"什么是公正?"或"什么是平等?"),这种倾向在当代的英美政治哲学中非常流行,是一种多余而无用的行为。波普尔主要感兴趣的是在一个无法为平等、公正、自由等术语提供最终定义的语境下找到问题并解决问题。如果有领导者或知识分子想要这样做的话,我们应该对他们持怀疑态度。他特别感兴趣的是知识的力量和局限性,因此也就关心统治者可能为进行社会改革所提供的恰当理由。鉴于此,波普尔在主流规范话语中一直是一个边缘人物,这就不奇怪了。毕竟,如果他的知识论的主张是正确的（即理性不可能揭示关于世界的某些真理），如果哲学不应该去关心公正、平等、自由等术语的定义这也是正确的，那么在英美传统领域的规范政治哲学家的重大担忧只不过就是毫无意义的错误而已。他们诉诸启蒙主义理性的错误概念，以便产生理想的政治术语定义，这是无用的，因为它们的逻辑性或说服力无法得到证明。

尽管如此，波普尔的思想在一些方面与英美政治理论家的思想比我们原本以为的，也比许多在这个传统领域的思想家们所想象的更加接近。例如，许多研究罗尔斯主义传统的哲学家同意波普尔的观点，即政治哲学家的主要任务是找到并试图解决真正的社会和政治问题。例如，像罗纳德·德沃金（Ronald Dworkin）这样的自由主义政治哲学家试图回答这样的问题——"什么是平等？"很显然，他们这样做主要是为了找到并解决真正的社会和政治问题。形形色色的自由主义的平等主义者在很大程度上受到社会和政治制度如何衡量和改善不公正的经济不平等的理论和实践问题的激发（如科恩[①]、德沃金[②]）。多元文化的自由主义者和政治自由主义者关注的诸多问题，包括解决总体上公平的自由民主制度可以如何适当地考虑到文化、民族、宗教的少数群体的不同利益的问题（如吉姆利卡[③]、拉兹[④]）。而国际公正领域中越来越多的政治哲学家开始普遍寻求解决复杂的实际问题的办法，包括减轻世界上贫困人口的贫穷和痛苦

①　Cohen,1997.
②　Dworkin,2000.
③　Kymlicka,1997.
④　Raz,1996.

（如博格①）。对于这些思想家而言，重点不在于为了抽象推理本身而去进行抽象推理，而是要以一种头脑清晰的、分析性的方式，将波普尔称之为理性主义传统的工具应用到具体的社会和政治问题上去，以便于解决这些问题。因此，关于其具体定义应在这些问题实际存在的本质的背景下进行讨论，并对其作出回应。当然，波普尔会强调任何此类解决方案的推测性的、假设性的性质；事实上他会主张推理需要在知识积累的背景下进行；他还会指出，提供的答案不应该被视为确定的真理。但是我们没有理由认为英美规范政治哲学家不会赞同波普尔的观点，即政治哲学（和任何其他学科一样）从本质上讲是一个解决问题的过程，而理性可以为具体的社会、政治、经济和法律问题提供解决方案。

　　波普尔还与许多当代英美政治哲学家一样反对目的论道德，即认为根据一项法令或一套制度在何种程度上符合或有助于实现事先确定的人人享有美好生活的概念，由此来决定这项法令或这套制度在道德上是对是错，这种做法是恰当的。大多数当代自由平等主义者、自由至上主义者、古典自由主义者、政治自由主义者和综合的自由主义者都支持这个主张（赫伯特·哈特在《法律概念》中，以及罗尔斯在《公正理论》中以不同方式提出），即功利目的论在道德上是有缺陷的，因为它会导致如压迫少数群体等不公正现象；他们也支持罗尔斯，提倡以自由主义的一种广义上的"道义论"形式来将其取代。波普尔的政治哲学通过对其核心假设提出一个不同的，也许更强大的认识论批判，巩固了自由主义对目的论的道德和政治制度的反对。其核心假

---

① Pogge,2007.

设是，任何道德理论若是根据一项法令或决策在何种程度上能实现某种所有人都能享有的未来总体利益来评价它是对是错，那么这样的道德理论不仅在道德上是不适当的，在认识论上也是不合逻辑的，因为这样的总体利益是不可能得知的。同样，波普尔的论证也有助于削弱道德结果论的某些更为激进的变种，即任何道德理论若是根据一项法令或决策的可能后果来评价其是对是错，那么它就会被以下事实所削弱：(1)为了知道最终后果是好是坏，需要对它们所致力于的目标有事先的了解(这是可能的，但由于理性的易谬性，难度很大)；(2)任何此类法令或决策的后果——尤其是长期后果——都无法确知。我们应该还记得，这就是波普尔致力于他所谓的"消极"功利主义而非"积极"功利主义的原因。他认为，我们能够也应该设法找出社会问题，并提出能带来有益结果的解决方案，但我们不应该试图建立美好生活的总体概念，不应该根据行为在何种程度上实现这个美好生活的概念来判断其对错。因此，我们行动的后果在我们的道德考量中是很重要的，但国家行为只能是为了减少损害，而不是为了促进特定的政治愿景，实施这样的国家行为才是合乎逻辑的。

最后，还有一个进一步的、更根本的主张，将波普尔与研究英美传统的当代政治理论家统一在一起，即关于政治和社会的规范性陈述既是有意义的，也是可能的。记得在波普尔写作的时期，分析哲学由维也纳学派的逻辑实证主义以及奥斯汀和赖尔等思想家的日常语言哲学所主宰。这些占主流地位的力量似乎共同排除了这样的观点，即作出关于政治或社会或道德等事物的规范性陈述是可能的。毕竟，逻辑实证主义者认为这样的陈述毫无意义，因此根本不能被描述为哲学陈述。而日常语言哲学家提出,政治概念的含义(以及关于政治或社会生活的陈述的规范性理由)不能从它们被使用的背景中分离,例如,日常语言哲学家提出,通过问这样一个问题,"什么是自由?"我们真正在问的是"个人在特定语境下以哪些方式使用'自由'这个词?"这种方法似乎排除了为这样的术语提供普遍定义的任何企图,因此,它意味着关于其重要性的规范性讨论(以及该如何保护或鼓励这些讨论)恰恰代表了关于这些术语的各种含义的一般对话。

　　逻辑实证主义和日常语言哲学的主导地位以及它们对规范性的排除,导致许多思想家如以赛亚·伯林[1]和彼得·拉斯利特[2](Peter Laslett)担心政治理论已死。波普尔可能并没有以他所声称的方式单枪匹马地摧毁了逻辑实证主义和日常语言理论,但他的确有助于打破它们对哲学的控制,并为一种以严谨分析为特征的哲学方法内部的规范性腾出了位置。波普尔反对归纳法科学模型,主张科学应该关心对关于世界的猜测性陈述进行证伪,而不是用归纳法推断一般规律,这体现了哲学可以(也应该)采取"科学"的方法,但这样做并没有排除规范性陈述的可能,也没有否认关于政治、社会、伦理或形而上学的陈述的哲学地位。波普尔的认识论提供了一种使形而上学、政治和道德陈述(以及规范性)与分析传统所具有的那种目的严谨和明确相适合的(有争议的)方式。因此,尽管他的影响常常被忽视,但我们还是可以公平地说,波普尔的思想有助于建立其他思想家(如H. L. A.哈特和约翰·罗尔斯)能够创作他们最著名的规范性

---

[1]　Berlin,1962.

[2]　Laslett,1965.

作品的哲学条件。

此外,波普尔重申政治哲学是寻求解决具体的社会和政治问题的办法,而不是追求最终真理或本质,这为理查德·罗蒂[①](Richard Rorty)等实用主义者铺平了道路,使他们能够提出对政治哲学中的基础主义的反对;为研究罗尔斯思想传统的英美政治理论家铺平了道路,使他们能够不依赖于真理的更广泛的描述就可以作出规范性主张。例如,在罗蒂的思想中,我们发现了波普尔式的主张,即哲学家不应该关心确定特定的真理,因为这些真理是无法确知的,相反,他们应该致力于使用他们目前可以支配的历史、分析和哲学工具,解决世界上的具体政治问题。罗蒂认为,对真理的追寻不仅毫无意义,而且令人们偏离了目标,寻求终极真理的哲学家必然会花太多时间寻找真理,以至于没有时间来解决世界上的人们所面临的真正的、长期的问题。因此,罗蒂式的实用主义者和波普尔一样,反对我们为了讨论哲学思想,而首先去找到这些思想的哲学基础(或本质),他们也和波普尔一样,主张社会和政治问题可以通过个人行动者的共同商议而得到解决。如罗蒂所说,政治哲学家真正的任务不是找到最终真理,而是要找到我们关于世界和政治的主张合乎逻辑的理由。波普尔和罗蒂一样,认为我们可以获得关于世界的知识,可以获得关于我们用以描述世界、理解世界的思想的知识,而无须首先揭露它们的本质或者——用罗蒂的话来说——这些思想得以建立的基础。因此,在波普尔和罗蒂看来,政治哲学的主要目标是在没有坚实基础或明确本质的情况下,找到政治原则的依据。所以,波普尔及实用主义者强调在拥有信息有限但

① Rorty,1989.

卡尔·波普尔

积极寻找共同问题的适当解决方案的个人行动者中共同协商和达成一致的重要性。

应该说,如今这不仅是实用主义者的目标,也是绝大多数研究英美传统的政治理论家的共同目标。如今越来越多的英美政治哲学家持有与实用主义者及波普尔相同的主张,即政治哲学的要务不是去揭示关于世界的特定真理,而是在关于真理问题存在深刻的,也许是不可解决的分歧的情况下,为共同的政治原则寻求辩护。在本章前面部分,我提到多元文化论作为政治和哲学问题的出现,并提到当代政治理论家们尝试解决这个问题所采取的一些方式。他们——特别是罗尔斯等政治自由主义者——共有的观点是,我们生活的世界对一些根本的问题,如生命的起源、人类的本性和我们在世界中的位置,有着严重的分歧。我们生活在一个有着不同宗教和道德观的社会中,其中有许多互不相容,但却被世界上亿万人视为极其重要的观点和价值。在这种情况下,任何认为政治哲学的主要目标是解决关于真理的问题,认为政治哲学应该试图以这样的真理为基础来为社会和政治安排与政策辩护的观念,都将注定失败,或者至少将是无结果的、偏颇的,不被许多人所接受。政治哲学不能也不应该试图解决关于真理的问题,自由主义政治哲学家尤其不该这样做,因为这样的事对于自由主义者而言,是该留给个人的道德良知来决定的。今天的大多数英美政治哲学家面对的主要问题可以说不是"什么构成了真理",而是我们应该如何找到公平的、可以为所有在其中的人所接受的、无论他们关于世界的基本想法是什么的政治原则、制度和政策。这是波普尔所坚持的一项主张,他也对此作出了重要贡献。政治哲学的要务对波普尔而言,如同对罗蒂等实用主义者、罗尔斯等政治自由主义者、扬等差异理论家、古特曼等审议民主主义者以及众多当代英美政治哲学家而言一样，不是揭示真理，以便为政治权力或者社会和政治制度的某些特定安排、某些系列政策提供某种统一的道德基础，而是在关于世界的真理上有着严重分歧的情况下，建立起一个具有包容性的政治制度。

我们不能轻易地把波普尔与剑桥学派及后现代主义、后结构主义或批判理论等联系起来。他没有占据如罗尔斯及其追随者那样的理论空间，尽管他的结论在他们的研究领域里具有持久的相关性。他不是许多人所理解的那种功利主义者，也不是目的论者，尽管他至少在一定程度上根据其产生的后果来评价社会改革提议的成功或失败。他不是一个相对主义者、民族主义者或共产主义社会的提倡者，但他认识到特殊的成员资格在整个历史上对那么多人曾有过强大的（往往是有害的）的控制。他不是严格意义上的保守主义者，也不是自由至上主义者，不是古典自由主义者，但他反对长期的社会、经济和政治规划，影响了许多与这些传统领域相关联的人。他不是社会主义者，但他相信国家制度可以而且应该减轻他认为许多人正在经受的严重贫困。他曾一度是一个马克思主义者，终其一生都一直尊重马克思对社会和经济思想的贡献，但最终将马克思视为对开放社会的目标的威胁。他支持启蒙运动所体现的理想，但猛烈抨击了许多启蒙思想家，他捍卫基于理性的政治学但同时宣称理性的局限性，他拥护知识的增长但主张某些知识是不可能获得的。在《开放社会及其敌人》中，他提出了关于战后社会民主的一个重要观点，发源于一个将被许多人用来将其摧毁的认识论。他不是像洛克、霍布斯、卢梭或康德一样的社会契约思想家。他的结论并非建立在关于人性或人的动机的具有争议性的主张之上。他没有明确关注政治理论家视为该学科核心的许多重要问题，如政治义务、政治权利和法律的来源等问题。他没有提供一个完整和彻底的政治学规范理论。许多哲学家强烈反对波普尔的认识论、社会和政治哲学，因此以推理错误或学风草率为由，将他的著作斥为错误的而予以否定。此外，确实有些重要问题波普尔很少或没有提及，而且他的哲学似乎也并不具备力量对这些问题加以解决。因此，绝大多数当代政治哲学家、政治学家、经济学家、社会理论家和社会学家不知道该如何处理波普尔，也就不足为奇了。他们因此决定对他不作处理，也就并不奇怪了。波普尔是一个博学者、一个离经叛道者。他的著作涉及如此多的主题，在如此多的领域引起争议，每个人都可能从他的著作中找到强烈反对的东西。他作品中的自相矛盾，他的直言不讳、往往显得好辩的写作风格，以及他在昙花一现的潮流中对自己坚信的原则顽强的固守，使我们很难将他在学术文献中定位，因此他一直是当代政治哲学的一个边缘人物。

波普尔哲学的当代关联性

结　　论

　　波普尔是为数不多的一个可以用名字作为形容词来描述其理论和方法（如陈述可以被描述为波普尔式的，或维特根斯坦式的，或罗尔斯式的）的思想家。但是不存在波普尔主义，就像存在马克思主义或柏拉图主义一样的主义——因为其理论没有可以集结支持者的实质性意识形态或规范性规划。当然这是预料之中的。波普尔对历史主义的反对，对实验法、零星社会改革以及人类知识的不确定性的支持，意味着他的著作不适合意识形态所激发的那种世界建立（或摧毁）。事实上，只要意识形态代表着关于社会和政治制度的理想目标的系列真理主张，那么，用波普尔的话来说，它们充其量天生就是脆弱的和偏颇的。在最糟糕的情况下，它们体现了其支持者怀有的错误愿望，想要预言人类朝着某个理想状态发展的未来道路——波普尔认为正是这种愿望使得暴政合法化。

那么，波普尔并没有给我们留下一个意识形态。他给我们的是一种方法，来弄清楚关于世界和我们自己，我们能够知道什么，不能知道什么；一种检验和评价那些统治我们或试图告诉我们该如何生活的人所提出的主张的方法。他没有给我们一个可以制定的政策清单，或者一个可以建立的制度蓝图。事实上，他认为，许多政治哲学家和活动家想要提供这种东西的愿望正是我们需要避免的。相反，他提供了一种方法来找出什么可能是适当的政策和制度，以及如何证明它们合理。由此，他提供了一个拥护个人自由、平等和理性的政治和社会愿景。波普尔认为，不论其具有何种特殊性，社会和政治制度都应该以鼓励思想自由和言论自由、保护个人免受暴政的方式来构建，使个人免受那些以为自己知道什么最利于人类的领导者的暴政、那些未能约束这些领导者权力的制度的控制，以及免受那些能够行使其经济权力来征服和操纵经济弱者或一无所有的人的"经济强者"的控制。他相信所有人都有能力通过理性的论证和同理心寻求在社会和政治事务的解决办法上达成一致，因此，他热切地信奉民主。他相信理性具有团结统一的特征，理性（得到恰当理解的理性）为打破封闭社会所具有的"我们"和"他们"的心态，为鼓励对世界上无论何地的所有人的普遍关心提供了手段。因此，他的政治学我们可以称之为世界主义的理性主义，即所有民族的所有人如果需要都应该得到帮助,世界上所有人都可以相互进行富有成效的对话,讨论政治和社会问题。他信奉开放社会:一个以自由思想和自由讨论为特征的政治社区;对人民负责的民主制度;不仅与近邻合作,而且与所有以知识、实验、真理、自由和平等为重要美德的人们合作的精神;反对所有的历史命运、共同命运、民族、非理性主义等有害思想,这些思想在历史上为领导者提供他们需要的哲学工具,以便剥夺个人的自由,操纵个人,分化个人,最终消灭个人。他相信个人有能力实现真正的改变,但也认识到改变的需求是渐进的而不是激进的,是逐步的而不是革命性的。波普尔在政治学和科学领域都相信真理来自于思想的碰撞。即使是最神圣不可侵犯的东西、最完美最迷人的理论,也必须被迫在对立的理论面前证明自己;没有任何理论可以超越批评,事实上,如果被认为可以超越批评,那它就会失去其解释力。正如牛顿关于物理科学的观点不能自称具有不容置疑的正确性一样,政治思想家和政治理论家的理论也应该被暴露在那些试图证伪它们的人们的批判眼光之下。波普尔在认识论领域的方法研究应用于社会和政治领域,就提供了一个理解哲学和国家的目标的真正创新方法,并立即提供了一个讨论"社会科学"的可能性的新视角。他相信,这样的东西确实是可能存在的,但是要将其建立则需要对科学有一个全新的理解。

参考文献

Adorno, T. W. (1973) *Negative Dialectics*. London: Routledge. (First published in German, 1963).

Adorno, T. W., H. Albert, R. Dahrendorf, J. Habermas, H. Pilot, & K. Popper (eds.) (1976) *The Positivist Dispute in German Sociology*. New York: Harper. (First published in German, 1969).

Agassi, J. (1993) *A Philosopher's Apprentice: In Karl Popper's Workshop (Series in the Philosophy of Karl R. Popper and Critical Rationalism*. Atlanta, GA: Editions Rodopi.

Arendt, H. (1951/2004) *The Origins of Totalitarianism*. Orlando, FL: Schocken Books.

Aron, R. (1957) *The Opium of the Intellectuals*. New York: Doubleday

Banbrough, R. (ed.) (1967) *Plato, Popper, and Politics: Some Contributions to a Modern Controversy*. Cambridge: W. Heffer & Sons.

Barry, B. (1995) *Justice as Impartiality: A Treatise on Social Justice, Vol. 2*. Oxford: Clarendon Press.

Beitz, C. (1989) *Political Equality*. Princeton, NJ: Princeton University Press.

Benhabib, S. (1992) *Situating the Self: Gender, Community, and Postmodernism in Contemporary Ethics*. London: Routledge.

Berlin, I. (1962) 'Does Political Theory Exist?' in P. Laslett & W. G. Runciman (eds) *Philosophy, Politics, and Society* (pp. 1–33). Series 2, Oxford: Blackwell.

Bevir, M. (1999) *The Logic of the History of Ideas*. Cambridge: Cambridge University Press.

Blundell, J. (1999) 'Introduction' in *The Road to Serfdom: The Condensed Edition* (pp. 14–24). London: Institute of Economic Affairs.

Burke, E. (1790/1986) *Reflections on the Revolution in France*. London: Penguin.

Brzezinski, Z. (1956) *The Permanent Purge: Politics in Soviet Totalitarianism*. Cambridge, MA: Harvard University Press.

Catton, P. & G. MacDonald (eds) (2004) *Karl Popper: Critical Appraisals*. London: Routledge.

Cohen, G. A. (2008) *Rescuing Justice and Equality*. Cambridge, MA: Harvard University Press.

Cohen, J. (1989) 'Deliberation and Democratic Legitimacy' in Alan Hamlin and Phillip Petit (eds) *The Good Polity* (pp. 17–34.). Cambridge, MA: Blackwell.

Cornforth, M. (1968) *The Open Philosophy and the Open Society: A Reply to Sir Karl Popper's Refutations of Marxism.* London: Lawrence & Wishart.

Crossman, R. H. S. (1959) *Plato Today.* 2nd edition. London: George Allen & Unwin.

Derrida, J. (1967) *Of Grammatology.* Baltimore, MD: Johns Hopkins University Press. (Originally published in French, 1967).

Duhem, P. (1954) *The Aim and Structure of Physical Theory.* Princeton, NJ: Princeton University Press.

Dworkin, R. (2000) *Sovereign Virtue: The Theory and Practice of Equality.* Cambridge, MA: Harvard University Press.

Edmonds, D. & J. Eidenow (2002) *Wittgenstein's Poker: The Story of a Ten Minute Argument Between Two Great Philosophers.* London: Faber.

Feyerabend, P. (1975/1993) *Against Method: Outline of an Anarchistic Theory of Knowledge.* London: Verso.

Fite, W. (1934) *The Platonic Legend.* New York: C. Scribner's Sons.

Fraser, N. (1997) *Justice Interruptus: Critical Reflections on the Post-Socialist Condition.* New York: Routledge.

Gamble, A. (1996) *Hayek: The Iron Cage of Liberty.* Cambridge: Polity Press.

Geuss, R. (1981) *The Idea of a Critical Theory: Habermas & the Frankfurt School.* Cambridge: Cambridge University Press.

Gray, J. (2000) *Two Faces of Liberalism.* Cambridge: Polity Press.

Gutmann, A. & D. Thompson (1996) *Democracy & Disagreement.* Cambridge: Cambridge University Press.

Habermas, J. (1971) *Knowledge and Human Interests.* Boston, MA: Beacon Press.

Habermas, J. (1976) 'A Positively Bisected Rationalism' in T. W. Adorno, H. Albert, R. Dahrendorf, J. Habermas, H. Pilot, & K. Popper (eds) *The Positivist Dispute in German Sociology* (pp. 198–225). New York: Harper and Row.

Habermas, J. (1989) *The Structural Transformation of the Public Sphere: An Inquiry into a Category of Bourgeois Society.* Cambridge: Polity Press. (Originally published in German, 1962).

Hacohen, M. (2000) *Karl Popper: The Formative Years, 1902 – 1945: Politics and Philosophy in Interwar Vienna.* Cambridge: Cambridge University Press.

Hart, H. L. A. (1961/1997) *The Concept of Law.* Oxford: Oxford University Press.

参考文献

Hayek, F. A. (1944) *The Road to Serfdom*. London: Routledge.

Hayek, F. A. (1960) *The Constitution of Liberty*. London: Routledge.

Hirschmann, N. (2003) *The Subject of Liberty: Toward a Feminist Theory of Freedom*. Princeton, NJ: Princeton University Press.

Horkheimer, M. (1997) *Dialectic of Enlightenment*. Revised edition. London: Verso. (Originally published in German, 1944).

Hume, D. (1748/2008) *An Enquiry into Human Understanding*. Oxford: Oxford Classics.

Jarvie, I. C. & S. Pralong (1999) *Popper's Open Society After 50 Years: The Continuing Relevance of Karl Popper*. London: Routledge.

Jarvie, I. C., K. Milford, & D. Miller (2006) *Karl Popper: A Centenary Assessment*. Aldershot: Ashgate.

Kauffman, W. (1959) *From Shakespeare to Existentialism: Studies in Poetry, Religion, and Philosophy*. Boston, MA: Beacon Press.

Kuhn, T. S. (1962) *The Structure of Scientific Revolutions*. Chicago, IL: University of Chicago Press.

Kymlicka, W. (1997) *Multicultural Citizenship: A Liberal Theory of Minority Rights*. Oxford: Clarendon Press.

Lakatos, I. (1976) *Proofs and Refutations*. Cambridge: Cambridge University Press.

Lakatos, I. (1978a) *The Methodology of Scientific Research Programmes: Philosophical Papers Vol. 1*. Cambridge: Cambridge University Press.

Lakatos, I. (1978b) *Mathematics, Science, and Epistemology: Philosophical Papers Vol. 2*. Cambridge: Cambridge University Press.

Lane, M. (2001) *Plato's Progeny: How Socrates and Plato Still Captivate the Modern Mind*. London: Duckworth.

Larmore, C. (2008) *The Autonomy of Morality*. Cambridge: Cambridge University Press.

Laslett, P. (1956) 'Introduction' in P. Laslett (ed.) *Philosophy, Politics, and Society*. Series 1, Oxford: Blackwell.

Levinson, P. (ed.) (1982) *In Pursuit of Truth: Essays on the Philosophy of Karl Popper on the Occasion of his 80th Birthday*. Atlantic Highlands, NJ: Humanities Press.

Levinson, R. B. (1953) *In Defence of Plato*. Cambridge, MA: Harvard University Press.

MacIntyre, A. (1996) *After Virtue: A Study in Moral Theory*. London: Duckworth.

Magee, B. (1973) *Karl Popper*. London: Penguin.

Mandeville, B. (1714/1988) *The Fable of the Bees: or, Private Vices, Public Benefits*. Indianapolis: Liberty Fund.

Marcuse, H. (1964) *One Dimensional Man: Studies in the Ideology of Advanced Industrial Society*. Boston, MA: Beacon Press.

卡尔 · 波普尔

Marx, K. (1932/1988) *Economic and Philosophic Manuscripts of 1844.* New York: Prometheus Books.

Menger, C. (1871/1981) *Principles of Economics.* New York: New York University Press.

Miller, D. (1994) *Critical Rationalism: A Restatement and Defence.* Chicago, IL: Open Court Publishing Company.

Miller, D. (1995) *On Nationality.* Oxford: Clarendon Press.

Mises, L. von, (1922/1951) *Socialism: An Economic and Social Analysis.* New Haven, CT: Yale University Press.

Mises, L. von, (1949) *Human Action: A Treatise on Economics.* New Haven, CT: Yale University Press.

Munz, P. (1985) *Our Knowledge of the Growth of Knowledge.* London: Routledge.

Nagel, T. (1991) *Equality and Partiality.* New York: Oxford University Press.

Nozick, R. (1974) *Anarchy, State, and Utopia.* New York: Basic Books.

O'Hear, A. (1980) *Karl Popper.* London: Routledge.

O'Hear, A. (ed.) (2004) *Karl Popper: Critical Assessments of Leading Philosophers.* 4 Vols. London: Routledge.

Parekh, B. (2005) *Re-Thinking Multiculturalism: Cultural Diversity and Political Theory.* 2nd edition. Basingstoke: Palgrave Macmillan.

Plamenatz, J. (1952/1967) 'The Open Society and Its Enemies,' *The British Journal of Sociology 3.* 264–73. Reprinted in R. Banbrough (ed.) (1967) *Plato, Popper, and Politics: Some Contributions to a Modern Controversy.* Cambridge: W. Heffer & Sons.

Pogge, T. W. (2007) *World Poverty and Human Rights.* Cambridge: Polity Press.

Polanyi, K. (1944/2001) *The Great Transformation: The Political and Economic Origins of Our Times.* Boston, MA: Beacon Press.

Popper, K. (1935/2007a) *The Logic of Scientific Discovery.* London: Routledge.

Popper, K. (1945/2006a) *The Open Society and Its Enemies 1: The Spell of Plato.* London: Routledge.

Popper, K. (1945/2006b) *The Open Society and Its Enemies 2: Hegel and Marx.* London: Routledge.

Popper, K. (1957/2005) *The Poverty of Historicism.* London: Routledge.

Popper, K. (1963/2007b) *Conjectures and Refutations: The Growth of Scientific Knowledge.* London: Routledge.

Popper, K. (1972/1979) *Objective Knowledge: An Evolutionary Approach.* Oxford: Oxford University Press.

Popper, K. (1974/2002) *Unended Quest: An Intellectual Autobiography.* London: Routledge.

Popper, K. (1977/2003a) *The Self and Its Brain: An Argument for Interactionism.* London: Routledge. With Sir John C. Eccles.

Popper, K. (1984/2000) *In Search of a Better World: Lectures and Essays from Thirty Years.* London: Routledge.

Popper, K. (1994a) *The Myth of the Framework: In Defence of Science and Rationality.* London: Routledge. Edited by M. A. Notturno.

Popper, K. (1994b) *Knowledge and the Mind-Body Problem: In Defence of Interactionism,* London: Routledge. Edited by M. A. Notturno.

Popper, K. (1994/2003b) *All Life is Problem Solving.* London: Routledge.

Popper, K. (2008) *After the Open Society: Selected Social and Political Writings.* London: Routledge. Edited by J. Shearmur & P. N. Turner.

Putnam, H. (1974). 'The "corroboration" of theories', in P. A. Schilpp (ed.) *The Philosophy of Karl Popper* (pp. 221–40). LaSalle, IL: Open Court.

Quine, W. V. O. (1960) *Word and Object.* Cambridge, MA: MIT Press.

Rand, A. (1943) *The Fountainhead.* Indiana, IN: Bobbs-Merrill Company.

Rawls, J. (1971) *A Theory of Justice.* Oxford: Oxford University Press.

Rawls, J. (1993) *Political Liberalism.* New York: Columbia University Press.

Raz, J. (1986) *The Morality of Freedom.* Oxford: Clarendon Press.

Raz, J. (1996) *Ethics in the Public Domain: Essays in the Morality of Law and Politics.* Oxford: Clarendon Press.

Rorty, R. (1989) *Contingency, Irony, and Solidarity.* Cambridge: Cambridge University Press.

Sandel, M. (1982) *Liberalism and the Limits of Justice.* Cambridge: Cambridge University Press.

Scanlon, T. M. (1999) *What We Owe To Each Other.* Cambridge, MA: Harvard University Press.

Schmitt, C. (1923/1988) *The Crisis of Parliamentary Democracy.* Boston, MA: MIT Press.

Schmitt, C. (1927/2006) *The Concept of the Political.* Chicago, IL: Chicago University Press.

Shearmur, J. (1996) *The Political Thought of Karl Popper.* London: Routledge.

Smith, A. (1789/2002) *The Theory of the Moral Sentiments.* Cambridge: Cambridge University Press.

Stokes, G. (1998) *Popper: Philosophy, Politics and Scientific Method.* Cambridge: Polity Press.

Tamir, Y. (1993) *Liberal Nationalism.* Princeton, NJ: Princeton University Press.

Taylor, C. (1958) 'The Poverty of the Poverty of Historicism,' *Universities and Left Review 4.* 77–78.

Waldron, J. (2004) 'Tribalism and the Myth of the Framework: Some Popperian Thoughts on the Politics of Cultural Recognition,' in P. Catton & G. MacDonald (eds) *Karl Popper: Critical Appraisals* (pp. 203–30). London: Routledge.

Wall, S. (1998) *Liberalism, Perfectionism, and Restraint.* Cambridge: Cambridge University Press.

Watkins, J. (1984) *Science and Scepticism.* Princeton, NJ: Princeton University Press, 1984.

Weimer, W. & D. Palermo (1982) *Cognition and the Symbolic Processes.* Vol. 2. Hillsdale, NJ: Lawrence Erlbaum Associates.

Wild, J. (1953) *Plato's Modern Enemies and the Theory of Natural Law.* Chicago, IL: University of Chicago Press.

Winspear, A. D. (1940) *The Genesis of Plato's Thought.* New York: S. A. Russell.

Young, I. M. (1990) *Justice and the Politics of Difference.* Princeton, NJ: Princeton University Press.

Young I. M. (2000) *Inclusion and Democracy.* Oxford: Clarendon Press.

参考文献

名词索引

(条目后的数字为原文页码)

Adler,Alfred 阿尔弗雷德·阿德勒 49—51,52

Adorno,Theodor 西奥多·阿多诺 29,54,57,114,120,138

Agassi,Joseph 约瑟夫·阿加西 96

analytical philosophy 分析哲学

  see Anglo-American political philosophy; logical positivism 参见:英美政治哲学;逻辑实证主义

  ordinary language theory 日常语言理论

Anglo-American political philosophy 英美政治哲学 139—48

  and essentialism 与本质主义 141—2

  Popper's congruence with 波普尔与其的共同性 142—8

  Popper's disagreements with 波普尔与其的分歧 140—2

  rejection of teleology 对目的论的反对

   see historicism, holism, teleology 参见:历史主义,整体主义,目的论

  anti-Semitism 反犹太主义 3,4,6,17,20,102

  Aristotle 亚里士多德 79,99

  as "unoriginal" "无独创性" 98

see also essentialism, teleology 也参见：本质主义，目的论

Arndt, Arthur 亚瑟·阿恩特 6

Aron, Raymon 雷蒙·阿隆 111

atomism 原子论 59, 61

Austin, John Langshaw 约翰·朗肖·奥斯汀 33, 144

Austria 奥地利

　Austrian liberalism 奥地利自由主义 3, 4

　Austrian Marxism 奥地利马克思主义 22, 51

　Nazi occupation of 纳粹占领 22—3, 103

Ayer, Alfred Jules 阿尔弗雷德·艾耶尔爵士 13, 21, 114

Bacon, Francis 弗朗西斯·培根 33, 40, 42, 123, 140

Barry, Brian 布莱恩·巴里 140

Beitz, Charles 查尔斯·贝茨 140

Benhabib, Seyla 塞拉·本哈比 116

Berlin, Isaiah 以赛亚·伯林 21, 111, 145

Boscovic, Rudjer 鲁杰尔·博斯科维奇 41

Bourdieu, Pierre 皮埃尔·布迪厄 138

Braithwaite, Richard Bevan 理查德·布莱斯维特 21

Buhler, Karl 卡尔·布勒 10

Burke, Edmund 埃德蒙·伯克 105—10

　and critique of French Revolution 对法国革命的批评 105—6, 123

　as different to Popper 与波普尔的分歧 108—9

　and fallibility of reason 推理的易谬性 106—7, 123, 124

　see also reason 参见：推理

名词索引

159

and representative democracy 代议制民主 107

similarities with Popper 与波普尔的共同点 107—10,123,124

    see also conservatism 也参见：保守主义

Cambridge School,The 剑桥学派 137—8,139

Carnap,Rudolph 鲁道夫·卡尔纳普 13,21

Cohen,Joshua 约书亚·科恩 29,140

Cold War Liberalism 冷战自由主义 26

collectivism 集体主义 121

    see also historicism 也参见：历史主义

Communism 共产主义 2,26—7,72,78

Comte,Auguste 奥古斯特·孔德 52—3,56,60,72,103

Condorcet,Marquis de 孔多塞侯爵 123

conservatism 保守主义

    ambiguity of 不明确性 98,105

    changing definition of 其定义的变化 105—11

    and gradualism 渐进主义 106,107

    and ideology 意识形态 105,107

    see also Edmund Burke,New Right 也参见：埃德蒙·伯克,新右派

conspiracy theory of society 社会阴谋论 84,116

    see also Karl Marx;critical theory 也参见：卡尔·马克思;批判理论

contextualism 语境主义

Cambridge School 剑桥学派

Copernicus 哥白尼 36,41,50

cosmopolitanism 世界主义 31,91,133

critical rationalism 批判理性主义 45,47,49,62,87—8,90

and democracy 与民主 90—1,114,119

see also democracy 也参见：民主

and evolutionary rationalism 与进化理性主义 124

see also Hayek and the "institutional method" 也参见：哈耶克和"制度化方法" 94—5,112

critical theory 批判理论 29,54,57,111—20,138

cult of incomprehensibility 不可理解性的狂热 119

culture 文化 55,133

and diversity 与多样性 133—6,142,146—8

death of political philosophy 政治哲学的死亡 145

democracy 民主

as best existing form of society 作为现有的最好的社会形式 119

Burke's definition 伯克的定义

see Burke 参见：伯克

compatibility with freedom 与自由的相容性 27—8

compatibility with Popper's epistemology 与波普尔的认识论的相容性 28

as deliberative 审议制民主 24,112—13,114,140

as an exemplar of critical rationalism 批判理性主义的典范 90—1

critical rationalism 批判理性主义

and historicism 与历史主义

see historicism 参见：历史主义

名词索引

161

Popper's ambiguous definition of 波普尔的模糊定义 27—8

deontology 道义论 143

Descartes,Rene 勒内·笛卡儿 33,40,41,123,140

disciplines,rejection of the separation of 反对学科分类

    see essentialism 参见:本质主义

Dollfuss,Englebert 恩格尔伯特·多尔福斯 20

Duhem,Pierre 皮埃尔·迪昂 33,97

Duhem-Quine thesis 迪昂-蒯因论题 97

Einstein,Albert 阿尔伯特·爱因斯坦 41,50

elitism 精英主义

    in Burke 伯克的精英主义 106

    as justifying constraints on free speech 为限制自由言论提供理由 70

    as justifying tyranny 为暴政提供理由 70—1

    see also historicism 也参见:历史主义

Enlightenment 启蒙运动 105—6,108,113,129,131,136,139—40,140

    see rationalism 参见:理性主义

epistemological optimism 认识论的乐观主义 40—1

epistemology 认识论 34—48

    and the human need for regularities 与人类对规律性的需求 10—11,40—1

    as a theory of the growth of knowledge 作为知识增长的一种理论 34—5

    and uncertainty 与不确定性 21,25,69—70

equality 平等 30—2

essentialism 本质主义 60—1

    Aristotelian form of 亚里士多德的形式 45,60,79

    and disciplinary boundaries 与学科界限 43—6,62

    see disciplines 参见:学科

    in political philosophy 政治哲学的本质主义 141—2

    and science 与科学 60

facts 事实

    as based on observation 基于观察的事实 18,35

    as distinct from theories 与理论相区别的事实 18,35

fallibilism 易谬主义

    see reason 参见:推理

falsifiability 可证伪性

    as criterion of scientific theories 作为科学理论的标准的可证伪性 18,37—9

    as criterion of social theories 作为社会理论的标准的可证伪性 49,108

    critique of 对其的批评 97

    see also Duhem-Quine thesis 参见:迪昂-蒯因论题

falsification(of theories),ascentral aim of science（对理论的)证伪作为科学的主要目标 18,37—9

Faraday,Michael 迈克尔·法拉第 41

Fascism 法西斯主义 2,8,72,78,131

Feigl,Herbert 赫伯特·费格尔 13,21

feminism 女权主义 116—17

Feyerabend,Paul 保罗·费耶拉本德 96—7

Fichte,Johann Gottlieb 约翰·戈特利布·费希特 9,13

    as 'windbag' "废话大王" 98

Foucault,Michel 米歇尔·福柯 114,138

Frankael,Otto 奥托·弗兰卡尔 23

Frankfurt School,The 法兰克福学派

    see critical theory 参见:批判理论

Fraser,Nancy 南希·弗雷泽 116,134

freedom 自由

    compatibility with democracy 与民主的相容性

    see democracy 参见:民主

    compatibility with equality 与平等的相容性 10,30—2

    as dependent on education 在教育上的独立性 8

    see also Open Society and Its Enemies 参见:《开放社会及其敌人》

French revolution 法国革命 105—6

    see also Burke 也参见:伯克

Freud,Sigmund 西格蒙德·弗洛伊德 9,49—51

Friedman,Milton 米尔顿·弗里德曼 97,125,129

Fries,Jakob Friedrich 弗雷德里希·弗里斯 102

Galileo 伽利略 36,50

gender 性别

    see feminism 参见:女权主义

German Idealism 德国唯心主义 13—14

Gilbert,William 威廉·吉尔伯特 41

globalization 全球化 131—2

Godel,Kurt 库尔特·哥德尔 13,21

Godwin, William 威廉·戈德温 123

Gomperz, Heinrich 海因里希·冈珀茨 10,12

gradualism 渐进主义

see conservatism; social engineering 参见：保守主义；社会工程

Gramsci, Antonio 安东尼奥·葛兰西 100

Gray, John 约翰·格雷 134—5

Gutmann, Amy 埃米·古特曼 140,147

Habermas, Jurgen 尤尔根·哈贝马斯 29,57,60,114,119,138

Habsburg Empire 哈布斯堡帝国 3,6,17

Haekel, Ernst 恩斯特·海克尔 81

Hahn, Hans 汉斯·汉恩 13

Hart, Herbert Lionel Adolphus 赫伯特·哈特·阿道弗斯 143,145

Hayek, Friedrich von 弗里德利希·冯·哈耶克 21—2,25,30,97,108,128,129

critique of social and economic planning 对社会和经济计划的批评 21—2,128

disagreements with Popper 与波普尔的分歧 125—7

on laissez-faire economics 关于自由放任经济学 21,122

praise for Popper 对波普尔的赞誉 21,25,122,125

Hegel Georg Wilhelm Friedrich 格奥尔格·威廉·弗里德利希·黑格尔 1,9,13,23—4,52—3,63,79,91,99,103,107,111,119

critique of Popper's analysis of 对波普尔分析的批评

165

101—2

and the dialectic 与辩证法 56

and history 与历史 79—80

as "illiterate charlatan" "不学无术的江湖骗子" 98—9

and nationalism 与民族主义 80—2

and the state 与国家 80—2

and totalitarianism 与极权主义 81

Heidegger, Martin 马丁·海德格尔 102

Hempel, Carl 卡尔·亨佩尔 13,21

Henniger, Josephine 约瑟芬·亨尼格 10

Heraclitus 赫拉克利特 73,80,102

Hesiod 赫西奥德 73

Hirschmann, Nancy 南希·赫希曼 116

historicism 历史主义 1,8,25

as anti-democratic 反民主的 71—2

and collectivism 与集体主义 52—3,68

as a critique of naturalism 对自然主义的批评 54—8

and culture 与文化 55

defined 定义 51—62

as elitist 精英主义的 67—8,70—1

see elitism 参见：精英主义

as epistemologically mistaken 认识论上的错误 71

as essentialist 本质主义的 60—1

as identifying a chosen people 确定选民的 52—4,70,81

as normatively objectionable 在规范上令人反感的 71

origins in Ancient Greece 起源于古希腊 73

卡尔·波普尔

166

see also Hesiod;Heraclitus;Plato 也参见:赫西奥德;赫拉克利特;柏拉图

as providing the basis for totalitarianism 为极权主义提供了基础 72—86

and the purpose of politics 与政治学的目的 53

and the purpose of social science 与社会科学的目的 53,61

as rejecting inductive science 反对归纳法科学的 54—9

and religion 与宗教 52

and social planning 与社会规划 66—70

and the subordination of the individual 与个人的服从 72,90,92

see also holism 也参见:整体主义

and theoretical history 与理论史

see theoretical history 参见:理论史

Hobbes,Thomas 托马斯·霍布斯 33,123

holism 整体主义

and historicism 与历史主义 59,67—8,72,90

see also historicism 也参见:历史主义

and politics 与政治学 72,118

in social science 社会科学中的整体主义 57,64,68,118

Horkheimer,Max 麦克斯·霍克海默 29,114,120,138

Hume,David 大卫·休谟 18,33,36—7,123

Husserl,Edmund 埃德蒙德·胡塞尔 102

identity politics 认同政治 113,133—6

see also culture 也参见:文化

ideologies 意识形态

as criticized by Popper 波普尔的批评 105,125,149—50

ideologism as distinct from pragmatism 与实用主义相区分的意识形态化 105,110,125

indeterminacy of 不确定性 129—30

individualism 个人主义

see methodological individualism 参见:方法论的个人主义

induction 归纳法 18

as basis for traditional science 作为传统科学的基础

see science;epistemology 参见:科学;认识论

and historicism 与历史主义

see historicism 参见:历史主义

problem of 归纳法的问题 36—9,69

institutional method 制度化方法

see critical rationalism 参见:批判理性主义

intervention 干预

and democratization 与民主化 136

social and economic 社会和经济干预 87,97,126

see also social engineering;laissez-faire 也参见:社会工程;自由放任

Jaspers,Karl 卡尔·雅斯佩斯 102

Jefferson,Thomas 托马斯·杰斐逊 123

justification 证明合理

see truth 参见:真理

Kant,Immanuel 伊曼努尔·康德 9,13,33

Kauffman,Walter 沃尔特·考夫曼 102

Kepler, Johannes 约翰内斯·开普勒 36,41—2,50

knowledge 知识

　growth of as public 公共知识的增长 43—5

　see also epistemology 也参见：认识论

　importance of a theory of 知识理论的重要性 33

Kolnai, Aurel 奥勒尔·科尔奈 101—2

Kraft, Julius 朱利叶斯·克拉夫特 10

Kraus, Karl 卡尔·克劳斯 9

Kuhn, Thomas 托马斯·库恩 29,96,97

Kymlicka, Will 威尔·金里卡 134

laissez-faire 自由放任 21,30,97,125—6,129

Lakatos, Imre 伊姆雷·拉卡托斯 96

Larmore, Charles 查尔斯·拉莫尔 134

Laski, Harold 哈罗德·拉斯基 25,26,97

Laslett, Peter 彼得·拉斯利特 145

Leibniz, Gottfried 哥特弗雷德·莱布尼茨 33

Levinson, Ronald 罗纳德·莱文森 99

libertarianism 自由至上主义 98,105,127—9

liberty 自由

　see freedom 参见：自由

Locke, John 约翰·洛克 33

Logic of Scientic Discovery《科学发现的逻辑》18

　see science 参见：科学

Logical Positivism 逻辑实证主义

　as critique of German Idealism 对德国唯心主义的批评

13—14

see German Idealism 参见:德国唯心主义

definition of 定义 15

demarcation of physics and metaphysics 物理科学和形而上学的划界 14—15,34,42

as dominant in analytical philosophy 分析哲学中流行的逻辑实证主义 144—5

rejection of metaphysics 对形而上学的反对 15

see metaphysics 参见:形而上学

Logik der Forschung《发现的逻辑》18,19,21,24,125

see Logic of Scientific Discovery 参见:《科学发现的逻辑》

London School of Economics 伦敦经济学院 21—2,25,26,29,96

Loos,Adolph 阿道夫·卢斯 9

Luxemburg,Rosa 罗莎·卢森堡 100

Mach,Ernst 恩斯特·马赫 9

MacIntyre,Alasdair 阿拉斯代尔·麦金泰尔 134

Magee,Bryan 布莱恩·麦基 103

Mandeville,Bernard 伯纳德·曼德维尔 123

Mannheim,Karl 卡尔·曼海姆 54—5,57,59,103

Marcuse,Herbert 赫伯特·马尔库塞 114

markets 市场

see laissez-faire 参见:自由放任

Marx,Karl 卡尔·马克思 1,10,23—4,52—3,56,60,63,79,98,99,103,107,111,129

see historicism;Marxism 参见:历史主义;马克思主义

as "false prophet" "假先知" 98

and historical determinism 与历史主义决定论 56,82—5

Marxism 马克思主义

critique of Marx's analysis of 对马克思分析的批评 100—1

and "false consciousness" 与"错误意识" 50—1,85

as historicist 历史主义的 51

unfalsifiability of 不可证伪性 49—51,52

see Austria;Karl Marx 参见:奥地利;卡尔·马克思

Menger,Carl 卡尔·门格尔 97

Menger,Karl 卡尔·门格尔 21

metaphysics 形而上学

see Wittgenstein; logical positivism; Vienna Circle; science 参见:维特根斯坦;逻辑实证主义;维也纳学派;科学

appropriate subject of philosophy 哲学的适当主题 16

importance to science 科学的重要性 16,18,40—2

Methodological essentialism 方法论的本质主义 60

see essentialism 参见:本质主义

methodological holism 方法论的整体主义

see holism 参见:整体主义

as distinct from methodological individualism 与方法论的个人主义相区分的 63—4,118

methodological individualism 方法论的个人主义 63—4,118,136

methodological nominalism 方法论的唯名主义 60,65

Mill,John Stuart 约翰·斯图亚特·密尔 33,52,56,72,90,103

Miller,David 大卫·米勒 134

Mises,Ludwig von 路德维希·冯·米塞斯 97—8

Monists,The 一元论者 6

Moore,George Edward 乔治·爱德华·摩尔 21

multiculturalism 多元文化论

　　see culture 参见:文化

myths 神话 40—1

Nagel,Thomas 托马斯·内格尔 140

National Socialism 民主社会主义

　　see Nazism 参见:纳粹主义

nationalism 民族主义 24,26,91—2,132—3

naturalism 自然主义 53—61

　　as denying human agency 否定人的能动性 55

　　and historicism 与历史主义

　　see historicism 参见:历史主义

Nazism 纳粹主义 2,23,72,78,102,131

　　European rise of 在欧洲的兴起 20,132

negative utilitarianism 消极功利主义 87

Nelson,Leonard 伦纳德·纳尔逊 9

Neurath,Otto 奥图·纽拉特 13,21

New Right 新右派 30

　　critique of post war consensus 对战后共识的批评 121—2

　　and Hayek 与哈耶克 122

　　see Hayek 参见:哈耶克

　　and political pragmatism 与政治实用主义

　　see pragmatism 参见:实用主义

卡尔·波普尔

New Zealand 新西兰

    see Popper, Karl 参见：卡尔·波普尔

Newton, Isaac 艾萨克·牛顿 18, 36, 41, 50

normative political philosophy 规范政治哲学

    see Anglo-American political philosophy 参见：英美政治哲学

normativity 规范性 144—5

Nozick, Robert 罗伯特·诺齐克 127

Oakeschott, Michael 迈克尔·奥克肖特 124

objectivity 客观性

    in politics 政治学中的客观性 91

    in science 科学中的客观性 46

open society 开放社会 86—95

    as compared to a closed society 与封闭社会相比较 95

Open Society and Its Enemies, *The*《开放社会及其敌人》1—2, 22, 23, 24, 25, 26, 28—9, 31, 33, 72, 97, 98, 104, 113, 119, 121

    contemporary neglect of 当代的忽视 1, 23, 135

    and education 与教育 8, 126—7

    in historical context 在历史背景下 131—2

    and "problem-solving" 与"解决问题" 11

    as statement of post-war social democracy 作为战后的社会民主陈述 111, 121, 129

    ordinary language theory 日常语言理论 33, 144

    Paine, Thomas 托马斯·佩恩 123

    paradigms, in science 科学中的范式

名词索引

173

see Kuhn 参见:库恩

Parekh,Bhikhu 海库·帕瑞克 134—5

Pedagogic Institute 教育学院 10

philosophy 哲学

    purpose of 哲学的目的 17—18,26,147

    see metaphysics; logicalpositivism; German Idealism; Wittgenstein 参见:形而上学;逻辑实证主义;德国唯心主义;维特根斯坦

    scope of 哲学的研究范围 12—19,23

piecemeal social engineering 零星社会工程

    see social engineering 参见:社会工程

Plamenatz,John 约翰·普拉梅纳茨 99

Plato 柏拉图 1,23—4,25,52,56,60,80,91,98,99,107

    and decay 与腐朽 73—5

    as defender of a closed society 作为封闭社会的捍卫者 76—7

    as defender of totalitarianism 作为极权主义的捍卫者 77—9

    and elitism 与精英主义 75—9,92

    and the Forms 与形式 73—4

    as historicist 作为历史主义者 78—9

    idea of justice 公正观点 73—9

    and race 与种族 76,78,107—8

    role of rulers is to arrest change 统治者的角色是阻止改变 73,75—6

Platonic astronomy 柏拉图的天文学 41

Pocock, John Grenville Agard 约翰·格伦维尔·波科克 137

Poincare, Henri 昂利·庞加莱 33

Polanyi, Karl 卡尔·波兰尼 9,98

political liberalism 政治自由主义 140,142

politics 政治学

  and historicism 与历史主义

  see historicism 参见:历史主义

  purpose of for Popper 波普尔认为的政治学的目的 89

Popper, Karl 卡尔·波普尔

  1927 thesis 1927 年论文 10—11,40

  and accusations of unscholarly behaviour 对其无学者风度行为的批评 98—100,101,103—4

  agreements with Hayek 与哈耶克的共识 21—2,25,28,125

  and Anglo-American political philosophy 与英美政治哲学 139—45

  attitude toward intellectuals 对知识分子的态度 12,16,17,120

  autobiography 自传

  see Unended Quest 参见:《无尽的探索》

  birth date 出生日 4

  and children's knowledge 与儿童的知识 10—11

  clash with Wittgenstein in Cambridge 在剑桥与维特根斯坦的冲突 26

  as critical of free markets 对自由市场的批评 125—6

名词索引

175

see laissez-faire 参见：自由放任

critique of Austrian Marxism 对奥地利马克思主义的批评 22

see Austrian Marxism 参见：奥地利马克思主义

critique of ordinary language theory 对日常语言理论的批评 33—4

see Ryle；Austin 参见：赖尔；奥斯汀

critique of Wittgenstein 对维特根斯坦的批评

see Wittgenstein 参见：维特根斯坦

demarcation of science from pseudo-science 科学与伪科学的划界 17

see science 参见：科学

early interest in psychology and epistemology 早期对心理学和认识论的兴趣 10—11

friendship with Hayek 与哈耶克的友谊 22,122

influence of Austrian progressive movement 奥地利进步运动的影响 24

and intolerant groups 与不宽容团体 27,30—1

job as cabinet-maker 任职木工 8

job as secondary school teacher 任职中学教师 11

job as social worker 任职社会工作者 8

knighthood 爵位 29

move to Buckinghamshire 移居白金汉郡 28

move to New Zealand 移居新西兰 21—3,103

on the nature of science 关于科学的本质 18—19

see science 参见：科学

卡尔·波普尔

as not engaging in critical rationalism 不涉及批判理性主义 104,119—20

critical rationalism 参见:批判理性主义

PhD thesis 博士论文 11

rejection of logical positivism 反对逻辑实证主义 16—17

see logical positivism 参见:逻辑实证主义

rejection of political radicalism 反对政治激进主义 29

school life 社会生活 5

and school reform 与学校改革 10—11

Simon and Jenny（parents）西蒙与珍妮（父母）3—4,4—5

and social and economic planning 与社会和经济规划 28,125—6

and student politics 与学生政治 6—7

support for Marxism 支持马克思主义 6—7

trip to England(1937) 英国之旅 21

turn from psychology to science 从心理学转向科学 11

and the University of Vienna 与维也纳大学 6,8

and the Vienna Circle 与维也纳学派

see Vienna Circle 参见:维也纳学派

wife 妻子

see Henniger 参见:亨尼格

positivism debate 实证主义辩论 57,115,119—20

see critical theory 参见:批判理论

postmodernism 后现代主义 138—9

poststructuralism 后结构主义 114,115—16

名词索引

post-war consensus 战后的共识 111,121

poverty 贫困 24

Poverty of Historicism, *The*《历史决定论的贫困》1—2, 21,23,34,93,97,103,104,131

and "problem-solving" 与"解决问题" 11

power 权力 115—17

pragmatism 实用主义

philosophical 哲学实用主义 145—7

political 政治实用主义 105,106,122

prediction 预言

as distinct from prophecy 与神灵预言相区分的 52, 61,63

in historicism 历史主义的预言

see historicism 参见:历史主义

in science 科学的预言

see science 参见:科学

in social science 社会科学的预言

see social science;historicism 参见:社会科学;历史主义

progress 进步 93—5

protest politics 抗议政治

see radicalism 参见:激进主义

psychologism 心理主义 11

Putnam,Hilary 希拉里·普特南 97

quantum theory 量子理论 42

Quine,Willard Van Orman 威拉德·冯·奥曼·蒯因 13,97

卡尔·波普尔

radicalism 激进主义 109,111,118—19,122

Popper's rejection of 波普尔的反对 111—20,124

see utopianism;social engineering 参见:乌托邦主义;社会工程

Rand,Ayn 艾因·兰德 127

rationalism 理性主义 33,40—1,122,123—4,131,140

as compatible with tradition 与传统的相容 124

evolutionary and constructivist forms of 进化论形式和建构主义形式 123—4,128

Rawls,John 约翰·罗尔斯 29,134—5,139,140,143,145

Raz,Joseph 约瑟夫·拉兹 134

Reagan,Ronald 罗纳德·里根 30

reason 推理

as an ability of all individuals 作为所有个人的能力 24,91,92

as able to provide guidance for social reform 作为对社会改革的指导 24,115,120

as embodied in institutions 作为制度中的体现 91—3

fallibility of 易谬性 21,38—9,62—3,68—70,91—2,106—7,108,118,123—4,136—7,140—1

as providing right to hold power 提供了执政的权利 106

relativism 相对主义 119,138—9

Rorty,Richard 理查德·罗蒂 145—6,147

see pragmatism 参见:实用主义

Rousseau,Jean Jacques 让·雅克·卢梭 52,56,60,72,80,111,123

Russell,Bertrand 伯特兰·罗素 21,25,26,33,97,114

Ryle,Gilbert 吉尔伯特·赖尔 21,33,144

Sandel,Michael 迈克尔·桑德尔 134

Scanlon,Thomas 托马斯·斯坎伦 140

Scheler,Max 马克斯·舍勒 102

Schelling,Friedrich Wilhelm Joseph 弗里德里希·威廉·
约瑟夫·谢林 9,13

Schlick,Moritz 莫里茨·石里克 11,12

Schmitt,Carl 卡尔·施密特 28,114

Schnitzler,Arthur 阿瑟·施尼茨勒 9

Schopenhauer,Arthur 阿图尔·叔本华 99,102

science 科学

    as concerned with the establishment of general laws 关
注普遍规律的建立 35

    as deductive not inductive 演绎的而非归纳的 18—19,
36—9,46—8

    see verifiability;induction 参见:可检验性;归纳法

    as distinct from pseudoscience 与伪科学相区分的 17—
18,34

    historical inaccuracy of inductive view 归纳法观点在历
史上的不准确性 39—42

    the importance of falsified theories 被证伪的理论的重要
性 37—8

    importance of metaphysics 形而上学的重要性

    see metaphysics 参见:形而上学

    inductive model defined 定义归纳法模型 35—6

the inference of theories from facts 从事实推断理论 35

and long-term prediction 与长期预言 35,38—9

method common to all disciplines 所有学科的共同方法 43—7

and objectivity 与客观性

see objectivity 参见:客观性

and observation 与观察 35—6

as only capable of short-term prediction 仅能进行短期预言 38—9

Popper's contribution to 波普尔对科学的贡献 96—7

Popper's view defined 定义波普尔的观点 46—8

scientific discovery 科学发现 41—2,47

scientism 唯科学主义 61

see naturalism 参见:自然主义

situational logic 情境逻辑 137—8

Skinner,Quentin 昆汀·斯金纳 137

Smith,Adam 亚当·斯密 123

social engineering 社会工程 25,64—5,66,68,87—8,108,121,124,128—9

social science 社会科学

as beginning in the identification of problems 从确认问题开始 48—9,62—3

growth of knowledge in 知识的增长 48—9

and historical laws 与历史规律 53—4,66—7

see historicism 参见:历史主义

Popper's methodology defined 波普尔定义社会科学的

方法论 48—66

    practical function of 社会科学的实践功能 64—5,69

    purpose of for Marx 马克思认为的社会科学的目的 83

    purpose of for Popper 波普尔认为的社会科学的目的 62—3,64,69

    unity of method with physical sciences 与物理科学的方法的统一 49

social technology 社会技术 4,24,32

Socrates 苏格拉底 9,23,98,100

Sorel,Georges 乔治·索列尔 100

Soros,George 乔治·索罗斯 129

Stalin,Joseph 约瑟夫·斯大林 78

Structure of Scientific Revolutions, The 《科学革命的结构》97

    see Kuhn 参见：库恩

Tamir,Yael 耶尔·塔米尔 134

Tarski,Alfred 阿尔弗雷德·塔斯基 13

Taylor,Charles 查尔斯·泰勒 102

teleology 目的论 143—4

Thales 泰勒斯 41

Thatcher,Margaret 玛格丽特·撒切尔 30,129

theoretical history 理论史 53,59

theories 理论

    as distinct from facts 与事实相区分的

    see facts 参见：事实

    as inevitably conjectural 不可避免地具有推测性 18,39

卡尔·波普尔

Thompson, Dennis 丹尼斯·汤普森 140

Tocqueville, Alexis de 亚历西斯·托克维尔 90

totalitarianism 极权主义 1,8,23,25,27,72—86

as undertheorized by Popper 波普尔认为理论不足 102—3

Tractatus Logico-Philosophicus 《逻辑哲学论》 12,14,17

see Wittgenstein 参见：维特根斯坦

tradition 传统 105—6,109,119,124

tribalism 部落主义 24,26,81,90,119,132

see historicism 参见：历史主义

truth 真理

as distinct from justification 与辩护理由相区分的 146

philosophy as the search for 哲学作为对真理的追寻 17—18,128,135,138,146,147

see philosophy; logical positivism; Wittgenstein; verifiability 参见：哲学；逻辑实证主义；维特根斯坦；可检验性

in science 科学中的真理 18,37—8,47—8,87,97,128

in social science 社会科学中的真理 55,65,86—7,90,128,135

tyranny of the majority 多数人的暴政 90,112

Unended Quest 《无尽的探索》 7,19,30

universalism 普遍主义 31,114—15,133

utilitarianism 功利主义 143—4

see negative utilitarianism 参见：消极功利主义

utopianism 乌托邦主义 21,25,64—5,67,86—90,110,126—7

名词索引

threat to individual freedom 对个人自由的威胁 21

verifiability 可检验性

of scientific theories 科学理论的可检验性 18,35—7

of truth claims 真理主张的可检验性 14—15,35

verisimilitude 逼真性 97

Vienna 维也纳

and anti-Semitism 与反犹太主义

anti-Semitism 参见：反犹太主义

and Austrian liberalism 与奥地利自由主义

see Austrian liberalism 参见：奥地利自由主义

before World War Ⅰ 一战之前 3—4

and the impact of World War Ⅰ 一战的影响 16,8—9,
19—21

interwar intellectual community 两次大战之间的知识界
12,17,19—21

and the Progressive movement 与进步运动 4,24

and social democracy 与社会民主 7—8

Vienna Circle,The 维也纳学派 12—19,25,42,43,119,144

defence of logical positivism 对逻辑实证主义的辩护 13

see logical positivism 参见：逻辑实证主义

dissolution of 解散 19—21

members of 成员 13

Popper's critique of 波普尔的批评 16—18,33

Popper's exclusion from 波普尔被排斥 12—13

and Wittgenstein 与维特根斯坦 17—18

Vienna Fabian Society 维也纳费边社 4

Waissman,Friedrich 弗里德里希·韦斯曼 13,21

Waldron,Jeremy 杰里米·沃尔德伦 29

Wall,Steven 史蒂芬·沃尔 140

Watkins,John 约翰·沃特金斯 96

Wild,John 约翰·威德 99

William,Frederick,of Prussia 普鲁士的腓特烈·威廉一世 99

Wittgenstein,Ludwig 路德维希·维特根斯坦 12,26

　　analytical and synthetic statements 分析和综合陈述 14—15

　　and the demarcation of physics and metaphysics 与物理科学和形而上学的分界 14

　　　see logical positivism 参见：逻辑实证主义

　　and language 与语言 14—15,17—18,45,138

　　and meaningfulness 与意义 14—15

　　and observation 与观察 14

　　Popper's attitude towards 波普尔对他的态度 17—18,26

　　on the scope of philosophy 关于哲学的研究范围 15,17—18,23,26

Young,Iris Marion 艾莉丝·马里昂·扬 116,134,147

KARL POPPER

PHIL PARVIN

MAJOR CONSERVATIVE AND
LIBERTARIAN THINKERS

Series Editor's Preface

Karl Popper was one of the most important and controversial thinkers of the twentieth century. Today he is best known for his contributions to the philosophy of science and the history of ideas. In the former Popper argued that only scientific theories that could be subject to falsification could make a contribution to knowledge; propositions that could not be falsified could not advance human understanding of the world. In the latter Popper traced the origins of twentieth-century totalitarianism to the ideas of Plato and Hegel whom he believed had provided the intellectual foundations for fascist and Nazi regimes that subjugated the rights of individuals to the pursuit of collective ends.

There were elements of Popper's thought, then, that were clearly libertarian or conservative in character: Popper embraced individual freedom and adopted a methodological individualist approach to his scholarly work; he believed in a dynamic, cos-mopolitan 'open society' characterized by free thought and expression and contrasted this ideal with the 'closed society' that was organized to facilitate the collective

I

pursuit of a social end determined by political elites; and he was sceptical of radical change that aimed to enact a pre-determined blueprint for the organization of society.

In other respects, however, Popper's thought does not fit so easily into the libertarian or conservative tradition. Popper's politics were recognizably social democratic: he believed in incremental social reform aimed at improving the lot of the poorest in society and was at ease with the Western European post-war welfare state; he believed the scope of the market should be limited, and had faith in the power of public reason emerging from democratic deliberation to guide the state in the effective amelioration of social problems. Popper's open society, then, was not a free market utopia, but a political community in which diverse people engaged with one another in constructive dialogue to seek political solutions to common problems.

As Phil Parvin of the University of Loughborough shows in this masterly account of Popper's work, Popper made important and enduring contributions to the libertarian and conservative traditions, but it would be a mistake to uncritically label him a conservative or libertarian. Rather, Popper was a scholar who contributed to a range of different fields without being shackled to one particular perspective or approach. It is in this context that we should understand Popper's contribution to libertarian and conservative thought.

This volume contributes to the *Major Conservative and Lib-*

ertarian Thinhers series by presenting Popper's thought in an accessible and cogent form. It is an outstanding work that provides a thorough account of Popper's life and work, considers the reception of Popper's work by his contemporaries, and then shows Popper's continuing relevance, in particular to twenty-first century Anglo-American political philosophy. This book will prove indispensable to those unfamiliar with Popper's ideas as well as more advanced scholars.

John Meadowcroft

King's College London

Contents

1 Intellectual Biography **1**

    Early beginnings **3**

    The Pedagogic Institute **8**

    Wittgenstein and the Vienna Circle **12**

    'A fighting book' **20**

    The later years **26**

2 Popper's Ideas **34**

    Popper's epistemology **36**

    From science to social science **49**

    From social science to politics **67**

    The Open Society **88**

3 Reception and Influence of Popper's Philosophy **97**

    Popper, Burke, and the fallibility of reason **106**

    Radical politics, radical philosophy **112**

    Popper and the rise of the New Right **122**

    A final word on ideologies **131**

4 The Contemporary Relevance of Popper's Philosophy **133**

    Conclusion **152**

1
Intellectual Biography

Karl Popper was on one of the most important philosophers of the twentieth century. His influence can be seen across many disciplines, and he wrote widely on subjects as diverse and complex as the philosophy of science and mathematics, music, history, psychology, politics, logic, and epistemology. He was not strictly a political philosopher, although his famous defence of individual liberty against the purported totalitarian tendencies of thinkers like Plato, and Hegel continues to represent an important contribution to Western political thought. His critique of historicism as an approach to understanding not only philosophy, society and politics, but music, science, and history itself has had an enormous and lasting effect on the conduct of debates in these areas. His approach to the appropriate conduct of the natural and social sciences still represents one of the most important contributions to epistemology and the philosophy of science made in the twentieth century. His application of this approach to all aspects of human inquiry, including politics, provided a new and provocative approach to understanding not merely politics and society, but the appropriate ends of philosophy.

Despite all this, Popper nevertheless remains a marginal figure in the history of political thought. Contemporary political theorists rarely engage with his ideas, and even more rarely encourage their students to study him.

Popper was controversial. *The Open Society and Its Enemies* and *The Poverty of Historicism*, his two most famous contributions to social and political theory, caused outrage among many philosophers, and derision among others. His books were criticized for lacking in scholarship, for denigrating the name of some of the most revered thinkers in the history of Western civilization, and for defending the simplistic liberal democratic bourgeois hegemony against more radical visions of society and politics. Popper's political thought was driven by a profound philosophical rationalism which was at odds with a lot of political philosophy of the time, and a belief in the need for social and political theory to be of *practical* help to legislators and policymakers which ran (and still runs) counter to the ideal theorizing popular among many analytical political philosophers, and the abstractionism of many postmodernists and poststructuralists. But it was also driven by a deep and clear moral sense. *The Open Society*, written during World War II when Europe seemed on the brink of falling to fascism, represents nothing less than a philosophical defence of Western civilization and the values upon which it was founded. It represents a vindication of the values of freedom, equality, and democracy, and a withering, visceral attack upon those who would deny these values in the name of national unity, or stability, or the good of all. Popper's language is often brutal, his arguments unmeasured by scholarly convention, and his attacks personal and devastating. His commitment to the open society was trenchant and unwavering, and his hatred for those throughout history whom he thought provided the Nazis, the Fascists with the philosophical tools to justify their evil, was obvious. Small wonder, then, that his work caused such controversy when it emerged, and why so many current philosophers are unsure as to what to do with it. His political prescriptions cannot be easily associated with any political ideology, although thinkers from all points on the political spectrum have tried to claim him for their own. And his epistemological views place him outside many of the dominant approaches to understanding society and politics. Popper's was an original, controversial, flawed, but important contribution to political thought which has stood the test of time, but which remains all but ignored by social and political theorists. In what follows, we will come to see more clearly what Popper had to say about politics, society, and philosophy, the controversy he caused, and the enduring implications his claims have for the contemporary study of society and its problems.

Early beginnings

Karl Popper's story begins in Vienna towards the tail-end of the Habsburg Empire. At that time, the city was the capital of a huge multi-ethnic empire, and nationalism was becoming an increasingly visible and important force in Austrian politics. Between 1867 and 1879 Austrian liberalism achieved a great many positive social and political reforms, including economic modernization and the expansion of public education, which would profoundly shape the social and political environment into which Karl Popper would later be born. But it also left a darker legacy that would come to dominate Popper's world. Austrian liberalism had an assimilationist and nationalist character: full citizenship was limited to those who 'exhibited the solid character of the German *Burger*' (Hacohen, 2000; 32). Vienna was, at that time, the 'most assimilated city in Europe' (Edmonds & Eidenow, 2002; 72). The city 'had the highest conversion rate of Jews to Christianity of any European urban centre', partly due to the pervasive anti-Semitism felt by many Jews (Edmonds & Eidenow, 2002; 72). As time went on, Austrian liberalism collapsed into German nationalism, as liberals sought to unify an increasingly fragmented middle class under a new and visceral political vision rooted in ethnicity. This vision became increasingly powerful, and increasingly detrimental to the lives and interests of Jews like Karl's parents, Simon and Jenny especially Jewish immigrants like his father (Jenny Popper had been born in Vienna). Like so many

3

other Jewish families living in the city, the Poppers renounced their membership of the Jewish community and converted to Lutheranism in 1900 but despite doing so, and despite adopting the work ethic and values of German *Kultur*, the Poppers-like most Jews-were never truly welcomed into mainstream society. The early liberal idea that one might acquire the qualities of 'the good citizen' through acculturation and hard work appeared to have been replaced by a newer appeal to ethnicity and race. Consequently, the Jews kept themselves to themselves, living, working, socializing, and marrying within a broadly cohesive and generally exclusive and excluded community.

Vienna at that time was also home to a radical progressive movement and the Poppers moved in the same circles as many of its most important members. Even before Popper's birth, radical progressives had ' rebelled against the social conservatism of mainstream liberalism and sought an opening for the workers. They opted for a bourgeois-proletarian alliance under the auspices of an enlightened bureaucracy that would promote social legislation, economic modernization, and scientific education' (Hacohen, 2000; 24). They sought a new leftist agenda, as a challenge to Austrian liberalism. They believed in the capacity of science and 'social technology' to resolve the problems of poverty and the unequal distribution of resources among the rich and the poor, and believed, therefore, that social justice required a scientific understanding of these problems (and their solutions). They established the Vienna Fabian Society in 1891, and the *Sozialpolitische partei* in 1896, and used these and other fora to campaign for universal male suffrage and welfare reforms and against Catholicism and anti-Semitism.

So it was that on 28 July 1902, Karl Popper was born into an imperial city divided along political, social, economic, and religious lines, into a newly Christian household, to parents who had given up their religion and embraced the dominant culture in order to succeed, but who were nevertheless con-

4

sidered with suspicion by the largely anti-Semitic majority. Nevertheless, Popper's parents had succeeded in climbing to the upper echelons of Viennese society. Simon Popper was a highly-paid lawyer who, together with his wife, two daughters and new son, lived in a huge 20-room apartment which provided enough space to house his family, his many books, secretary's and servants' quarters, as well as offices for the various charitable organizations that he ran. In his *Autobiography*, Popper described his father as 'more of a scholar than a lawyer', with interests in poetry, history, and philosophy. His book collection, so large that it spilled from his library and into the rest of the apartment, apparently contained around 14, 000 works, including those of Plato, Bacon, Descartes, Spinoza, Nietzsche, Locke, Kant, and Mill, as well as the 'standard authors of German, French, English, Russian, and Scandinavian literature' (Popper 1974/2002; 6); it included a large history collection, classical works, contemporary philosophy and literature, and recent Viennese publications on politics, social reform, and psychoanalysis, as well as the works of Charles Darwin.

Popper's immediate family, as well as those members of the progressive movement which his parents were a part of, encouraged in him an early appreciation of knowledge, scholarship, and culture. He described himself as a 'bookish' child, 'rather priggish' and a 'softy'. From a very young age, young Karl was fascinated by philosophical issues, and his inquiry into these issues was encouraged. He wrote that, at the age of 8, he became much exercised by the nature of infinity, and at 12 or 13 he was enquiring as to 'the problems of the origin of life, left open by Darwin, and whether life is simply a chemical process' (Popper, 1974/2002; 12). And he claimed that it was at the age of 15 that he stumbled across an idea that would later inform his most important mature philosophy: the 'problem of essentialism'.

Popper described his school life as 'boring in the extreme'. Despite his teachers' best efforts, he found his lessons to be nothing but 'hours and hours of torture' and a 'waste of time'. Born into a family and a social milieu which valued critique and engagement with conventional wisdom, Popper hated the way teachers attempted to 'drill' knowledge into their students. He sought a more reflective and interactive way of learning, one which would allow students to develop their critical faculties, rather than accept what they were told uncritically. This view would become strengthened in the years during and after World War I, as he himself came to challenge many of the views he had held up to that time.

He was 12 when the war broke out. He recalled the day well. A socialist family friend Athur Arndt often took him to meetings of the Monists, an association of progressive socialists dedicated to the 'scientific reform of philosophy, education, and the law', where the young Karl would learn about the progressive cause and discuss political reform (Hacohen, 2000; 42). Popper was on a hike with the Monists when he first heard the news that Archduke Franz Ferdinand had been assassinated; war was declared one week later, on his birthday. The war was to have a profound and irrevocable effect both on the Austro-Hungarian empire and Popper. The social, political, and economic divisions which predated the war (between the rich and the poor, the Jewish minority and the Christian majority, the liberals and the progressives) were exacerbated and politicized. As a consequence, Viennese society became much more fragmented and reactionary. As the war started to go badly, immigrants (many of whom were Jews) flooded into Austria. Anti-Semitism rose, and Jewish refugees were viewed by many as parasites. Severe food and fuel shortages increased social tensions, culminating in strikes and demonstrations. Social and economic chaos, coupled with huge and devastating losses from the Front, conspired to make the situation untenable. By the time the Armistice was signed in October 1918 (marking the end of the Habsburg empire) Viennese society had altered radically.

Young people at this time were becoming increasingly politicized,and Karl Popper was no exception. At around the same time that Popper was rebelling against the authority embodied in the Austrian school system he was rebelling too against those ideas which dominated political discourse at the time. In 1918,Popper left school(against the wishes of his parents)and enrolled as an unmatriculated student at the University of Vienna. He also became involved in student and youth politics and embraced communism as a means to end the conflict, poverty,and prevailing social unrest. This sympathy for communism would prove short-lived, however, and would be extinguished in 1919 at a student demonstration organized by communists like himself at which a number of students were shot and killed by the police. In *Unended Quest*,he wrote of being'shocked by the brutality of the police,but also by myself. For I felt that,as a Marxist,I bore part of the responsibility-at least in principle. Marxist theory demands that the class struggle be intensified in order to speed up the coming of socialism. Its thesis is that although the revolution may claim some victims,capitalism is claiming more victims than the whole socialist revolution' (Popper,1974/2002;33). The shootings took place a few days before Popper's 17th birthday and he claimed that by the time he was 17 he had become an anti-Marxist. ' I realized the dogmatic character of the creed and its incredible intellectual arrogance,' he wrote. ' It was a terrible thing to arrogate oneself to a kind of knowledge which made it a duty to risk the lives of other people for an uncritically accepted dogma,or for a dream which might turn out not to be realizable. It was particularly depressing for an intellectual who could read and think. It was awfully depressing to have fallen into such a trap. ' (Popper, 1974/2002; 34). Popper was particularly 'revolted' by the 'intellectual presumption of some of [his] Marxist friends and fellow students, who almost took it for granted that they were the future leaders of the working class'. They had,he said,'no special intellectual qualifications. All they could claim was some acquaintance with Marxist literature-though not even a thorough one, and certainly not a critical

7

one. '(Popper,1974/2002;35).

We can,perhaps,glimpse in these statements echoes of what was to come. In *Unended Quest* Popper praised the workers of Vienna and their political movement,while at the same time rejecting the'historicist ideas of their social democratic leaders as fatally mistaken' (Popper, 1974/2002; 35). Their leaders were able to inspire in them a sense that they were embarked upon a mission no less important than the liberation of mankind from poverty,from hunger,and from oppression. It was a movement premised on the education of the workers-the provision of those intellectual resources necessary for individuals to 'emancipate themselves and thus to liberate mankind' (Hacohen, 2000; 36). The progressive aim of establishing education as something that all people should have access to(regardless of whether they are rich or poor) stayed with Popper, who advocated the state provision of education for all in *The Open Society*. The idea,therefore,that freedom and equality could be secured by state institutions which provided people with the ability to take their lives(and their political destinies)into their own hands lived on in his later work and formed an important theme in his critiques of totalitarianism and fascism, and the historicist doctrines on which he believed they were built. Self-emancipation through knowledge,social reform through human agency,a hatred of poverty,injustice and oppression;Popper's view was that it was possible to hold all these ideas while rejecting Marxism.

The Pedagogic Institute

Popper sought his own solutions to social problems,while also seeking a practical and professional career that would have seemed somewhat alien to his intellectual friends. In 1922, at the age of 20, Popper passed his *matura* (a school-leaving exam),allowing him to become a fully matriculated student at the University. Two years later, he passed a second *matura* from a teacher-training college. This was at the same time as he was also learning to become a cabinet maker, as a carpenter's apprentice. At that time, teaching posts were rare and carpentry did not agree with him, and so he changed jobs, and spent some time as a social worker for neglected children. Popper appeared to be drifting. The social, political, and economic upheavals of the war and the revolution destroyed old certainties and created an environment in which settled patterns of life were disrupted. This emerging sense of uncertainty was reflected in the intellectual and artistic movements of the time. With the dissolution of established traditions in the wake of social and political conflict, Vienna became the

city of Ernst Mach and the theory of the fluctuating and uncertain self; of Freud and the power of the unconscious; of Schoenberg and the ousting of conventional tonality in favour of the twelve tone system. Here within a single period were Arthur Schnitzler's literature on the interior monologue and of the sexual drive as the prime mover of human relationships; AdolfLoos and the stripping away of ornament for ornament's sake in architecture;... and Karl Kraus and his attack on linguistic forms-clichés, metaphors-that disguised realities in politics and culture. (Edmonds & Eidenow, 2002, 76)

The new and uncertain social order provided Popper with a developing political sense of what he thought needed to be done to rebuild society along more humane and just lines, but precious little guidance as to what he should *do* with his life. Meanwhile, his interest in politics and philosophy endured and intensified. He fell under the influence of Karl Polanyi, a respected social theorist who argued for a non-Marxist form of socialism, and Leonard Nelson, a radical Kantian philosopher and cosmopolitan who argued for the establishment of an international legal system and the adoption of a 'Socratic method' in teaching the young. Together, Polanyi and Nelson had a profound effect on Popper; Polanyi showed that a commitment to social justice was not incompatible with bourgeois economics (and hence, that socialism need not be revolutionary, or aim at the socialization of the workforce), and Nelson's work on Kant, and his conception of a 'critical philosophy' which held Socrates and Kant as exemplars of reasoned philosophical inquiry (who were betrayed by the likes of Hegel, Fichte, and Schelling), provided crucial elements to Popper's developing philosophy of knowledge and politics, and provided new insights into the relationship between freedom and egalitarianism.

In 1925 the City of Vienna established the Pedagogic Institute an autonomous institution linked to the University, aimed at encouraging reform of the primary and secondary school system. Popper was one of several social workers who were admitted to the Institute. He described his years there as ones devoted to studying, reading, teaching, and writing, but not publishing. He taught classes in psychology and, through doing so, met Karl Buhler, Professor of Psychology at the University. In his second year, he met Heinrich Gomperz, Professor of Philosophy at the University, whose work on epistemology would greatly influence him, and Julius Kraft, with whom he shared a non-Marxist understanding of socialism and with whom he often discussed the failings of Marx. It was also at the Institute that Popper would meet Josephine Henniger, whom he would later marry.

It was at the Pedagogic Institute that Popper first became interested in psychology and epistemology. Through conversations with Buhler, Gomperz and Kraft, Popper was able to develop his earlier general concerns about the way in which children were being taught in Vienna at that time. He became increasingly consumed by questions about how individuals acquire knowledge of the world, what form this knowledge took, and what limits there might be to obtaining it. His 1927 thesis 'Habit and the Experience of Lawfulness'-submitted in order to complete his two years at the Institute-explored the relationship between logic and psychology, focusing primarily on the ways in which children acquire knowledge. He argued that children are naturally conservative in that they prefer order to disorder. Consequently, he believed, children try as far as possible to impose order on the world by understanding it in terms of regularities. This idea-that human beings seek to impose regularity on their lives and upon the world in which they live by deriving overarching laws(of nature, of history, of tradition, of nation) later assumed a pivotal place in Popper's mature political philosophy. Popper conceived the thesis as a 'Kantian critique of the limits of scientific pedagogy', and he used it to criticize many of the trends in educational reform that were dominant at the time (and which the Institute had been established to encourage). The result was a paper which questioned the idea that children could be educated into becoming critical thinkers, and which sought to provide a general description of the process by which children acquired knowledge by appealing to the standard inductive method of scientific inquiry, rather than psychology. Popper extended these themes in his PhD thesis which he submitted a year later. The thesis, entitled 'On the Methodological Problem of Cognitive Psychology' sought to resolve 'the problem of the boundaries among psychology, logic, and epistemology' by providing some criterion of 'demarcation' between epistemology and psychology (Hacohen, 2000; 63). Popper claimed that he was unhappy with his thesis, and described it in his autobiography as 'a kind of hasty last minute affair' (Popper, 1974/2002; 87). Nevertheless, his examiners (Karl Buhler, and Moritz Schlick) passed it with distinction. Whether Popper was happy with it or not, the thesis marks Popper's break with psychology and his turn towards logic and science. Popper's PhD represented an argument against psychologism (the idea that all knowledge can be understood in terms of subjective thought processes), and a development of the claim (made by Buhler) that 'we do not think in images but in terms of problems and their tentative solutions' (Popper, 1974/2002; 86). This claim-that human beings are principally problem solvers-reappears in Popper's later work, including *The Poverty of Historicism* and *The Open Society*. The turn to science was more or less completed a year later when, in 1929, at the age of 26, Popper qualified to teach mathematics and physical sciences at secondary school level. His thesis (submitted in order to graduate) was on the history and foundations of geometry, and included some of his earliest thoughts on scientific rationality and progress.

Wittgenstein and the Vienna Circle

Despite not being a member of the academy, Popper continued to move among some of the most talented academics in Europe, especially in the fields of epistemology, science, and mathematics. Interwar Vienna was home to a lively and intense intellectual community of scholars from many different disciplines, both within the academy and beyond it. Even before the outbreak of the World War I, Vienna had always been known for its literary, academic, and cultural life found in the coffee shops and meeting places along the *Ringstrasse*. Intellectuals and activists would meet and argue and, over 'a coffee, a glass of water and perhaps a strudel, an article would be written, an argument renewed, a play reviewed, an introduction made' (Edmonds & Eidenow, 2002; 58). Popper was always sceptical-if not contemptuous-of this intellectual scene, viewing it as a self-indulgence among the affluent, and dominated by passing intellectual fads and fashions. Popper once remarked that Wittgenstein's *Tractatus* (which he loathed) 'smelled of the coffee house'.

Popper may not have been a regular at the coffee houses of Vienna, but he was greatly influenced by other academic gatherings, especially in the years during and immediately after the submission of his PhD. Heinrich Gomperz, for example, ran an informal discussion group on the history of ideas, in which academics from a range of disciplines would discuss historical and philosophical issues. Through Gomperz, Popper was invited to attend these meetings and, in fact, it was perhaps his performance at one such meeting that kept him from becoming a member of the more important and influential Vienna Circle, convened by his PhD examiner Moritz Schlick. Schlick-who also attended Gomperz's discussion group from time to time-had never been a great admirer of Popper (the fact that he passed Popper's PhD thesis with distinction was apparently more to do with his respect for Buhler than Popper's work). When Popper used the session to viciously attack Ludwig Wittgenstein-one of Schlick's heroes and the intellectual father of the Vienna Circle-Schlick left halfway through in disgust and denounced Popper's critique as a caricature. Whether that moment was decisive or not, no invitation was made to Popper to join the Circle.

Popper appeared to revel in his exclusion from the Vienna Circle, and was always proud of the fact that he was never welcomed as a member. Otto Neurath, a member of the Circle, once described Popper as the group's 'official opposition', a role that Popper relished. Popper would spend most of his career attacking the philosophical foundations of the Circle, and developing arguments against many of its most influential members. And influential they were. The Vienna Circle, established by Schlick was one of the most important academic groups in interwar Europe. Regular members of the group-which drew leading thinkers in the fields of philosophy, logic, mathematics, the social sciences, and the natural and physical sciences-included such luminaries as Rudolph Carnap, Otto Neurath, Hans Hahn, Kurt Godel, Friedrich Waissman, and Herbert Feigl. Often joined by international visitors like V. W. O. Quine from America, A. J. Ayer from Britain, Alfred Tarski from Poland, and Carl Hempel from Berlin, the meetings of the Circle were a veritable who's who of philosophical and scientific talent. The raison d'etre of the Circle, and the ideology which bound this eclectic group of thinkers together, was the idea that the methods of the physical sciences should be applied to philosophy. Their stance was most obviously opposed to German Idealism-embodied in the work of Hegel,Fichte,Schelling,and Kant-which held that there were things about the world which could not be known through observation and that, consequently, the scientific method could not yield true or complete knowledge about the world. The German Idealists thus held that philosophy and science were separate endeavours, that there were genuine questions which could not be answered by science (like questions of metaphysics, ontology, ethics, and theology), and that philosophy was uniquely suited to resolving these issues. The members of the Vienna Circle,on the other hand,believed that philosophy should learn from science,and that philosophy would always be subordinate to science as the means by which knowledge about the world might be meaningfully pursued and acquired. Their principal aim, therefore, was to demarcate 'physics' (that is, what could be known scientifically) from 'metaphysics'(which could not). The criterion of demarcation was drawn from Wittgenstein's *Tractatus Logico Philosophicus*(1921), which became the Circle's bible.

In the *Tractatus*, Wittgenstein explored the relationship between language and reality and argued that this relationship was a *descriptive* one; the world is the totality of facts which exist around us,and we use language to *describe* this world. There are, therefore,two ways in which a statement might be said to be meaningful; it must either be verifiable through observation (in the sense that it meaningfully describes something that can be seen or experienced in the world), or 'analytical' in the sense that its meaning is derived entirely from the logical relationship of the particular words used. Statements or utterances which do not intelligibly describe some fact in the world, and which are also not logical statements which derive their meaning from the internal structure of the statement itself, are *meaningless*. For example,the statement'a rectangle has four sides'is *analytical* (and, hence, meaningful) in the sense that its meaning is

14

derived from the words used in that order, not because it necessarily tells us something *true* about the world. It is a tautology: its meaning is derived from the logic of the statement itself. Similarly, a statement such as 'that shoebox is rectangular' is meaningful in the sense that it can be verified through observation and experience. However, a statement such as 'God made that shoebox' is neither analytical not verifiable, and hence, is meaningless.

Philosophy, then, for Wittgenstein (and the Vienna Circle), was not the search for truth but the search for meaning: the search for statements about the world which were either logically meaningful in their own right or gained their meaning through verification. Consequently, metaphysical statements such as 'The mind and body are distinct' or 'God is the prime mover of the Universe' were considered meaningless. They are not 'untrue' or 'wrong', they are merely beyond the scope of philosophy to resolve. While *science* determines what is true, *philosophy* should concern itself with determining the meaning of words, and of the utterances that they compose. This approach was named 'logical positivism', and it embodied a radical approach to understanding the purposes and limits of philosophy. For if the principal criteria of demarcation between the meaningfulness and non-meaningfulness of statements was whether they could be verified through an observation of the real world, or whether they were meaningful in terms of their own internal logic, then it was not merely *metaphysical* statements which were consigned to the rubbish bin but all statements which fail the verification test, such as those of aesthetics, ethics, politics, and theology. Claims such as 'Beethoven was a better composer than Mozart', or 'All human beings should live virtuous lives', or 'God gave human beings rights' are meaningless, because none of these claims are analytical (in Wittgenstein's sense) or empirically verifiable. Thus, the Vienna Circle believed that Wittgenstein's philosophy of language had laid bare the real content and aims of philosophy, and provided the criteria by which one might determine which questions or statements were important and legitimate, and which were meaningless and redundant.

Popper agreed with the broad claim made by the logical positivists that science and philosophy might complement one another. After all, he shared the logical positivists' commitment to rationality, reason, and intellectual inquiry, and believed that it was important to distinguish between real knowledge and subjective opinion. He was, for example, supportive of Carnap's pleas for 'rationality, [and] for greater intellectual responsibility'. Carnap, he said, 'asks us to learn from the way in which mathematicians and scientists proceed, and he contrasts this with the depressing ways of philosophers: their pretentious wisdom, and their arrogation of knowledge which they present to us with a minimum of rational, or critical, argument' (Popper, 1974/2002; 100). Again, we can sense Popper's disdain for the philosophers in their coffee houses, so many of whom felt they could pontificate on the nature of reality without having to trouble themselves with providing evidence for their claims. The logical positivists' attitude was 'the attitude of the enlightenment', and Popper claimed to feel very much at one with the Vienna Circle's claim that philosophers (like anyone else) should limit themselves to what can be established through reason and rational argument, and that one should be sceptical of bold assertions of philosophical truth that could not be criticized rationally.

But Popper was not a logical positivist, and was not a member of the Vienna Circle, even though many believed that he was. Indeed, he was keen to disassociate himself from the Circle. Popper rejected the creed of the logical positivists because their aim was to debunk metaphysics, aesthetics, ethics, and other branches of philosophy as meaningless and redundant. They sought to demarcate physics from metaphysics, in order to consign the latter to uselessness. But Popper was deeply critical of this view, primarily because he felt that many of the most innovative *scientific* discoveries in history began as *metaphysical* statements. 'Scientific research,' he argued, 'is probably impossible without... "metaphysical" faith in sometimes hazy theoretical ideas' (Popper, 1935/2007a; 38). Moreover, he argued, 'all observation involves interpretation in the light of our theoretical knowledge... pure observational knowledge, unadulterated by theory, would if at all possible, be utterly barren and futile' (Popper, 1963/2007b; 30). Metaphysics was not useless, he believed; rather, it represented the basis for many claims which would go on to become scientific. Scientific knowledge was more advanced than metaphysical knowledge, he believed, and scientists 'may exclude, in a piecemeal fashion, the remaining metaphysical elements in theories, by demarcating them through testability' (Hacohen, 2000;247). So metaphysics was not meaningless, but rather an important aspect of scientific discovery. Popper therefore believed that, in seeking to consign metaphysics to the rubbish bin, the logical positivists 'failed to notice that they were throwing their *scientific* theories on the same scrapheap as the "meaningless" metaphysical theories' (Popper, 1963/2007b; 349). Consequently, the task was not to demarcate physics from metaphysics, but to demarcate 'science' from 'pseudo-science'; that is, to work out which areas of knowledge fell within the realm of science and which did not.

So for Popper, the problem with the logical positivism of the Vienna Circle was that they were trying to demarcate the wrong things for the wrong reasons. But that was not all. He also believed they were using the wrong criteria of demarcation. The Circle were besotted with Wittgenstein; they read the *Tractatus* line by line (more than once) in their meetings, over the course of a year; they pored over every nuance and detail; Moritz Schlick, along with several other members of the Circle, developed a personal relationship with Wittgenstein and formed an informal discussion group at which they would gain the benefit of the great man's wisdom. Popper loathed him. He considered his whole philosophy to be mistaken and, worse, entirely contrary to what philosophy should be about. Wittgenstein became Popper's nemesis. His

17

central claim that there are no such things as philosophical 'problems' only philosophical 'puzzles' arising from the use of language, and that philosophy was about the pursuit of meaning rather than truth, embodied everything that Popper hated about the self-indulgence of philosophers. For someone who grew up in a city divided by anti-Semitism, poverty, and conflict, who lived through World War I and witnessed the destruction of the Habsburg Empire, the food and fuel shortages, and the revolution first hand, the claim that there were no philosophical 'problems', only 'puzzles', smacked all too obviously of the cosseted world of the coffee house, the fashionable affluent classes, and the irresponsible fripperies of the rich and idle. Popper believed that real philosophical problems existed and that it was the role of the philosopher to seek resolutions to these problems. He believed that philosophy was the search for truth, not meaning. This sense-that philosophers should concern themselves with the resolution of concrete problems that exist in the world-informs every aspect of Popper's philosophy, from the questions he took to be important, to the way he sought to resolve them. The key was not to demarcate between what was meaningful and what was not, but between what provided grounds for knowledge and what did not.

Popper had begun this project in his PhD thesis, and in his 1929 thesis on geometry. But it was in 1934, with the publication of *Logik der Forschung* (later translated as *The Logic of Scientific Discovery*) that Popper famously outlined his alternative theory of demarcation, and his critique of the foundations upon which logical positivism were built. What Popper proposed was nothing less than the re-interpretation of science not as an inductive process, but a deductive one. The problem with the logical positivists, he claimed, was not that they sought to apply the methods of the physical sciences to philosophy, but that they had a mistaken understanding of what science was, and how it should be understood. Popper believed that this error was shared by many scientists, who on the whole clung to Newton's idea that it was possible to extrapolate generalizable laws of nature from specific experiments or tests. Popper criticized this view by criticizing the inductive method on which it was based, and turning it on its head. He did so by applying a Humean scepticism towards induction itself, and defining science as a deductive process. Building on his claim that scientific discovery often begins in metaphysical claims, Popper argued that the inductive process of discovery (in which scientists move from facts to general theories) should be inverted: scientific discovery begins with the statement of theories which are either confirmed or falsified by facts or other theories. On this view, the truth of any particular theory (however compelling) is always conjectural and hypothetical, never irrefutable or concrete. A scientific theory is a claim about some aspect of the world and, hence, represents an invitation to others to test and falsify its core assertions. If it can stand firm against these attempts, then its claim to truth remains valid(but still hypothetical, as it may be falsified in the future). If it cannot, then it is abandoned. Scientific discovery is thus a process of building and falsifying theories through a process of trial and error. The result was a genuinely new approach to the philosophy of science which had implications for the pursuit of knowledge outside of the scientific community, and which had the potential to empower philosophers and social scientists (as well as scientists) to engage with fundamental problems by employing the same approach. The point was not to determine what was scientific and what was not in order to renounce the latter; rather, it was to provide a broad theory of epistemology, within which it was possible to determine what appropriately belonged to the realm of science and what did not. Consequently, Popper's approach reclaimed non-scientific forms of philosophy as valid pursuits. It also solved many of the problems faced by the Vienna Circle by providing a 'deductive science that was empirical but not inductive, testable and confirmable but not certain, demarcated from metaphysics by falsifiability but not deeming metaphysics meaningless. Science left space for epistemology, methodology, and "nonscientific" philosophy' (Hacohen, 2000; 199).

'A fighting book'

In his *Autobiography*, Popper proclaimed logical positivism dead by his own hand. Logical positivism, he said, collapsed under the weight of 'insuperable internal difficulties. Most of these difficulties had been pointed out in my *Logik der Forschung*. Some members of the Circle were impressed by the need to make changes. Thus the seeds were sown. They led, in the course of many years, to the disintegration of the Circle's tenets' (Popper, 1974/2002; 99). But, as Popper also pointed out, the Circle had begun to dissolve even before its tenets. Interwar Vienna had been becoming increasingly inhospitable to intellectuals, especially those who held left-wing sympathies, or were Jewish. The economic depression which began in 1929 further divided an already tense society, and ushered in an era of right-wing extremism. A dramatic fall in industrial production, a weakened trades union movement, and a doubling of unemployment between 1929 and 1932 brought economic hardship to many and fresh political challenges to the coalition government. Post-war inflation reached unprecedented levels, wiping out long term savings, and throwing many families into poverty (Popper's father lost his savings in this way). Anti-Semitism, already a visible force in Viennese society-became more vicious and widespread. All Austrian political parties used anti-Jewish imagery in their propaganda, and the Jews bore the brunt of public hostility in the wake of economic chaos. As Hacohen puts it, in the 'Bourgeois imagination, the Jew embodied capitalism, socialism, and the republic, all at the same time' (Hacohen, 2000; 294).

The early 1930s saw the rise of the National Socialists, as the 'white collar German middle class, the civil servants, the

German intelligentsia, the non-Jewish professionals, and the petty bourgeoisie' all became supporters of the Nazi cause (Hacohen, 2000;296-7). The German National Socialists came to power in Berlin on 30 January 1933, and within three months the leader of the Austrian coalition government(which opposed the Nazis) had suspended parliamentary democracy and declared presidential rule. The move was accompanied by a raft of repressive measures, including press censorship, the outlawing of strikes, and the banning of mass public demonstrations. When the socialists failed to stage a fight back, it was clear that a pivotal moment had been reached. In 1934 Englebert Dollfuss (prime minister, and head of the coalition government) created a one party state, and was assassinated by the Nazis on 25th July of that year.

With political and economic tensions reaching boiling point, and threats of German occupation in the air, the philosophers, scientists, and mathematicians of the Vienna Circle joined the doctors, bankers, artists, film-makers, and others in their flight from Austria. Carnap moved to Prague and then joined Godel at Princeton, Menger moved to the University of Notre Dame in Indiana, Hempel went to New York via Brussels and Chicago, Feigle went to Minnesota via Iowa, and Friedrich Waissman moved to Cambridge and then Oxford. Neurath-the most politically active of the Circle-left Vienna for Holland, before settling for the rest of his life in Britain.

Popper left Vienna for New Zealand in 1937, whereupon he took up his first full-time lectureship at Canterbury University College. This was preceded by an extended lecture tour of England during which he met many of the leading lights of British academic life, including A. J. Ayer, Isaiah Berlin, Gilbert Ryle, Bertrand Russell, R. B. Braithwaite, and G. E. Moore, and spoke at many universities on topics arising from *Logik der Forschung*. His most pivotal meeting, although he may not have realized it at the time, was with Friedrich von Hayek, an Austrian émigré economist, and Professor at the London School of Economics. Hayek invited Popper to present to a seminar that he ran at the LSE, and it was at this meeting that Popper chose to develop a number of ideas that he had been toying with about the methodology of the social sciences. The paper, entitled ' The Poverty of Historicism ' would later become the book of the same name, and would see Popper apply many of the arguments he had made in *Logik* about science and epistemology to the study of society and politics. Hayek had read *Logik* and was greatly impressed by it. Popper's rejection of social, economic, and political planning proved congenial to Hayek, whose brand of *laissez-faire* free-market economics emerged out of his concerns about epistemological uncertainty. Hayek and Popper worried about similar things: the threat to individual liberty posed by utopian political ideologies; the uncertain nature of human knowledge; the fallibility of reason; the impossibility of knowing another individual's interests more fully or more rationally than the individual him/herself knew them; and, perhaps most of all, the need to ensure that the state did not overstep its bounds, or claim legitimacy in some goal which was valid for all individuals. Hayek and Popper made quite an impression upon one another; an impression which would stay with Hayek sufficiently for him to support Popper in his move to the LSE after the war.

By the time he left for New Zealand, upon returning to Vienna after his sojourn around England, Popper was all but ready to formulate his major contribution to political philosophy. The pieces were nearly all in place. Born into a city of intellectuals and surrounded by progressive socialists, and having lived through the disintegration of all that he had once taken for granted in the destructive energies of war, revolution, and internal conflict, Popper's journey to *The Open Society* had been a slow but inexorable one. Popper was furious at the arrogance of the Austrian Marxists, who failed to notice that interwar economic strife was not leading to socialist revolution, but fascism, and a reactionary politics of hatred and division. He believed that the socialists had deluded themselves: rather than change their tactics in response to the events that were unfolding around them in the 1930s, they remained blinded by their ideology and the false prophecies of Marx that capitalism would end and be replaced by communism. Rather than face the truth, they carried on regardless, interpreting all events and developments as stages on the road to communism. Their hopes were in vain, however, and Popper believed that their failure was not merely a failure of Austrian socialism, but of socialism more broadly. When Popper arrived in New Zealand, his separation from Vienna was merely geographical. His mind was on the political and social world he had left behind. When, in March 1938, the Nazis occupied Austria, Popper heard that many of his family and friends had fallen to the new regime; many were arrested, interrogated and never heard from again, or taken to concentration camps or prison. His mother died in May 1938, and his sister escaped to Paris in June, without money or passport. 'Other relatives and friends were scrambling to leave the country, to England, France, anywhere-even New Zealand' (Hacohen, 2000; 345). According to Hacohen, Popper, with his friend Otto Frankael, did what he could to organize immigration permits for Austrians to come to New Zealand, but there were many obstacles to doing so.

In the face of such overwhelming horror and uncertainty, Popper's mind turned from natural science to politics. Unlike Wittgenstein, who believed that philosophy could have nothing to say about political or social problems, Popper felt that philosophy as *he* understood it could contribute to the fight against tyranny, and against the rising tide of fascism. With the outbreak of World War II, Popper put aside what was to become *The Poverty of Historicism* and began work on another book which would draw on many of its central themes. Together these books would represent Popper's 'war effort'. *The Open Society*, especially, he described as a 'fighting book'.

Given the contemporary neglect of *The Open Society* by political philosophers, it is easy to underestimate how radical and important the book was at the time of its publication. Popper's aim was nothing less than to trace the origins of the totalitarian ideologies which dominated world politics at that time,and had produced the greatest evils that the world had ever known. His conclusion was that these origins could be traced back to some of the most celebrated and revered figures in the history of Western civilization. Prior to *The Open Society*,Ancient Greece had been largely held by classicists and historians as the seat of enlightened democracy and culture, and Plato, its most notable and eloquent voice, as an embodiment of reason and humanity. Hegel-whose philosophy was considered controversial and difficult-was nevertheless considered a philosopher of major significance. Popper found them all guilty of paving the way for the tyranny and evil found at the heart of fascism and Nazism:Plato was painted as a racist, and a self-aggrandizing betrayer of Socrates who hated freedom, Hegel a clown and a fool who dressed his ridiculous and hateful ideas in an impenetrable cloak of baffling complexity and who pandered to the political leaders of his time in return for money. The message of the book was clear: that in the work of these great figures,and others who shared their method,we find the justification for tyranny,for murder, for racial politics, for tribalism, for evil-we find the closed society. And in his response, we can glimpse ideas traceable right back to his childhood in Vienna-we can see the influence of the progressives in Popper's rejection of nationalism as being exclusionary and 'closed', his belief in the capacity of individual human beings to change the society in which they live,that the state should aim to alleviate poverty through the implementation of humane social policies, and that it was possible to view science and social technology as a means of understanding social problems and responding to them. We can see his commitment to the ability of individuals to reason pro-ductively about their lives,and about the world in which they live,and that it was important for the state(and for teachers)to recognize and encourage this ability. And most obviously, we

24

can see his ideas, expressed in *Logik* and countless other essays and lectures, about knowledge, the process by which individual human beings come to know about the world in which they live, and about the limits to that process which place necessary and inevitable checks on what states can do, and the justifications they can provide for their actions.

The *Open Society* brought Popper immediate attention, both good and bad. Many derided his scholarship and accused him of caricaturing and misrepresenting the views of Marx, Plato, and Hegel. Despite his support for state intervention in economic markets in the interests of alleviating poverty, the provision of public services and education for all (regardless of income), his rejection of social, economic, or political privilege, his avowal of a deliberative form of democracy open to all, and his commitment to social change through debate and critical engagement on fundamental political assumptions, Marxists condemned him as an establishment figure and an apologist for capitalism. State socialists like Harold Laski supported Popper's conclusions, however, as did many other socialist academics and activists, including Bertrand Russell-an intellectual inspiration to both Popper and to the Vienna Circle-who proclaimed his attack on Plato's philosophy as 'brilliant'. Popper's aim was to 'destroy the unreal and metaphysical gulf that separates reasonable and liberal people in the various camps on the left', and to bind these disparate groups together in a common cause against totalitarianism (Popper, Letter to Alfred Braunthal, 12 December 1943; quoted in Hacohen, 449). But his book became popular with the Right, too. One of its biggest champions was Popper's friend Hayek, who was so impressed that he set out to get Popper a job at the LSE on the strength of it. Popper's defence of piecemeal social engineering in place of utopian planning, and his critique of historicism in politics and the social sciences, fit well with Hayek's general scepticism about epistemological certainty, and his views as to the spontaneity of social and political institutions. Popper's argument was more hospitable to economic interventionism and social planning than Hayek's, but nevertheless, Hayek was impressed by the application of Popper's scientific theory to social and economic questions and believed that he would be the perfect candidate for a position in logic and scientific method at the School. Hayek's efforts paid off, and Popper arrived in Britain on 5 January 1946, following the end of hostilities in Europe, to take up his post at the LSE. In 1949, he was appointed Professor of Logic and Scientific Method, a post he held for 23 years.

The later years

His first few years at the LSE'were exhilarating. He was a rising star. *The Open Society* threw him overnight into the public eye. At the LSE he drew large audiences, competing with Laski for popularity'(Hacohen, 2000; 523). Invitations to speak were plentiful. One meeting in particular has become the stuff of legend. On 25 October 1946, Popper presented a paper to a meeting of Cambridge's Moral Sciences Club, attended by a number of leading philosophers, including Bertrand Russell and one Ludwig Wittgenstein. Popper had been asked to present a short paper on 'some philosophical puzzle'. Popper chose to present a paper not-so-innocently entitled 'Are there any philosophical problems?', and used the session to provide a trenchant and sustained critique of Wittgenstein's idea that philosophy was a search for meaning in linguistic puzzles, rather than a search for the resolution of concrete problems. Differing views exist as to what actually transpired during the meeting (Popper's own recollections on the matter have been shown to be unreliable), but what can be gleaned from the testimony of those present is that Wittgenstein challenged Popper to provide examples of philosophical problems rather than puzzles. Popper suggested induction, infinity, and the validity of moral rules. Wittgenstein dismissed these examples and, in his frustration, began toying with a poker that he had taken from the fire in the room(as, apparently, was his habit). When challenged to provide an example of a moral rule, Popper said 'Not to threaten visiting lecturers with pokers', at which point (according to Popper as well as a number of others present), Wittgenstein threw down the poker and left the room. The accuracy of all this is difficult to ascertain, but it is certainly clear that Popper relished the opportunity, finally, to face his nemesis and show his philosophy to be mistaken. It was not a view that Wittgenstein was used to hearing.

The Open Society cut across ideological divides and united many liberals and socialists against nationalism, tribalism, and tyranny, and in support of individual freedom, equality, and reason. The book became a classic text in what became known-somewhat pejoratively-as 'cold war liberalism'. Popper joined with other post-war liberals in trying to convince the trades unions and the socialists that capitalism had been replaced by totalitarianism as the enemy of the people. The cold war hostility towards communism mandated a consensus among liberals, socialists, and libertarians against the common enemy, and Popper's defence of piecemeal social engineering and democracy provided a rallying point.

As time went on, however, Popper's attitude towards democracy began to change. Mass support for fascist and illiberal parties around the world led him (and other post-war liberals) to worry about the compatibility of freedom and democracy. Post-war liberals became increasingly sceptical of the claim that democracy was the best way of securing individual freedom. Popper remained an advocate of democracy, but chose to redefine it as a thin rather than substantive idea. He did not think that it was based on the idea that the majority should rule, or that decision-making power should be devolved down to the citizen body, or that the citizen body need necessarily participate in political activity; indeed, Popper held that public opinion was an 'irresponsible form of power' and a 'danger to freedom if it is not moderated by a strong liberal tradition' (Popper, 1963/ 2007b;476). Rather, it was merely a system of checks and balances which allowed for the peaceful removal of tyrants. Popper therefore seemed to subordinate democracy to liberalism. In doing so, critics have suggested that Popper was moving to the political right(Hacohen).

This view was strengthened, perhaps, in the light of Popper's later pronouncements concerning liberal tolerance, which he believed mandated the silencing of illiberal, intolerant groups: '[A]ny movement preaching intolerance places itself outside the law', he argued, and hence, could reasonably be suppressed (Popper, 1945/2006a; 292-4). Such suppression was seen as a last resort, however, and post-war liberals generally favoured open dialogue as the means by which differences might be resolved and diverse interests represented. Critics claimed that such a view was idealistic and, again, represented a move towards conservatism, as dominant majorities would always marginalize the needs of minority groups. The picture of democracy that Popper presented in *The Open Society* and in later essays was seen by some as too abstract, and insufficiently attentive to the power held by majorities, and the lack of power held by minorities, to shape the political agenda and to voice their concerns. And there was a more fundamental problem: how could Popper's theory of knowledge and discovery, which was premised upon constant refutation, debate, and critique, possibly yield the kind of agreements and compromises necessary in politics? Conservative thinkers like Carl Schmitt have suggested that in the face of unresolvable disagreement and never-ending democratic dialogue, real decisions are in fact made by powerful elites behind closed doors. Popper's defence of an idealized deliberative democracy failed to provide a compelling defence against such a charge, and hence, his defence of democracy has been considered by some to be a de facto defence of elite rule.

In 1950, Popper moved to a house in rural Penn, Buckinghamshire, on the outskirts of London. Despite continuing to work on political matters, especially the relationship between liberalism and socialism, Popper's mind returned to the philosophy of science. With increased seclusion, those political ideas that Popper developed did indeed seem more conservative, although the application of ideological labels to Popper's political vision is difficult, as we will see. His 1954 essay 'Public opinion and liberal principles', quoted earlier, was indicative of this, as were his essays 'Toleration and Intellectual Responsibility' and 'What Does the West Believe in?', in which he extolled the virtues of liberal democracy as the best form of government ever invented. He was effusive in his praise of Hayek's *The Constitution of Liberty*, published in 1960, which forced Popper to confront the tensions in his own work between his defence of social engineering and his support for a limited state. His response was to become much more sceptical about state intervention and to cling more strongly to the emancipatory power of democracy and liberty as a grounds for piecemeal social reform.

The years following the publication of *The Open Society* were a time of professional triumphs and personal change. He was elected as a Fellow of the British Academy in 1958 and knighted in 1965. In the same year, the City of Vienna awarded him the *Geisteswissenschaften Prize*, and would later celebrate his 80th birthday with symposia and awards. He was elected as a Fellow of the Royal Society in 1976. However, Popper became even more isolated from his fellow philosophers, many of whom he believed were engaged in irrelevancies. Although his appearances at the LSE became less regular, his influence remained strong. Following the publication of Thomas Kuhn's groundbreaking *The Structure of Scientific Revolutions* in 1962, Popper responded with 'The myth of the framework', in which he provided a trenchant critique of Kuhn's 'incommensurability of theses' argument, a strident critique of cultural and political relativism, and a defence of political deliberation and reason which resonates with the work of later liberal thinkers like John Rawls, Jeremy Waldron, and Joshua Cohen.

Popper became increasingly separated not merely from the

LSE but from the world at large. His furious critique of critical theory, and his angry denunciation of such theorists as Jurgen Habermas, Theodor Adorno, and Max Horkheimer, seemed to cement his move to the Right, and distanced him from a lot of what came to be associated with Leftist politics during the 1960s and 1970s. Similarly, his claim that people needed to work with existing political institutions and practices in order to reform them from the inside rather than challenge them directly seemed at odds with the growing tendency among supporters of the Left to adopt more direct, radical approaches to social change, like forming protest movements or participating in demonstrations. The political and social climate in the 1970s brought out his conservative sympathies even more starkly: he often raged against the 'New Left, the British public health system,... and the British labour unions' suicidal tactics' (Hacohen, 2000; 540). However, it was clear that Popper's knowledge of world affairs was sketchy. 'When, in his final years, he watched a little television, he was horrified by both the programs and the media's power, and suggested controlling them in ways which violated liberal principles. ' (Hacohen, 2000; 540). The failures of British socialism in the 1970s appeared the last straw for Popper, who had been increasingly convinced by Hayek and others of the potential tensions between the principles of individual freedom and equality. By 1974-and perhaps earlier-Popper's transition from progressive socialist, to communist, to social democrat, and finally to conservative liberal, was, for many, obvious and complete. Looking back on this journey in this *Autobiography*, Popper eloquently states why he gave up on socialism and its promise of equality. 'I remained a socialist for many years, even after my rejection of Marxism,'he wrote,

and if there could be such a thing as socialism combined with liberty then I would be a socialist still. For nothing could be better than living a modest, simple and free life in an egalitarian society. It took some time before I recognized this as no more than a beautiful dream; that freedom is more important than equality, that the attempt to realize equality endangers freedom; and that, if freedom is lost, there will not even be equality among the unfree. (Popper, 1974/2002; 36)

Read at face value, this paragraph seems to support the popular notion that Popper ended his political journey as a libertarian, or as what had become known as the conservatism of Margaret Thatcher, Ronald Reagan, and the New Right. But the story is not so simple. True, Popper's rejection of socialist equality in this passage is emphatic, but his political philosophy (both early and late) is characterized by a search for a humane society in which freedom and equality might coexist *together*. True, he defends individual freedom, a limited state, and reasonable discussion as a means of resolving cultural and ethnic differences; and true, he argues that there may be grounds for not tolerating illiberal groups, denying that certain unreasonable claims or ideas need to be excluded from public debate, and that liberalism and democracy may not be entirely compatible. But these are ideas that are now shared by many contemporary egalitarian liberals, who are neither conservatives nor libertarians. He may have remained a committed individualist at a time when political discourse was becoming dominated by talk of groups, movements, and social activism, but the claim that individuals (and not groups) should be considered the principal actors in a democratic state does not necessarily imply conservatism. Indeed, such a position is entirely compatible with non-socialist understandings of equality, and has been advanced by many liberals who claim to be interested in supporting both freedom *and* equality. Popper's rejection of equality in the above passage is thus curious: despite his worries about the capacity of socialism to establish equality, he did not seem to give up on the idea of equality per se. At no point in his early or late political philosophy does he defend a society in which individual freedom is considered the only virtue to be encouraged; he defends a vision of society as 'open' rather than 'closed', a vision in which the capacity of *all* individual human beings to live free and flourishing lives is celebrated and nurtured, and in which arbitrary distinctions between the'deserving'and the'undeserving', the'worthy'and the'unworthy', are rejected and replaced with an appeal to cosmopolitanism and universalism. At the heart of Popper's critique of irrationalism in *The Open Society*, after all, was that it assumed 'the inequality of men'. It cannot be denied that 'human beings are, like all other things in our world, in very many respects very unequal,' he argued. 'Nor can it be doubted that this inequality is of great importance and even in many respects highly desirable. But all this has no bearing on the question whether or not we should treat men, especially in political issues, as equals, or as much like equals as possible: that is to say, as possessing equal rights, and equal claims to equal treatment; and it has no bearing upon the question of whether we ought to construct political institutions accordingly. "Equality before the law"is not a fact but a political demand based upon a moral decision' (Popper 1945/2006b; 259). The paradox that runs throughout Popper's political thought, then, and an important issue that crops up time and again in his discussion of it, is this central relationship between equality and freedom, and the extent to which his original progressive vision of an egalitarian society free from poverty might be reconciled with a society premised upon individual freedom(from the state, from others, and from one's own ignorance).

By the time Popper died on 17 September 1994, many believed that he had abandoned this project, but in fact, his commitment to the values which underpin his old egalitarianism were still evident. True, he moved away from social technology as an appropriate response to resolving political problems, and voiced concerns about mass democracy; he united with cold war liberals who sought to champion liberal principles on the world stage, and his politics became increasingly defined in reaction to Soviet excesses and the spread of illiberal groups who threatened freedom. But despite all this, his commitment to

Karl Popper

individual freedom, the possibility of advancing knowledge through human endeavour, and his distrust of assumed knowledge and authority were unwavering. In Popper's later politics, as in his earlier work, we find a hatred of tribal and nationalist conservatism, a rejection of privilege, and a genuine belief in the capacity of all people—if given the chance and the right resources—to free themselves from the grip of ignorance, tyranny, and the inequalities of wealth and power which thwart their lives. It is this belief—in the enlightenment, in reason, and in the equal dignity of all human beings—which is so relevant to contemporary politics and philosophy, and which resonates with so much contemporary political theory in the twenty-first century.

Intellectual Biography

2
Popper's Ideas

Popper wrote widely and prolifically over the course of his long career, on a range of diverse subjects. His principal interest, however, and the mission which drove and unified his work in areas as divergent as music, history, logic, mathematics, science, social science, and politics, was the 'problem of cosmology: the problem of understanding the world—including ourselves, and our knowledge, as part of the world' (Popper 1935/2007a; xix).

Popper believed that this was the central problem of philosophy. In arguing as much, he saw himself as belonging to a long and noble tradition of rationalist philosophers for whom the pursuit of knowledge (about the world and, importantly, about knowledge itself) was of crucial importance. From 'Plato to Descartes, Leibniz, Kant, Duhem and Poincaré; and from Bacon, Hobbes, and Locke, to Hume, Mill, and Russell, the theory of knowledge was inspired by the hope that it would enable us not only to know more about knowledge, but also to contribute to the advance of knowledge', and *scientific* knowledge in particular. It was a hope that Popper shared. And in sharing it, he set himself against the logical positivists of the Vienna Circle and 'ordinary language' philosophers like J. L. Austin and Gilbert Ryle who both, in their own ways, held that philosophy was primarily the study of language. 'Most of the philosophers who believe that the characteristic method of philosophy is the analysis of ordinary language seem to have lost the admirable optimism which once inspired the rationalist tradition', he wrote. 'Their attitude, it seems, has become one of resignation, if not despair' (Popper, 1935/2007a; xxii).

Popper's philosophy should be read as an attempt to counsel against this despair, and to overturn what he saw as the flawed philosophical doctrines which cause it. We have already mentioned some of them in Chapter 1 (the rejection of psychologism, logical positivism, Wittgensteinean linguistic philosophy, and the idea that philosophy is appropriately understood as the search for meaning rather than the resolution of concrete problems in the world), and we will discuss several more in the chapters which follow. Popper's aim was to establish an *epistemology*—a theory which would explain the status and growth of knowledge in the world, and which could be applied to all areas of human endeavour in which knowledge is sought. It was not, as it was for the logical positivists, to demarcate 'physics' from 'metaphysics' in order to junk the latter, but to demarcate science from pseudo-science (that is, to demarcate scientific theories from those theories which purported to be scientific but in fact were not). His conclusions were radical and far-reaching, and informed not only his work on science, logic, and mathematics, but politics and social science too. It is not possi-ble to provide an exhaustive treatment of Popper's philosophy of science here, as this book is principally concerned with his political philosophy. I will therefore flesh out some of the ideas described in the previous chapter, in particular those aspects of his epistemology which bear most importantly upon his poli-tical philosophy, before discussing the ways in which he applied these ideas first to the study of society (in *The Poverty of Historicism*) and then to politics (in *The Open Society and Its Enemies*). Having done so, I will, in Chapter 3, discuss some of the ways in which his political views changed in the years following the publication of *The Open Society*.

Popper's epistemology

Popper believed that 'the central problem of epistemology has always been... the problem of the growth of knowledge. And the growth of knowledge', he argued, 'can be studied best by studying the growth of scientific knowledge' (Popper, 1935/ 2007a; xix). So how, and by what method, does scientific knowledge grow? How are scientific discoveries made?

According to the traditional view, science is an *inductive* process in which scientists begin by collating and systematizing observations about the world in order to extrapolate from their observations overarching laws of nature. These laws of nature can in turn be used to *explain* the world (by verifying certain claims about it), and to *predict* future events. Consequently, science begins in the *observation* of certain natural properties or behaviours (in elements or chemicals like, say, lead, or water, or hydrogen, or in physical objects like wheels or propellers or atoms). In particular, it begins in the observation of particular, isolatable properties or behaviours via scientific experiments. The results (observations) gathered during these experiments are used to infer generalizable laws. It is therefore an important job of the scientist to establish the appropriate circumstances in which the observations might be made and tested in ways which do not lead to unintended or tainted consequences. Scientific *theories* are thus *inferred* from observed *facts* about the world, which are gathered through a process of repeated experimentation and empirical testing under controlled conditions. The resultant theories have a *predictive* and *verificational* quality: by isolating and observing the specific behaviour of specific objects (for example, the effect of gravity upon a falling apple), it is possible to *verify* (or *prove*) the truth of a claim about the world (e. g. the statement 'apples do not fall upwards'), and *predict* future events (e. g. 'if I were to release my grip on this apple, it would fall downwards '). Theories can be *proven*, or *justified*, by appropriately observed facts, and scientific progress is driven by, and measured in terms of, the growth in the number of such theories. The more the theory can explain in this way—the more universal its applicability—the more important it is considered.

This view of the scientific method—as an inductive process of establishing general laws of nature from specific, observable facts—has a long and illustrious pedigree, is generally held by the majority of scientists, and is held to be exemplified in the work of many of the greatest scientists in history, including Galileo, Copernicus, Kepler, and Isaac Newton. Newton's observation of something as small and insignificant as a falling apple, for example, allowed him to develop a general theory of universal gravitation which further allowed him to explain the movement of the planets, and predict their future progress, with great success and precision. The groundbreaking significance of Newton's theory for many lay primarily in the fact that it was rooted in observations of particular events or properties, but could be applied to all physical objects. From specific observations of specific objects, Newton was able to derive laws of nature which were generalizable and universal, and which could therefore contribute to a broad and far-reaching system of rules concerning the basic structure of the universe. Scientists before and after have employed an inductive method in their search for truth about the world and the wider cosmos in the hope that their observations will allow them to derive similarly universal and generalizable laws, capable of both explaining and predicting events.

Popper believed that this traditional understanding of science was fundamentally flawed. His reasons were various. *First*, he argued that the inductive method relies on a fundamental philosophical and logical impossibility, namely, that the ' truth of... [a] theory could be logically derived from the truth of certain observation-statements' (Popper, 1963/2007b; 251). Popper argued, on the contrary, that '[n]o rule can ever guarantee that a generalization inferred from true observations, however often repeated, is true' (Popper, 1963/2007b; 71). He did so by appealing to Hume's critique of induction in his *Enquiry into Human Understanding*. In that book, Hume states that there are no valid arguments allowing us to establish 'that those instances, of which we have had no experience, resemble those, of which we have had experience'. Consequently, Hume states, 'even after the observation of the frequent or constant conjunction of objects, we have no reason to draw any inference concerning any object beyond those of which we have had experience'; thus we should not 'form any conclusion beyond those past instances, of which we have had experience' (quoted in Popper 1963/2007b; 55—6). In other words, the fact that something has happened in the past, even a hundred or a thousand or a million times, does not mean it will happen in the same way in the future: repeated observations of a particular event under particular circumstances cannot *prove* inconclusively that it will always occur in the way we expect, or at all. We cannot predict the future by examining the past, however sure we are that we have observed the past correctly, and identified regularities or trends in it.

This claim led Popper to a radical conclusion: that the long-standing view that scientists should seek to derive generalizable laws of nature from specific events or facts in the world is mistaken and futile. Moreover, he concluded, the problem of induction implies that any theories we develop can never be scientifically *proven*-they can only be *falsified*. The statement 'All swans are white' cannot be *proven* by observing any number of white swans, but it can be decisively *falsified* by observing one non-white swan. The claim 'The fortress is impregnable' cannot be *proven* by any number of unsuccessful attempts to breach its defences, but it can be decisively *refuted* by a single successful attempt. And the theory that the sun will not rise in the morning unless a sacrifice is made to the sun god (as the Aztecs believed) cannot be *proven* by any number of successful sacrifices, but can be decisively *refuted* by the fact of the sun rising when no sacrifice was made. Facts cannot *prove* a theory to be true, but they can show it to be *false*. And once shown to be false, a theory comes to represent a genuine contribution to knowledge: we can state what *is not* true much more definitively than we can state what *is* true, and consequently, refuted statements are valuable. They are not useless (as the traditional view holds); for Popper the refutation of a theory represents a real advance in scientific knowledge which should be celebrated and valued because finding out that a theory *cannot* be true is an important step in what *is*, or *can be*, true. Useless theories, on the other hand, are those theories which cannot be falsified. Given that it is not possible to provide irrefutable proofs, or certain truths, in the realm of science (given the problem of induction), theories framed *as if* they were irrefutable truths, and which admit no possibility of falsification, are thus unscientific and unhelpful. Consider, for example, two statements:

(a) Because we have provided this sacrifice, it will rain tomorrow.
(b) Because we have provided this sacrifice, it will rain in the future.

What makes (a) a possible candidate for the truth (and hence, *scientific*) and (b) *unscientific* is that (a) can be refuted while (b) cannot. That is, we may not *currently* possess the requisite knowledge to refute it, but it is framed in such a way that we *may* one day do so. Statement (a) is precise while (b) is imprecise. Statement (a)'s precision means that it can be tested (by waiting until tomorrow to see if it rains), while (b)'s imprecision means that it cannot: we can spend generations waiting for it to rain but, given that it is possible to do so infinitely, we will never know if it will or not. Consequently, (b) is incapable of adding anything to our knowledge of the world, while (a) is capable of doing so (although it still may not be true). Popper believed that predictions (in science as elsewhere) are important and possible, but that they must be precise and, hence, falsifiable, rather than general and unfalsifiable. They also need to be short-term. Reason can be predictive, but it is necessarily limited and fallible. No individual or group of individuals can foresee all the various long-term consequences of particular actions or reactions by reasoning about them; consequently, predictions must be tentative and short-term, rather than radical and long-term. Science cannot and should not seek to establish theories which prove certain things about the world(that is, which *verify* the truth of a statement or claim)—rather, it should seek to eliminate error in those falsifiable theories which currently exist. Moreover, the fact that theories cannot be *proven* to be true, means that all existing theories—however compelling or persuasive or universally applicable—must be considered inherently conjectural and hypothetical; as no hypothesis can be proven, it remains forever a *hypothesis* (unless it is ever shown to be false, in which case it is abandoned).

Secondly, and relatedly, Popper disputed the philosophical and historical accuracy of the view that science begins in *observation*. Popper believed, on the contrary, that science begins with the proposal of *theories* concerning particular *problems*. This represented an inversion of the traditional inductive understanding of science; while inductivists held that science moves from observations (or facts) to theories (or general laws), Popper argued that science in fact begins with the identification of *problems* about which we propose *theories* which may in turn be *falsified* by other theories or observations. This connects with the point raised in Chapter 1: that, for Popper, the growth of knowledge arises out of our confrontation with real problems rather than, say, the meaning of linguistic statements. Science, he held, was not an *inductive* process, but a *deductive* one: scientists identify certain problems in the world, propose theories to resolve them, and then seek to falsify these theories. If they can falsify them, then they are abandoned (except for any residual elements which stand up to testing); if they cannot, then the theory stands while they continue to seek refutations based upon what is currently known: such theories cannot be considered true, but they may be considered hypothetically true, or potentially true. That is, facts are not used to prove theories, and they are not considered a source for general laws of nature, rather, they are used to deduce whether or not a particular theory can be correct given what is currently known about the world. Science, then, does not begin in observation, but in the positing of *theories* about *problems*.

Again, the implications of this for our understanding of science are radical and far-reaching. It has become an assumed truth that science is (and should be) characterized by a dispassionate, clinical detachment from the world, and understood as a process of observation, experimentation, and collation of results in a controlled environment. This, Popper believed, was characteristic of a particular brand of the rationalist tradition exemplified by Bacon and Descartes, who argued that in order to understand the world we must first 'purge our minds of all conjectures or guesses or prejudices' which might taint our findings, and reveal truth by the light of our reason alone (Popper, 1963/2007b; 19). It was also, as we saw in Chapter 1, the view of the logical positivists. Popper, on the other hand, believed that scientific discoveries do not arise from the barren application of reason in the world, but precisely in those conjectures and guesses and prejudices which Bacon, Descartes, and the logical positivists urged us to put aside. 'Science must begin... neither with the collection of observations, nor with the invention of experiments,' Popper argued, 'but with the critical discussion of myths' (Popper, 1963/2007b; 66). Human beings are inclined to impose order upon the world and their lives by trying to explain them, and in particular, by trying to explain them in terms of regularities or trends on which they can depend, and which can be used to explain current events, and predict events in the future. This is true of children (as Popper argued in his 1927 thesis, written at the Pedagogic

Institute), and of adults too; it is evident in our desire to establish overarching natural laws, but also in our construction of other myths and narratives which provide order and context to our lives: for example, myths of nation, religion, culture, history. These myths and conventions are important in that they set the initial framework within which scientific investigations are conducted. 'Observation is always selective', Popper argued. 'It needs a chosen object, a definite task, an interest, a point of view, a problem' (Popper 1963/2007b; 61). It is not the job of the scientist to collect random observations about the world, but to solve problems by attempting to falsify those conjectural solutions (or theories) which already exist. In science as elsewhere, we 'cannot know: we can only guess. And our guesses are guided by the unscientific, the metaphysical (though biologically explainable) faith in laws, in regularities which we can uncover' (Popper 1935/2007a; 275). Scientists cannot merely *look* (or listen, or hear, or feel), they need to know what they are looking *for*, and how they might look *effectively*. Similarly, they cannot merely *create*: they need some context of ends (some problem requiring a solution) which can guide them. 'No amount of physics will tell a scientist that it is the right thing for him to construct a plough, or an aeroplane, or an atomic bomb', Popper wrote. 'Ends must be adopted by him, or given to him; and what he does *qua* scientist is only to construct means by which these ends can be realized' (Popper 1963/2007b; 483). Theory thus 'dominates the experimental work from its initial planning up to the finishing touches in the laboratory' (Popper 1935/2007a; 90).

Furthermore, for Popper, the idea that scientific discovery begins in *observation* rather than the proposal of *theories* (often rooted in myths and metaphysical ideas) is simply not true of some of the most significant advances in the history of cosmology. 'For it is a fact', Popper wrote, 'that purely metaphysical ideas... have been of the greatest importance for cosmology. From Thales to Einstein, from ancient atomism to Descartes's speculations about matter, from the speculations of

Gilbert and Newton and Leibniz and Boscovic about forces to those of Faraday and Einstein about fields of forces, metaphysical ideas have shown the way' (Popper, 1935/2007a; xxiii). 'Copernicus's idea of placing the sun rather than the earth in the centre of the universe', for example, 'was not the result of new observations but of a *new interpretation* of old and well-known facts in the light of semi-religious Platonic and neo-Platonic ideas' concerning the pre-eminence of the sun in the natural order. Thus, he says, the Copernican revolution in astronomy did not 'start with observations, but with a religious or mythological idea' (Popper, 1963/2007b; 253—4). Similarly, Kepler's claim that the planets held an elliptical orbit around the sun and that their velocities changed throughout their journey did not arise from observations, but from a desire to prove the *pre-existing* theory that the planets held a circular orbit and travelled at a constant velocity. And Einstein's quantum theory was incredibly speculative and abstract, and could not—Popper believed—be appropriately said to be based upon specific observations at all. Therefore, if the claim—shared by many scientists, in addition to the logical positivists of the Vienna Circle—that science is rooted principally in an accumulation of sense-experiences (or observations) and, hence, is inimical to metaphysical theorizing were correct then none of these theories, as well as countless others, could be understood as truly 'scientific'. The irony of the position advanced by the logical positivists, then, was that they held science to be pre-eminent over philosophy (and sought to demarcate valid and invalid philosophical enquiry by appealing to the inductive scientific method) only to define science (and, therefore, their understanding of philosophy) 'in such a way that it [became], by definition, incapable of making any contribution to our knowledge of the world', and unable, too, to include many of history's most important scientific discoveries (Popper, 1935/2007a; xii).

Science is therefore no enemy of metaphysical theorizing, because metaphysics and settled conviction often provide the springboard for scientific discovery by providing guidance as to what questions the scientist should ask, and how she should ask them. But science *does* represent the means by which we might know *which* metaphysical positions—or which *aspects* of a particular position—are worthy of support. 'Once put forward,'he argued, none of our metaphysical conjectures 'are dogmatically upheld. Our method of research is not to defend them, in order to show how right we were. On the contrary, we try to overthrow them. Using all the weaponry of our logical, mathematical, and technical armoury, we try to prove that our anticipations were false—in order to put forward, in their stead, new unjustified and unjustifiable anticipations, new "rash and premature prejudices" as Bacon derisively called them' (Popper, 1935/2007a; 278—9). Many metaphysical theories will contain erroneous or mistaken claims, but these can be revealed and refuted through critical engagement and perhaps empirical testing. Science(on Popper's understanding) provides the critical tools capable of making metaphysical positions more helpful (by removing those aspects of them which can be shown to be mistaken), but it should not be considered the enemy of these positions, or of metaphysics in general.

Popper thus believed that in solving the problem of induction by reconceptualizing the growth of knowledge as a non-inductive process of testing and discussing theories critically, he had provided a more persuasive answer to the original problem of demarcation posed by the logical positivists of the Vienna Circle. Remember, their claim (with which Popper had a great deal of sympathy) was that philosophy would benefit from the rigour characteristic of the physical sciences, and that the methods of the physical sciences should therefore be applied to philosophy. For the logical positivists, this meant working out which aspects of the *discipline of philosophy* were compatible with—or could be brought within—the methods characteristic of the *discipline of science* (understood in the traditional, inductive way). The scientific method therefore provided a solid basis for demarcating between physics and metaphysics, or science and non-science, and hence, valid and invalid philosophical questions. Popper rejected all of this, turned the inductivist method on its head, and argued that the growth of scientific knowledge proceeded in the same way as knowledge in any other field, and in fact, *relied* on other fields of inquiry. Scientific discovery, like the growth of knowledge in other areas, is unpredictable, often complicated, messy, and problematic; it does not always follow a set pattern and, even if it does, it is not clear that we could predict this pattern beforehand; and it emerges from a process of trial and error, and of rational, critical discussion among a community of peers. The growth of knowledge—in science as elsewhere—is thus a *public* process. Knowledge does not grow merely as a result of those private and isolated endeavours of individual scientists, for example; it grows out of the public discussion and critique of the theories proposed by these individuals. All knowledge (including, but not limited to, *scientific* knowledge) thus grows out of the ongoing critical engagement with problems among individual human beings across many disciplines.

This is what Popper meant when he stated that there was no method peculiar to science: knowledge, in all areas of human endeavour, grows out of the process of individuals engaging with one another over the possible resolution of problems, and the falsification of those theories that already exist. Consequently, Popper was deeply distrustful of the inclination—common in modern academic life, and implicit in the view of the logical positivists—of dividing the search for knowledge into particular disciplinary realms, each governed by their own methodologies and conventions and accepted practices. The urge to create disciplinary sub-divisions of this kind, he believed, arbitrarily fragmented a process of epistemological discovery which should be considered broadly uniform across all disciplines. 'The belief that there is such a thing as physics, or biology, or archaeology, and that these "studies" or "disciplines" are distinguishable by their subject matter which they investigate, appears to me to be a residue from the time when one believed that a theory had to proceed from a definition of its own subject matter', he wrote. 'But subject matter... [does] not... constitute a basis for distinguishing disciplines. ' The portioning up of the general quest for knowledge into discreet disciplinary fields is really little more than a matter of administrative convenience. All such ' classification and distinction is a comparatively unimportant and superficial affair. *We are not students of some subject matter but students of problems*. And problems may cut right across the borders of any subject matter or discipline' (Popper 1963/ 2007b; 88). While some differentiation among disciplines is sometimes helpful, then, members of these disciplines should understand that they are all involved in the same process of discovery, using broadly the same methodology. Questions such as ' What is philosophy?' or ' What is economics?'are redundant, self-indulgent, and merely an off-shoot of the Wittgensteinean desire to search for the meaning of words, or the Aristotelian need to understand phenomena in terms of their ' essences '. Philosophers, scientists, and economists should not seek to determine the'essence'of their discipline, by distinguishing its methodology from that of others, rather, they should confront problems by adopting a critical attitude towards all existing ideas and theories, and by proposing and falsifying theories through a process of rational, critical discussion—a discussion which is not limited to one set of disciplinary concerns, but which ranges across all disciplines and subject areas. *Scientific* discoveries, for example, may spring—and have sprung—from *religious* theories, or mathematics; and *political* innovations might spring(and have sprung)from theories generally thought to be the preserve of economists, or psychologists, or sociologists. What is important is that those engaged in all these fields do not seek to ring-fence their own endeavours, but instead engage enthusiastically in a critical engagement with these theories(and their proposers)with an open mind. Popper called this ' critical rationalism '; the tradition, drawn from the Greeks, 'of [the] free discussion of theories with the aim of discovering their weak spots so that they may be improved'; the idea that individuals from all disciplines should engage with one another over the resolution of problems in the world and that, in these discussions, they should adopt 'an attitude of readiness to listen to critical arguments and to learn from experience' (Popper, 1963/2007b; 67). Critical rationalism is thus fundamentally 'an attitude of admitting that *"I may be wrong and you may be right, and by an effort, we may get nearer to the truth"*' (Popper, 1945/2006b; 249).

In arguing as much, Popper believed that he had provided not just a more coherent definition of the physical sciences, but a broad epistemological theory which could explain the growth of knowledge not just in science, but in all fields and all disciplines. Popper's deductive method suggested that scientists and philosophers who were committed to contributing to our understanding of the world should see themselves as engaged in a common project, rather than different projects which are defined by different methodologies and subject-matters. Scientists and philosophers are (or should be) in the business of confronting and proposing solutions to problems, and engaging with others in critical dialogue about the efficacy or coherence of existing theories as well as the theories that they themselves have proposed. Doing so ensured scientific objectivity. 'The naïve view that scientific objectivity rests on the mental or psychological attitude of the individual scientist, on his training, care, and scientific detachment, generates as a reaction the sceptical view that scientists can never be objective.' But scientific objectivity does not depend upon the psychology of the individual scientist; rather, it is the 'public character of science and its institutions which imposes a mental discipline upon the individual scientist, and which preserves the objectivity of science and its tradition of critically discussing new ideas' (Popper 1957/2005; 144). The idea that knowledge grows as a consequence of public debate among members of all disciplines and all fields ensures honesty and full disclosure among those involved. Popper's epistemology did not seek to demarcate a distinct scientific method, then, as no such thing really existed; rather, it provided a criterion for judging whether a particular theory or claim should be under-stood as capable of contributing to our understanding of the world (in any field, regardless of the subject-matter).

Pulling these various ideas together, then, we can see why Popper's conception of science (and of the growth of knowledge in general) was, and remains, so controversial. In place of the traditional view of science (as an *inductive* process which extrapolates *general laws* or hypotheses about the world from specific *observations*, and which have the capacity to *prove* that statements about facts are *true*), Popper suggested that science should be understood as a *deductive* process whereby theoretical solutions to *problems* are proposed and then falsified through critical discussion of the facts, or other theories. Hence, *unfalsifiable* theories are not scientific. No theory can be decisively *proven*, but they can be decisively *falsified*, hence, the scientist should not seek proofs, but rather falsifications, of scientific theories, through public engagement, debate, and empirical testing. Some theories will be easily falsified, others will not; however, it is the repeated and successive attempts to falsify existing theories and to replace them with others, which drives forward the process of scientific discovery, and increases our aggregate knowledge of the world. On this view, science becomes characterised as a trial and error process of conjecture and refutation. Individuals propose (often bold) theories about particular problems in the world, and in doing so invite others to falsify these theories. Scientific discovery requires the adoption of a critical attitude towards problems and their hypothetical solutions, and is born out of critical dialogue among a community of individuals:

The advance of science is not due to the fact that more and more perceptual experiences accumulate in the course of time. Nor is it due to the fact that we are making ever better use of our senses. Out of uninterpreted sense-experiences science cannot be distilled, no matter how industriously we gather and sort them. Bold ideas, unjustified anticipations and speculative thought, are our only means for interpreting nature:... our only instrument for grasping her. (Popper, 1935/2007a; 280)

Scientific discovery is not clean and tidy; rather the history of science, 'like the history of all human ideas, is a history of irresponsible dreams, of obstinacy, and of error' (Popper 1963/2007b; 293). Rather than seek generalizable proofs of great and general *truths* through the bare application of reason, we should seek to remove *error* through a critical engagement with existing theories, ideas, traditions, and narratives, by testing them against what we ourselves have found out and what others have similarly thought and discovered. Understanding science as the accumulation of certain truths about the world 'hampers not only the boldness of our questions, but also the rigour and integrity of our tests. The wrong [or "traditional"] view of science betrays itself in the craving to be right; for it is not the *possession* of knowledge, of irrefutable truth, that makes the man of science, but his persistent, recklessly critical *quest* for truth' (Popper 1935/2007a; 281). His broad conclusion, then, was that we should 'give up on the idea of ultimate sources of knowledge, and admit that all knowledge is human; that it is mixed with our errors, our prejudices, our dreams, and our hopes; that all we can do is to grope for the truth even though it be beyond our reach' (Popper 1963/2007b; 39).

From science to social science

It is often thought that Popper developed a 'philosophy of science' and then applied this philosophy to the social sciences.

But as we have already seen, Popper's aim was in fact slightly different. It was not merely to develop a philosophy of science: it was to provide a theory of epistemology which would explain, and contribute to, the process by which our knowledge of the world might grow, or, rather, it was to develop a theory about 'the development of human thought in *general* and of scientific thought in *particular*'(Popper 1963/ 2007b; 421). Hence, Popper did not seek to *apply* his 'philosophy of science' to society and politics; rather, he sought to provide a general explanation of the process by which understanding of the world might be gathered, which was *as true* of science as it was of social science or politics.

Broadly speaking, therefore, Popper believed that the growth of knowledge in the social sciences should be understood as progressing in roughly the same way—according to the same *logic*—as in the physical sciences. Social scientific inquiry should begin in the identification of social and political problems, and should seek to resolve these problems through a trial and error process of conjecture and refutation aimed at eliminating error in those theories and practices which currently exist, and in those hypothetical solutions offered by others. It is not the role of social theory to make generalizable and long-term prophecies about the future course of history, but—as it is in the physical sciences—to resolve specific problems in ways which might be criticized and tested by others, and to work out whether those solutions already in operation(and embodied in social and political institutions, and social practices) are the right ones. In the social sciences, as in the physical sciences, then, knowledge grows as a consequence of adopting a critical(a 'critical ratio-nalist') attitude towards social and political problems and their hypothetical solutions, and engaging critically with others about existing theories and ideas.

Popper thus proposed that the physical and social sciences are characterized by a 'unity of method'. That is, he argued that 'all theoretical or generalizing sciences make use of the same method, whether they are natural or social sciences', namely, the trial and error process of conjecture and refutation of falsifiable hypotheses about existing problems, conducted among a community of individuals who have adopted a critical rationalist attitude towards existing ideas, theories, and practices(Popper 1957/2005; 120). Theories about society— about *social problems*—thus need to be falsifiable in the same way as do theories about problems commonly assumed to be in the province of the physical sciences. And just as Popper believed that falsifiability was the appropriate criterion for demarcating scientific from non-scientific theories in the physical sciences, so he believed that it did so also for social scientific theories, and theories in other fields too. In arguing as much, Popper believed that he was able to reveal the weakness (or, at least, the non-scientific character) of many theories which purport to be scientific (and hence, purport to add to human knowledge), but which do not. Three such theories were Adler's theory of 'individual psychology', Freud's theory of psychoanalysis. The problem with these theories, for Popper, was precisely that they were *unfalsifiable*: it was impossible to refute them. What impressed the Freudians, and the Adlerians was, he argued, precisely the *explanatory power* of their theories, indeed, 'they appeared to be able to explain practically everything that happened within the fields to which they referred'. The study of them seemed to open

your eyes to a new truth hidden from those not yet initiated. Once your eyes were thus opened you saw confirming instances everywhere; the world was full of *verifications* of the theory. Whatever happened always confirmed it. Thus its truth appeared manifest; and unbelievers were clearly people who did not want to see the manifest truth; who refused to see it, either because it was against their class interest, or because of their repressions which were still 'unanalysed' and crying out for treatment. (Popper 1963/ 2007b; 45)

Popper's Ideas

We see in these theories, therefore, the error in taking verification by observation/experience as the demarcation between scientific theories and non-scientific theories (in the realms of the physical sciences, as well as the realms of the social sciences and psychology), and the folly of (inductively) extrapolating theories from facts: namely that the facts can often prove anything that the theorist likes, and hence they prove nothing. What made the theories of individuals like Copernicus, Kepler, and Galileo important *scientific* theories, Popper believed, was that they could be shown to be *false*. Even Newton's theory of universal gravitation and dynamics was *falsifiable*, as was shown by Einstein. But even Einstein could not have falsified Freud's theory of psychoanalysis or Adler's 'individual psychology' because no appeal to the facts or rival theories could ever undermine them. Any patient of Freudian psychoanalysis who felt that their behaviour could not be explained by some combination of repressed urges of one kind or another was merely considered 'in denial' and in need of further treatment. It is important to understand Popper's critique of historicism in detail, as it is fundamental to his ideas about the appropriate conduct of the social sciences and the practice of politics.

Popper described historicism as, broadly speaking, 'the doctrine that history is controlled by specific historical or evolutionary laws whose discovery would allow us to prophesy the destiny of man' (Popper 1945/2006a; 4). It therefore embodies the view that 'a truly scientific or philosophical attitude towards politics, and a deeper understanding of social life in general, must be based upon a contemplation and interpretation of human history' (Popper 1945/2006a; 3). It is, he said, an 'approach to the social sciences which assumes that historical prediction is their principal aim, and which assumes that this aim is attainable by discovering the "rhythms" or "patterns", the "laws" or the "trends" which underlie the development of history' (Popper 1957/2005; 3). Historicism, then, is an approach to understanding society and politics by understanding social and political phenomena as products of historical forces; as things which have *origins*, which are thought to develop towards their own internally defined endpoints or goals, and which exist in their current form as the culmination of historical events. Consequently, the study of social and political institutions, norms, and conventions cannot be undertaken in abstraction from the historical forces and conditions which brought them into the world. The study of politics and society is, on this view, little more or less than the study of *history*.

This view, Popper believed, was a popular and pernicious one, in human history, the history of political thought, and in what passed for social and political discourse at the time. Some of the oldest and most obvious examples of historicism, he thought, were those religions which identify a 'chosen people' whose role is to function as 'the selected instrument of [God's] will', and who, in assuming this role correctly, 'will inherit the Earth' (Popper, 1945/2006a; 4). In such doctrines, the laws of historical development are laid down by the will of God, and it is the role of the chosen people to do what they can to hasten the inevitable coming to fruition of the prophecies foretold in their holy texts. Religious and secular forms of historicism thus share the same broad features, Popper argued: they are collectivist, in the sense that they speak in terms of groups rather than individuals (they speak, for example, of 'peoples' or 'nations' or 'races' or 'classes'), and the ends they prophesize are always distant and remote. For although we may have a good idea of what we are striving for, 'we will have to go a long way before we reach it. And the way is not only long, but winding, leading up and down, right and left. Accordingly, it will be possible to bring every conceivable historical event well within the scheme of interpretation' (Popper 1945/2006a; 5). Like the claims of the Freudian psychoanalyst, the Adlerian psychologist, then, religious doctrines which foretell the destiny of a chosen people are unfalsifiable, and hence, cannot contribute to human knowledge.

Popper believed that the history of the social and political sciences was littered with thinkers who had adopted the historicist approach. Thinkers with philosophical and political conclusions as diverse as Plato, Hegel, Rousseau, Mill, and Comte were embracing the historicist method—indeed, he believed. And for Hegel, the 'chosen people' was 'the nation', and the laws of historical development described the dialectical progression of the nation (understood as the embodiment of the Spirit) towards freedom, or self-realization. The view that Hegel (and, consequently, Hegelians) shared with other historicist thinkers, then, was that human societies are products of impersonal and overarching laws of historical development, and that this fact determined the appropriate conduct of the social sciences, and the appropriate character of politics. It also allowed those capable of knowing the laws of history to predict the future of humankind. The point of the *social sciences*, for the historicist, was to reveal those historical laws of development which determine the nature and content of society (and hence, our social relations with one another, our social attitudes, and the implicit social norms which govern and regulate our lives) at any given time. The point of *politics*—and the correct role and responsibility of political institutions like the state—was primarily to set the conditions appropriate for the realization of those goals or ends determined by the historical laws of development. Popper developed his own approach to social science out of an engagement with historicist ideas. Therefore, for the remainder of this section, I will discuss the implications of the historicist approach for the study of *society* (and Popper's critique of it), before going on to discuss its *political* implications in the next section.

I have already mentioned that, for Popper, historicism is characterized primarily by the claim that it is the appropriate role of the social scientist to seek those *historical* laws which determine the nature and content of society and, hence, that sociology is little more or less than the study of *theoretical* history. Historicism thus embodies a fundamental rejection of the idea that the methods of the natural and physical sciences can be unproblematically employed in the social sciences. Historicists argue that the methods of the physical sciences cannot hope to yield insights into social and political life, for four principal reasons.

First, historicists reject the idea that it is possible to infer generalizable, immutable laws governing social and political life in the way that natural scientists believe it is possible in the physical sciences. The overarching aim of the physical scientist, historicists claim, is to derive general laws governing the structure of the universe, and the behaviour of physical elements, which are not rooted in any particular historical period and which are, therefore, considered timeless. 'Physical laws, or the "laws of nature,"[the physical sciences tell us], are valid anywhere and always; for the physical world is ruled by a system of physical uniformities invariable throughout space and time. Sociological laws, however, or the "the laws of social life" differ in different places and periods' (Popper, 1957/2005; 4). While the historicist might concede that there are certain trivial regularities that it is possible to identify in the character of social life which might extend beyond any one particular historical period, they hold that it is not possible to identify more substantive (and therefore, useful) laws which stand independent of the historical period in which they are observed. ' A method which ignores this limitation and attempts a generalization of social uniformities will, according to historicism, implicitly assume that the regularities in question are everlasting' (Popper 1957/2005; 5). Such a theory will deny that 'society ever develops; or that it ever changes significantly; or that social developments, if there are any, can affect the basic regularities of social life' (Popper, 1957/ 2005; 5—6). Historicists therefore argue that instead of adopting the 'methodologically naïve' view that we can simply import the methods of the physical sciences into the study of politics and society, we should take seriously the *historically rooted* nature of social relations. Similarly, the idealism of Hegel and his more recent supporters—so vehemently opposed by the logical positivists as well as Popper—embodied a rejection of the notion that 'truth' could be discovered via science, claiming instead that truth was itself a historical phenomenon which could only be revealed via an engagement with those historical laws from which it emerged. To understand society, these and other historicists argued, we must approach the study of social relations as historical phenomena—produced by historical forces, shaped by historical circumstances, and understandable as products of history itself, rather than as things which can be rendered intelligible in abstraction from their origins. Importantly, we should take seriously the importance of *culture*, and the ability of human beings to shape the future of the society in which they live. Historicism holds that the search for timeless social laws leaves no room for *activism*, that is, the possibility that individual members of society might, through conscious will or accident, shape their own future and the future of their society. Innovation and creativity only exist within—and are defined by—the general structure of overarching laws which govern social life for all time and it is therefore these laws, not human beings themselves, which determine the character of social and political life, and the course of social change.

Now this may sound confusing, given that we have already suggested that it is characteristic of historicism that its defenders *do* seek overarching laws of history. It is important, therefore, to re-affirm that, for Popper, the aim of historicism is not to discover the laws of any one particular historical period and then to assert that these laws must hold for all historical periods; rather, it is to discover those more general laws which determine the *transition* from one historical period to another. That is, historicism seeks laws of *historical development*. For example, a social scientist may look at contemporary capitalist society and identify certain laws which hold within it (e. g. the law that increased demand for a scarce resource raises the market value of that resource). This will be a law which holds true in capitalist societies, but it may well not hold true in societies (in history or in other parts of the world) which order their economies differently: for example, feudal societies or planned economies. Hence, it is not possible to speak of universal, trans-historical laws of the kind mentioned above, because these laws will only hold in certain societies at certain times. We cannot speak meaningfully of, say, laws of economics which extend across all historical periods; rather, we can only speak of the laws of economics of the capitalist period, or the economics of the feudal period, and so on. What the historicist seeks, therefore, is not the extrapolation of generalizable, trans-historical laws of social behaviour from specific observations of one particular period, but the deeper laws which determine how, when, and why one historical period becomes another. What rendered Marx's theory of historical materialism so powerful and radical, for example, was not that it merely identified the past existence of distinct historical epochs, each characterized by their own social, economic, and political norms and institutions, but that it also provided an overarching explanation of how and why each period gave way to the next and, hence, how the present system would give way to further epochs in the future. Similarly, Hegel's dialectical conception of history did not merely delineate those historical epochs that had already existed, it provided a means of predicting how history would develop in the future, and the ends to which history itself was inevitably headed. And, Popper believed, we can find similar claims in the work of Plato, Comte, Mill, Rousseau, and all those other historicists who have written on the social sciences: common to all of them, he argued, was the idea that the role of sociology was to derive general laws or 'uniformities' in history which could explain the development of successive historical periods and, hence, the *origins* of each set of social relations which characterize them.

A *second*, and intimately connected, criticism that historicists make of adopting the methods of the natural sciences in the study of society is that the principal means of obtaining reliable knowledge in the physical sciences is wholly inappropriate in a social and political context. Physical scientists infer general laws through an observation of the behaviour of physical elements. They introduce ' artificial controls, artificial isolation, and thereby [ensure] the reproduction of similar conditions, and the consequent production of certain effects' (Popper,1957/2005;7). The idea that it is possible to observe social and political phenomena in this way and derive general laws from these observations which exist for all time is absurd, they believe. This is because the structure of inference that works in the physical sciences breaks down in a social and political context. In the physical sciences, it is possible to observe certain behaviours and to infer from this that under the same conditions the same elements/processes would behave/occur in the same way. Hence, it is an important aim for the physical scientist to stipulate and then isolate the specific conditions necessary to test specific behaviours and hypotheses. That is, she conducts experiments aimed at providing specific answers to specific questions which can then provide a basis for a general law. Historicists argue, however, that no such inferential relationship can exist when studying society. Popper illustrated this historicist contention with reference to Mannheim's *Man and Society* but, it becomes clear in his later war of words with Habermas and Adorno during the 'positivism debate' in the 1960s, he also identified it as a belief shared by critical theorists. It is not possible to isolate social and political phenomena in the way that it is possible to isolate physical elements, the claim goes, and so ' social experiments' will always produce indeterminate results. Furthermore, he argued that historicists like Mannheim, Adorno, and Habermas held that any social experiments must be necessarily radical and holistic. The components of society cannot be broken down and examined in isolation, and hence, social experiments should not seek to do so. The subject-matter of the social sciences (i. e. people) is too complex and too changeable to be compatible with the physical sciences' need for objectivity, control, and the dispassionate isolation of individuated subjects. So observation and experimentation, while perfectly valid and intelligible with regard to the gathering of knowledge in the physical sciences, cannot provide the *social* scientist with the unambiguous, objective knowledge that they would need in order to infer generalizable laws for all time and for all people. Also, as we mentioned earlier, historicism holds that the inference that 'in similar circumstances, similar things will happen' is only really applicable within particular historical periods. Cultures change and ideas develop; as a consequence, each new historical period may well represent a genuinely new system of relations, ideas, and assumptions of a like that has never been seen before. Consequently, there are no observable, transhistorical 'similar circumstances' in the past which one might look to in order to make sense of the present or the future. As Popper put it, in a

world described by physics nothing can happen that is truly and intrinsically new. An engine may be invented, but we can always analyse it as a rearrangement of elements which are anything but new. Newness in physics is merely the newness of arrangements or combinations. In direct opposition to this, social newness [for the historicist] is an intrinsic form of newness... For in social life, the same old factors in a new arrangement are never really the same old factors... This is held [by historicists] to be significant for the consideration of the development of new stages or periods in history, each of which differs intrinsically from the other. (Popper, 1957/2005;9)

There is no more important a moment in the study of social life for the historicist than the birth of a genuinely new period of history. And historicists believe that the methods of the physical sciences hold no key to understanding such a change, or even rendering such a change intelligible.

A *third*, and related, feature of historicism is its *holism*. The methods of the physical sciences are, historicists claim, *atomistic*: they study particular elements in particular circumstances. They are also *ahistorical* in the sense that they do not examine the historical characteristics of the object in question, but merely its behaviour under certain conditions. This approach is entirely appropriate to the physical sciences, they argue. Although it may be interesting to explore, say, the history of the solar system, it is not necessary to do so in order to understand its present state. This is because its present state is 'independent of the history of the system. The structure of the system, its future movements and developments, are fully determined by the present constellation of its members... [T]he history of the structure, although it may be interesting, contributes nothing to our understanding of its behaviour, of its mechanism, or its future development' (Popper, 1957/2005; 16). Social groups, however, are very different. Historicists believe that social groups should never be understood as mere aggregates of persons. Social groups are more than the mere sum of their total members, and more also than the sum total of personal relationships which exist among its members at any one time. For historicists like Mannheim, it is crucial to understand that 'all social groups have their own traditions, their own institutions, their own rites. Historicism claims that we must study the history of the group, its traditions, and institutions, if we wish to understand and explain it as it is now, and if we wish to understand and perhaps explain its future development' (Popper, 1957/2005; 16). Again, therefore, we note the historicist idea that to understand society, we must understand the *history* of the *group*. This is why, for the historicist, sociology is merely a form of theoretical history: to understand social life in any particular historical period, it is necessary to examine the overall character of the social group as a whole, and its historical origins. One should not merely examine the individuals which constitute this group at any one time; one should instead take as the subject the internal dynamics and character of the group *as a whole*.

Karl Popper

60

Fourthly, Popper claimed that historicists throughout history, from Plato to Comte, Rousseau, and Habermas, were united in their claim that social scientists should adopt a *methodologically essentialist*, rather than a *methodologically nominalist*, approach to understanding society. Popper's rejection of essentialism was noted in the section above regarding his claims concerning the folly in seeking the 'essence' of particular academic disciplines in the interests if splitting them off from one another. However, these terms need further explanation in the current context. Popper understood methodological essentialism as an approach to science founded by Aristotle, which states that in order to explain something one must 'penetrate its essence'. 'Methodological essentialists', Popper argued, 'are inclined to formulate scientific questions in such terms as "what is matter?" or "what is force?" or "what is justice?", [or, as in the discussion earlier about disciplines, "what is philosophy?" or "what is science?"] and they believe that a penetrating answer to such questions, revealing the real or essential meaning of these terms, and thereby the real or true nature of the essences denoted by them, is at least a necessary prerequisite of scientific research, if not its main task' (Popper, 1957/2005; 25). Methodological nominalists, on the other hand, seek no such fundamental answers. Rather, they frame their questions in terms of how things behave under certain conditions. From what we have already discussed, it is clear that historicists impute a methodological nominalism to the physical sciences, and with good reason. There is indeed a strong trend of methodological nominalism in the physical sciences. Physics, for example, does not attempt to define the 'essence' of light or gravity, rather, it observes how these things behave in certain conditions. Historicists believe that this is inadequate for the study of society and that, in order to understand social life, we must understand its internal dynamics, its structure, its history, and its origins. We must therefore do more than merely observe the behaviour of its members; we must get under its skin, and go beyond a mere description of its surface behaviour. We must seek its *essence*. We need to get to grips with the group's culture, and the way in which this culture has developed throughout history.

Considered together, then, these four characteristic features of historicism provide a general methodology for the social sciences which stands utterly opposed to that defended by Popper. It is *essentialist* and *holistic*, in the sense that social scientists should seek to understand the essential nature of the social group as a whole, rather than the *particular* relations or interactions that occur among *individual* members of that society. It collapses the distinction between the study of society and the study of the *history* of society; to study society is simply to study its history and no more. And, despite rejecting the naturalistic conceit that it is possible to establish generalizable social laws from observed behaviour within particular historical periods, historicists nevertheless cling to the worst aspects of the inductive method in claiming that it is possible to reveal overarching laws of historical development which can *prophesize* the long-term future of society history, and the fate of humankind. Popper thus identified both anti-naturalistic and pro-naturalistic doctrines in historicism: historicists rejected the methodological nominalism, atomism, ahistoricism, and the primacy of observation and experiment which they saw in the methods of the physical sciences, but crucially retained other aspects of the natural scientific method which suited their purposes: primarily, the idea that the social sciences could and should infer general social (i. e. historical) laws capable of predicting long-term future events.

Popper pointed out, however, what many readers will already have noticed: that all the historicists' criticisms of the scientific method are in fact criticisms of the traditional, inductive view of science that Popper sought to undermine. They represent a critique of what we might call 'scientism' in social theory. Consequently, their general position (that it was not appropriate to use the methods of the physical sciences in the social sciences) was, for Popper, premised upon a fundamental misunderstanding of science and, hence, what it would *mean* to adopt the scientific method in the study of society. The problem with the historicists, for Popper, was not that they believed that the inductive model was inappropriate to the study of society (indeed, Popper agreed with this claim), but that they drew the wrong lessons from this point, and proposed a mistaken alternative to it. Their claim, remember, was that the inductive method is indeed appropriate for the study of physical and natural phenomena, but that it is not appropriate for the study of social phenomena. They, like the logical positivists and others, were therefore in the business of drawing boundaries between disciplines on the basis of their various subject-matters, and the methodologies appropriate to each, in ways which were anathema to Popper. The historicists accepted unquestioningly the supremacy of the inductive method in the physical sciences; their claim was that natural scientists should do their thing, and social scientists should do theirs. Popper, of course, disagreed. He argued that the inductive model did not represent an appropriate method by which to study society, but only because he thought that the inductive model did not represent an appropriate method by which to study *anything*. He thus agreed with the historicists that social scientists should abandon the inductive model, not so that they could replace it with historicism, but so that they could replace it with a more coherent conception of science and the scientific method.

In place of historicism and scientism, Popper defended a conception of the social sciences built around his conception of critical rationalism, that is, one rooted firmly in his wider epistemological ideas which emphasised the clash of ideas, the fallibility of reason, and the gradual step-by-step reform of social and political life on the basis of rigorous testing, critique, and debate. Its characteristic elements stand opposed to historicism, and are thus:

(1) The principal purpose of the social sciences is to identify and attempt to resolve social problems by proposing theories about them, and subjecting these and other theories to a rigorous process of refutation and testing, in circumstances of epistemological uncertainty. It is not the role of the social scientist to make long-term, general *prophecies* about the future historical development of society, or to justify social and political reform by appealing to unfalsifiable social and historical laws, or to reveal the 'end of history', Hegel, and others did. Because there are no laws of historical development which can be inferred from specific observations, social scientists cannot make predictions above and beyond what is supported by the sum total of knowledge already in existence. They must base their predictions and theories on the information available, because that is all there is. Human actions will often lead to unexpected outcomes. Social reforms initiated in good faith will have unintended consequences. Political activity will lead to unforeseen events and unpredictable conclu-sions. Consequently, the 'main task of the theoretical social sciences' is not to prophesize the future of human develop-ment, but to 'trace the unintended social repercussions of intentional human actions' (Popper, 1963/2007b; 460). Social life is 'not only a trial of strength among opposing groups [like classes or nations]: it is action within a more or less resilient or brittle framework of institutions and traditions, and it creates... many unforeseen reactions in the framework, some of them may even be unforeseeable (Popper, 1945/ 2006b; 105). Consequently, predictions in the social sciences, like predictions in the physical sciences, should only be short-term, limited, and falsifiable; *prophecies* of the kind indulged in by historicists are none of these things, and so are unscientific and cannot represent contributions to knowledge.

(2) The appropriate objects of social enquiry are not laws of history or social groups, as Hegelians, and other historicists contend,

but observable social institutions and arrangements, and the actions and interactions of *indivi-dual human beings*. The social sciences should thus be 'methodologically *individualist*' rather than ' methodologically *holistic* '. Society should be understood as an aggregate of *individuals*, and the actions of *individuals* within this system should be understood to count. Historicism subordinates the individual to society; it is interested not in the specific actions of individual human actors, but in the general social laws governing the actions of all members of society at any one time. Far from emphasizing the capacity of individuals to shape society according to their own collective will, as is their professed intention, the historicists present a conception of society in which the actions and thoughts of individual human beings are stifled by history and determined by historical forces over which they have no control, and from which they are powerless to escape. Historicists thus fall into the same trap as those inductivists who believe that it is possible to infer generalizable laws in the study of human societies.

(3) The social sciences have an important practical function: through the endeavours of individual social scientists, who have adopted the appropriate critical rationalist attitude towards social problems and the theories in common currency in social scientific discourse, and who have engaged in critical discussion and debate with others about these matters, it is possible to furnish legislators with the theories they need to reform society in a way that is humane, just, and compatible with individual freedom. Social science provides a guide for social reform. Reforms must be short-term, gradual, and *piecemeal*, rather than long-term, radical, and *utopian*, for all the reasons mentioned in point 1, above. Instead of trying to resolve all the problems of society in one fell swoop by appealing to some overarching plan rooted in revealed knowledge about the true nature or purpose of social and political institutions, social scientists should identify specific problems and seek to resolve them through

a process of conjecture and refutation. By engaging in such a process, problems might be identified, examined, and resolved in a *piecemeal* fashion, as theories are proposed, debated, tested, and, perhaps, rejected in a constant search for error. It is thus the principal role of social scientists to determine the purpose of existing social and political institutions, to evaluate whether they are successfully achieving their purpose, and, if they are not, to propose new and bold alternative arrangements.

(4) The social sciences should be 'methodologically *nominalist*' rather than 'methodologically *essentialist*'. It is not the role of the social scientist to trace the historical origins of particular social relations, or to grasp the *essence* of a particular society, but to identify genuine social problems and work out how they might be resolved. According to Popper's wider epistemology, the purpose, legitimacy and effectiveness of existing social institutions (and the theories justifying and explaining them) are inevitably conjectural; the role of the government or some other social institution may change in response to wider changes in our understanding of the world and individual members of society and, hence, no institution or arrangement is set in stone as legitimate for all time. Similarly, no particular set of social institutions might appropriately claim its legitimacy in some projected future goal for all humanity: arguments in favour of particular arrangements and institutions (and, hence, these arrangements and institutions themselves) must remain conjectural, and may be falsified by empirical or theoretical challenges. The aim of the social sciences is thus not to build grand theories about the nature of society and politics, or to search for the origins of social relations, and it is not to seek certain and irrefutable *truths* about the nature of society and its development, but to eliminate *error* in those theories about society and politics which have been proposed by testing them against the sum total of all the knowledge (derived from all the various

'disciplines') that bear upon that issue.

In summary, then, we can see that Popper's vision of the social sciences was rooted firmly in his wider views about epistemology: knowledge in the sciences, the social sciences, and elsewhere, grows in the same way and according to the same logic. Popper shared with the historicists the view that the inductive model was inappropriate for the study of society, but fundamentally disagreed with their alternative. He saw the historicists as seeking a new form of social inquiry concerned primarily with foretelling the future of humanity by identifying laws of history (which determined the nature and appropriate structure of social relations, and the actions of those individuals within it) and examining the culture of society as a whole, in order that they might structure society according to a fixed plan or blueprint. Popper, on the other hand, believed that both the historicist and inductive approaches should be replaced with his own approach which emphasized trial and error, conjecture and refutation, and piecemeal social reform guided by the elimination of error in existing theories about society and its problems. In social science, then, as in the physical sciences, the driving thought for Popper was that we can learn from our mistakes. By identifying problems, proposing solutions, and debating these problems critically with others who are as ready to listen to rational arguments as we are, we can identify the incoherences and falsehoods in existing theories just as we can identify failures in existing practices and institutions, and in doing so we can work out how best to identify and resolve social problems through a process of piecemeal social reform.

From social science to politics

Popper's views about the appropriate role and responsibilities of social and political institutions represent an inversion of the historicist position, and a rejection of all the normative, epistemological, and methodological foundations upon which it is built. The aim of the historicist, remember, was to study society in such a way as to reveal those historical laws of development which determined its nature and shape. Having done so, historicists could consult these underlying historical laws in order to infer the future development of society. Once sufficient knowledge of society had been gained—knowledge, that is, of its culture, its underlying history, and the complex web of subjective interactions and assumptions which combine to create the social whole—it was possible for the historicist to work out not only how society had got to where it had, but where it was heading. The historical laws of development therefore provided historicists not only with the key to understanding the past, but the tools necessary to prophesize the future. By appealing to past examples and events, and by understanding the nature of human beings and the particular social and historical context in which they live, historicists held that it was possible to predict with relative certainty the outcome of political proposals and decisions. Furthermore, having identified what brings new social and historical periods into being—that is, what social, political, economic, and legal conditions need to hold in order for society to move from one period to another—historicists felt able to use this knowledge as an appropriate justification for social and political reform. Once one understands that society develops according to objective historical laws, and that history requires certain conditions to be in place in order for society to move to the next stage, then it becomes straightforwardly obvious that social, economic, and political change should be geared towards the bringing about of those conditions conducive to either ushering in the new era, or protecting society from such change. Social reform is thus viewed by historicists as a tool by which society might either be made ready for the birth of a new era, or protected from moving into this new, and worse, state of affairs.

Importantly, then, Popper believed that historicist politics was fundamentally *utopian* and *elitist*. It was *utopian* in the sense that historicist social science is not merely a passive process of understanding and interpreting the laws of history; it is both *active* and *purposive*; it embodies a desire to discover not just what society looked like in the past, but where it is heading and, importantly, where it *should* be heading, and how it might get there. Historicism therefore demands that ' we must determine our ultimate political aim, or the Ideal State, before taking any practical action. Only when this ultimate aim is determined, in rough outline at least, only when we are in possession of something like a blueprint of the society at which we aim, only then can we consider the best ways and means for its realization, and to draw up a plan for rational action' (Popper, 1945/2006a; 167). Social engineering, or the process of social reform with a view to solving social and political problems, is thus a *holistic* and *collectivist* endeavour; it aims at nothing less than the wholesale restructuring of society in order that it might bring about, or protect, an idealized form of politics in line with historical laws. A utopian form of social engineering holds that we need to know the ends or goals to which we strive before engaging in social reform; it would be *irrational* for us to implement a policy or set of reforms without first knowing why we are doing so, and what we wanted that policy to achieve. We thus work out what kind of society and politics we want to have, and then do those things (determined by the historical laws of development) which help to bring that society and politics about.

Utopian social engineering thus 'recommends the reconstruction of society as a whole' with the aim of bringing about radical and very long-term changes in our social and political arrangements, in line with a distant idealized conception of how we should all live and what society should look like. But, Popper argued, such a view is rendered incoherent by the fact that we cannot predict with certainty the outcome of our actions or decisions in the way that the historicists believe we can. This, again, is because reason is fallible; we may think can provide a successful plan for the achievement of some future society, and that we can foresee all potential problems along the way, but we cannot. The practical and long-term consequences of our decisions are, as we saw in point (1) in the previous section, 'hard to calculate, owing to our limited experiences'. Historicism 'claims to plan rationally for the whole of society,' but 'we do not possess anything like the factual knowledge which would be necessary to make good such an ambitious claim. We cannot possess such knowledge since we have insufficient practical experience in this kind of planning, and knowledge of facts must be based on experience. At present, the sociological knowledge necessary for large-scale engineering is simply non-existent' (Popper, 1945/2006a; 171). The idea that we can (and should) *plan* what a society should look like in advance and then implement social reforms in accordance with this plan, is a fallacy, Popper believed. 'Only a minority of social institutions are consciously designed, while the vast majority have "grown" as the undesigned results of human actions... [and] most of the few institutions which were consciously and successfully designed... do not turn out according to plan... because of the unintended social repercussions resulting from the intentional creation' (Popper, 1945/2006b; 103). Hence, as we mentioned in the previous section, it should not be considered an important role of the social sciences to understand society such that its future can be rationally planned and predicted; rather, given that this process is ultimately doomed to failure, it should 'study the unwieldiness, the resilience or the brittleness of the social stuff, of its resistance to our attempts to mould it and work with it' (Popper, 1945/2006b; 104). The reason we cannot predict with certainty the outcome of our decisions, or what long-term social and political conditions we should aim for, is precisely because it is impossible for us to infer such things from present circumstances or events. The reason we cannot plan the future in response to the past, and the reason we cannot justify social and political reform by appealing to the an

70

idealized future(attainable via a proper grasp of the historical laws of development) is because such an approach would require the adoption of an *inductivist* method which Popper believes is mistaken and incoherent: it requires too much of reason. The best we can do given the problem of induction, and the inability of reason to provide absolutely certain knowledge of the long-term future consequences of our actions and initiatives, he believed, is to admit that utopianism cannot provide the blueprints or the certainty that historicists require, and adopt instead his idea of *piecemeal social engineering* in its place, which does not require the inductive inference of historical laws, but which is rooted instead in our experience of the world—limited and short-term as it is—and is consistent with his wider epistemological ideas about the growth of knowledge.

We will discuss piecemeal engineering in more detail a little later in this and the next chapter. Before doing so, it is important to deal with Popper's second critique of historicist politics: that it is *elitist*. Popper felt that the historicist approach to politics was *elitist* in the sense that it presupposed that power should lie in the hands of those who could see and understand the laws of development and, hence, who could know the future of humankind, the inevitable outcome of social and political decisions, and how best to establish the Ideal State. It was thus, Popper believed, a vindication of centralized planning, and the coalescence of power in the hands of those who possessed the requisite knowledge to implement social and political reforms in ways which would bring about the creation of new historical periods. This argument, he said, has been used by dictators and tyrants throughout the ages to ignore the expressed wishes of the people, to oppress them, to brutalize them, and to claim that they were only doing so for their own good, and in pursuit of a goal that only the tyrant could see or understand. We see in this claim the earlier point that historicism embodies the notion of a 'chosen people'. Popper believed that it was characteristic of all forms of historicism that knowledge of history(and hence, what needed to be done in order to make sure history progressed in the right way) did not belong to everyone, but to a few. And as political power should rightfully belong only to those who possess this knowledge it followed that historicism represented an argument for the consolidation of power in the few, and provided the justification for this few to do whatever they wanted to do, all the while claiming that their actions were justified by the goals that only they could understand, and that their views and ideas were right even if others refused to agree.

Furthermore, Popper believed that the elitism and utopianism at the heart of historicist politics conspired to silence free expression, thought, and any criticism of those in charge. The reason for this, he said, was that the kind of long-term, large-scale, profound social reforms which were the stuff of historicist politics would 'cause considerable inconvenience to many, and for a considerable span of time. Accordingly, the Utopian engineer will have to be deaf to many complaints; in fact, it will be part of his business to suppress unreasonable objections... But with it, he must invariably suppress reasonable criticism also' (Popper, 1945/2006a; 169). Those with access to the privileged information contained in history are not only able to determine what should and should not be done, they also possess the power to determine what is reasonable and unreasonable criticism. Without access to this privileged information, the ignorant majority have little or no grounds on which to criticize the actions of their rulers, to engage in meaningful debate about the appropriate ends of social and political institutions, or to judge the legitimacy or illegitimacy of those who rule them. They simply do not possess the requisite knowledge to make such judgments or to engage meaningfully in debates about what the state should do, or the goals to which it should be committed.

Historicism is thus, for Popper, *epistemologically* mistaken, and *normatively* objectionable; it is premised upon the false *epistemological* assumption that it is possible to infer historical laws of development, and it is *normatively* objectionable in the sense that it appeals to these historical laws in order to justify the oppression of the general population by leaders who, and who alone, are privy to their secrets. Moreover, given that any goals to which the ruling elite are committed are necessarily long-term and, hence, unlikely to be achieved in the lifetime of the present ruler or dictator, it is crucial that successors to the dictator are *appointed* rather than *elected*. Holding free and fair elections, and allowing the people to decide who rules them, may well result in the election of a ruler who does not, and cannot, possess the requisite knowledge to govern in a way that brings about the Ideal State. Hence, democratic elections—and with them any notion of popular sovereignty or accountability—are rejected in favour of a system which allows the ruling elite to appoint their successors and, hence, to perpetuate its unassailable dominance over the people across generations.

Popper thus believed that historicism provided the philosophical justification for *totalitarianism* in that it placed ultimate and unchecked power in the hands of a ruling elite that need not justify itself to anyone for any reason. It rendered democratic politics impossible by denying the people the requisite resources they needed to form their own political judgments and the requisite democratic institutions or mechanisms necessary for them to elect or remove from power those who ruled them. It took away the ability of the people to criticize their rulers. And, importantly it subordinated the good of the individual to the good of society as a whole. All these things find their modern expression in Nazism, Fascism, and hence, he argued that historicism has provided the normative and philosophical foundation for some of the most heinous and oppressive regimes in the history of the world. These are, of course, powerful claims. But what rendered them even more powerful, however, and what made *The Open Society and Its Enemies* such an explosive and controversial book, was that having argued that the seeds of modern *totalitarianism* lie in *historicism*, he then argued that the seeds of *historicism* lie in the work of some of the most revered and celebrated figures in history. Thus it was that Popper laid the blame for the rise of modern totalitarianism at the door of a diverse range of thinkers who had, up to that point, been acknowledged to be some of the most important and humane voices in the development of Western social and political thought. So how did he come to such a conclusion?

Although he identified historicist tendencies in Mill, Comte, and Rousseau, Popper spent the majority of *The Open Society* tracing the development of historicism—and hence, modern totalitarianism—through the work of Plato and Hegel. Its earliest incarnation, he argued, was in the philosophy of ancient Greece, in particular the ideas of Hesiod, who 'made use of the idea of a general trend or tendency in historical development' (Popper, 1945/2006a; 7). This tendency, he believed, was one of physical and moral degeneration. He identified it, too, in the work of another Greek philosopher, Heraclitus, who claimed that the world was not *static* (as was the dominant view at the time) but rather characterized by constant *change*. Importantly, Heraclitus's view of history and change contained within it an important idea that would come to characterize all later historicist thought—that the world was not only in a constant state of change but that this change proceeds according to some 'inexorable and inevitable *law of destiny*'(Popper, 1945/2006a; 10).

For Popper, this view was most fully and obviously expressed by Plato. Popper believed that Plato's vision of the world embodied elements from both Hesiod and Heraclitus, in that he held that the world is characterized by change, and that, moreover, this change brings with it moral and physical degeneration. Societies are not static, Plato believed. They change, and in changing they tend towards decay and corruption. Therefore, he held that the principal role of a just state is to arrest all change and, hence, to protect the polity from descending into corruption. In a long and impassioned deconstruction of Plato's claims concerning justice and the qualities which characterise just and legitimate leaders, Popper argued that Plato's entire political vision was aimed at halting the development of history and maintaining stability and unity at virtually any cost. The key to understanding this, Popper claimed, was Plato's theory of the Forms. Plato believed that all existing earthly phenomena had an ideal Form which could not be truly or completely achieved in the real world. Any existing physical object is merely the flawed physical embodiment of the Form of these things, which existed in some idealized past. Consequently, any existing *state* would be merely an imperfect copy of the Form of the state, existing in an idealised and pristine past. Therefore, for Plato, the historical development of all things is little more than their continued journey *away* from their ideal and perfect Form (in the past) *towards* a more corrupted and flawed version.

Popper continued that, for Plato, the just state is one charac- terized primarily by unity and peace. The Form of the state is unified and harmonious, and unthreatened by vested interest or conflict. The Form of the ruling regime is one which can secure this unity for all its members. Hence, the just state is one which is as unified and harmonious as possible, as unthreatened by internal conflicts as it can be, and governed by political lead- ers who have the requisite strength and knowledge to do what is necessary to secure social and political conditions which are as much like their Forms as possible: perfect, unified, and unchanging. Plato is clear that the worst fate that can befall any society is that it allows any room for disunity. So much is proven in his sketch of the history of the state, in which he claims (in a move thought by Popper to be characteristic of all historicists) to have identified a series of distinct social and political periods which, for Plato, were brought about by the introduction of unharmonious tendencies and disunifying events into the otherwise harmonious state. Plato believed that the most just state was that of a *Kingship*, in which political power was held by the 'wisest and most god-like of men'

(Popper, 1945/2006a; 40). However, without careful protection, such a state inevitably descends into *Timocracy*— the rule of the nobles who seek honour and fame—as a result of individual ambition and greed for power. As some members of society become envious of those with power, they seek to gain power and distinction through the acquisition of economic and social resources; ability to rule becomes associated less with wisdom and more with wealth, until, after some time, Timocracy collapses into *Oligarchy*, whereby the rich pass a law which 'disqualifies from public office all those whose means do not reach the stipulated amount' (Popper, 1945/2006a; 42). Oligarchy in turn exacerbates conflicts and enmities between the rich and the poor until, finally, civil war breaks out between the two classes. The poor, greater in number than the rich, overthrow their rich oppressors and divide power equally among themselves, ushering in a period of *Democracy*. This period of democratic rule is short-lived, however, and is replaced by *Tyranny*, upon the emergence of a 'popular leader who knows how to exploit the class antagonism between the rich and the poor within the democratic state, and who succeeds in building up a bodyguard or a private army of his own. The people who have hailed him first as a champion of freedom are soon enslaved; and then they must fight for him in "one war after another which he must stir up... because he must make the people feel the need of a general"' (Popper, 1945/2006a; 44). Each new stage in this historical journey of the state from its most just manifestation to its most abject is brought about by destabilising tendencies, motives, and emotions among its members. Greed, vested interest, emotion, passion: these things throw the state off balance and, hence, need to be guarded against if justice is to reign. Consequently, Plato argued, the state should be purged of those things which inflame these subversive passions and tendencies and, hence, the role of the political rulers is, as far as possible, to banish from society the possibility of change and disunity by quelling internal dissent, establishing a strict division of labour, and centralising power among a ruling elite who had undergone a rigid programme of indoctrination and training so that they might rule effectively (and without concern for personal advancement or ambition).

Plato's claim that the just state should be protected against disharmony thus allowed him to justify enormous and egregious violations of individual freedoms in the aim of 'arresting change', Popper believed, and presented a picture of the just state as one which had a moral duty to intrude upon any and all aspects of human life in the interests of rooting out potential sources of disunity and instability. It also allowed him to justify the accumulation of all political power in the hands of those capable of seeing the realm of the Forms (and, consequently, the form of the state). For Plato did not believe that everyone was capable of knowing what the ideal state should look like, and specifically argued that only that elite class of philosophers capable of seeing and understanding the Form of the state should hold political power. Furthermore, the qualities necessary to understand the nature of the ideal state could be shaped by social and political life, but they could not be instilled in those who were not born with them. Consequently, the ability to rule was something that people were either born with or not: those born with the intelligence and insight to see the Form of the state should hold power; those who are not born with this insight should not.

For Popper, Plato's republic represents the apotheosis of the closed society, and a destruction of all those principles and ideals upon which a truly just (i. e. open) society should be based. It is characterized by a ruling elite—defined as a *race*— whose ability to wield political power is determined by birth. It embodies the widespread and profound suppression of *individual* free thought and opinion in the interests of maintaining the stability of the *group*, the destruction of any distinction between *public* and *private* through the politicization of all aspects of all lives within the republic, and a radical, politically-enforced *division of labour*. the state, Plato believed, runs best when its people are confined to roles that have ascribed to them by birth, are discouraged to think beyond the confines of these roles for any reason, and are denied the capacity to participate in the governance of their own republic or their own lives lest they cause disharmony, disunity, or change. People should do what they were born to do: those born with the skills to mend shoes should mend shoes, those born with the skills to build ships should build ships, and those born with the skills to rule should rule. Democracy is a corrupted and debased form of politics because, among other things, it places power in the hands of those who do not have the skills or the knowledge to be able to wield it appropriately (i.e. in pursuit of ends located in the realm of the Forms, which only certain people can see). In Plato, therefore, Popper identified that claim that, for the good of society as a whole, it is crucial that individuals do not seek to better themselves, or seek to stray beyond the confines of their ordained role in society, or to learn new things, in case they start to ask questions, to challenge authority, or do anything other than obey the master race of Guardians who watch over them.

In all this, Popper believes, Plato shows himself to be an enemy of freedom and the individual, and, hence, of an open society, founded upon liberal principles. He denies that all individuals, by virtue of their basic humanity, are in some sense equal, and equally capable of rational thought and action. He denies that people should be free to live their lives according to goals and values that they themselves have considered, and deemed worthwhile, rather than goals which have been forced upon them by birth (or, more accurately, by those powerful few who are able to define what skills people have and which they do not). He denies that there is any conceivable area of human life which should be considered beyond the reach of the state: our goals, our ideals, our very thoughts themselves must be controlled in the interests of the greater good. He denies that individuals might together converge on the appropriate response to moral or political questions through free discussion and democratic debate: instead, the answers to these kinds of questions are located in an idealized past, and are *revealed* or *discovered* by those who have the ability to do so, and then communicated to those too ignorant to know where to look. He denies that political leaders should draw their authority from the consent of the people, and hence, that the leaders must justify their actions in ways in which the people to whom they are accountable find agreeable and intelligible: instead, they draw their authority from an ideal vision of society to which only they are privy. And he denies the central liberal idea that as far as possible the state should support all individuals in their desire to live their own lives in their own way, and only act in those ways which are consistent with, and in defence of, the ability of all individuals to pursue their own freely chosen ends without coercion or constraint: instead, he believes that the state should at all times remain vigilant against individuals developing their own ideas, pursuing their own goals, questioning their rulers, or doing anything to upset the order and harmony imposed upon them from above.

Plato's conception of the ideal state is, on this view, nothing less than totalitarianism—a state in which a minority assumes complete control of the majority, with the help of the military, and justifies the oppression and mistreatment of the people by appealing to a mythical future good for all human beings which only they can see, and which—therefore—only they can bring about. Understood thus, Plato's ideal republic does indeed share profound similarities with modern totalitarian states like Soviet communism under Stalin: the destruction of the family, the rejection of private property (for its tendency to cause conflicts), the suppression of art in the name of maintaining social harmony, the politicization of individuals' private lives in the interests of suppressing dissent, the denial of democracy or the idea of selfrule, the denial of individual freedom in the name of collective stability, and the constant, all pervasive, and dominating exercise of power among a chosen elite legitimated not by democratic or popular sovereignty, but by a utopian goal that only this elite could see or understand. To Popper, Plato's ideal republic represented little more or less than a system premised upon the domination of the racially inferior masses (who are denied education or the resources to challenge or to question the status quo) by the racially superior minority (who are indoctrinated, brain-washed, and purged of all individuality in order that they might rule without concern for personal status).

Popper was explicit in drawing the link between Plato's conception of justice and modern totalitarianism. He believed that the vision of the ideal state presented in Plato's work represented a direct philosophical pre-cursor to the modern totalitarianisms of Soviet communism, Italian fascism, and German Nazism. We can certainly see that it bore all the hallmarks of *historicism* (in terms of its politics and its sociology). Plato's sociology was *collectivist* and *holistic*, in that he believed that society should be understood not merely as a collection of individuals, but as an organic whole; his approach was *essentialist*, in the sense that he believed that it was crucial to grasp the fundamental essence of society before concluding as to how it should be structured; and his idea of justice was premised upon a conception of history as progressing according to discreet periods or epochs, brought about by identifiable social and political conditions.

These are claims that Plato shared with many historicist writers throughout history, but most obviously with the idealist writings of Hegel. However, while Popper felt that Plato's historicism was *pessimistic*, in that it presented historical development as a journey away from social harmony (and hence, justice) towards disharmony (and injustice), he described the historicism of Hegel as *optimistic*. Hegel believed that history progresses in a series of periods or *epochs* according to fixed laws of development, but—unlike Plato— believed that each stage in the development of society represents a *positive* step in the evolution of human social and political relations. Hegel, like Plato and Aristotle, adopted a methodologically *essentialist* approach to understanding society and the state: that is, like Plato and Aristotle, Hegel believed that it was crucial to grasp the fundamental essence of the state in order to work out how it had developed in the past, and how it might develop in the future. And like Aristotle, Hegel believed that natural phenomena developed towards a final cause or *telos*. The reason that Hegel was more optimistic about historical development than Plato, Popper argued, was because he understood the ideal form of the state to exist in the essence of each historical embodiment of the state in the world, rather than in some idealized past. For Hegel, therefore, the ongoing development of history served to further *reveal* the hidden or latent essence (and hence the ideal form of the state) in each successive historical period and therefore brought humanity closer to realizing it; it did not, as Plato believed, take humanity further *away* from it. Hegel's historicism is thus *optimistic* in the sense that the essences hidden within all phenomena (including the state) are 'self-moving; they are self-developing, or, using more fashionable terms, they are "emerging" and "self-creating". And they propel themselves in the direction of an Aristotelian "final cause", or, as Hegel puts it, towards a "self-realizing and self-realized cause in itself"' (Popper, 1945/2006b; 40). Hegel thus shared with Heraclitus and Plato the idea that the world was in a state of flux, but unlike them concluded that this was a good thing; Hegel's world of flux represented a 'state of "emergent" or "creative evolution"; each of its stages contains the preceding ones, from which it originates; and each stage supersedes all previous stages, approaching nearer and nearer to perfection. The general law of development is thus one of progress' (Popper, 1945/2006b; 40); the process by which the essences of all things are systematically revealed through the dialectical clash of ideas.

Despite the optimistic strain of Hegelian historicism, Popper argued that Hegel's philosophy was little more than 'the fertilizer to which modern totalitarianism owes its rapid growth' (Popper, 1945/2006b; 63). The reason for this, he thinks, is that we find in Hegel all the arguments and philosophical suppositions which would later be used by totalitarian dictators around the world to centralize power in the hands of an all-powerful state. Behind what Popper clearly viewed as purposefully obtuse and jargon-ridden prose, Hegel's theory of history was little more than a story about the rise of nationalism, and the journey of the State towards totalitarianism. Like Plato, he argued, Hegel envisages the state as an organism and, ' following Rousseau, who had furnished it with a "general will" Hegel furnishes it with a conscious, thinking essence, its "reason" or "Spirit". This Spirit. . . is at the very same time the collective *Spirit of the Nation* that forms the state' (Popper, 1945/2006b; 41). Thus to understand the State, we must understand its essence or Spirit, and to do *that* we must understand its history. ' The Spirit of the nation determines its historical destiny; and every nation that wishes "to emerge into existence" must assert its individuality or soul by entering the "Stage of History", that is to say, by fighting the other nations; the object of the fight is world domination' (Popper, 1945/2006b; 41).

Popper therefore identified in Hegel the idea that history develops according to overarching laws of development, and that the prime mover of history—its ' chosen people'—is the *nation*. History is the movement of the nation from a brutish, lawless rabble to a galvanized, militarized unity under the state. History is thus the march towards the nation-state; the all-powerful state being the Idea which is slowly but surely revealed within the essence of each successive historical epoch by dialectical leaps of will and imagination, until it is revealed entirely and the development of history ceases. Thus, in Hegel, we see the claim that ' the Nation State is. . . the absolute power on earth', and, as in Plato, we can see the exultation of the closed society over the open society.

Given its core assumptions, Popper believed, it was relatively easy for disciples of Hegel like Haekel to use Hegelianism to justify a particularly odious form of nationalism based on race. And in Hegel's exaltation of the nation state as the purest expression of freedom, and his claim that '"the State is... the basis and centre of all the concrete elements in the life of a people: of Art, Law, Morals, Religion, and Science"' Popper saw the defence of the totalitarian state whose 'might must permeate and control the whole life of the people in all its functions' (Hegel quoted in Popper, 1945/2006b; 68). Hegel's philosophy thus embodies all the worst excesses of historicism in its essentialism, holism, collectivism, and its subordination of the freedom and the interests of the individual to the good of the whole, and to the inexorable march of history. In his valuing of human passion and will, and of blood and war, Hegel—for Popper—did more than anyone to let loose on the world the destructive energies of nationalism and tribalism, and can be held responsible for furnishing tyrants and dictators ever since with the philosophical resources they needed to justify their corrupt and bankrupt appeal to tribal politics and to shun the open society characterized by freedom, equality, reason, and individuality.

We find similar criticisms in Popper's treatment of Marx. Popper had vastly higher regard for Marx than Hegel (or, it seems, for Plato). For while Plato and Hegel were committed to a conception of politics driven by, and shaped according to, historical laws of development, they nevertheless believed that the historical process could be changed or guided by human intervention. Having identified what caused the state to develop towards injustice, for example, Plato outlined all the various ways in which it was possible for human actors to *stop* this process. Similarly, Hegel's dialectics were driven by *people*—their ideas, their passions, the conflicts between them—and, hence, for him history was a story of the development of human ideas and the national traditions which shaped them. For Marx, however, there was very little room for

Popper's Ideas

human beings to affect the development of history at all. Marx's inversion of Hegel's idealism took the laws of historical development out of the hands of human beings entirely and located them instead in wider,impersonal economic forces. He subscribed to a social and historical *determinism*:

> if there was to be a social science,and accordingly,historical prophecy, the main course of history must be pre-determined, and neither good-will nor reason had the power to alter it. All that was left to us in the way of reasonable interference was to make sure,by historical prophecy,of the impending course of development, and to remove the obstacles in its path. (Popper,1945/2006b;94)

As Marx himself put it in *Das Kapital*, when 'society has discovered the natural law that determines its own movement,... even then it can neither overleap the natural phases of its evolution, nor shuffle them out of the world by a stroke of the pen. But this much it can do;it can shorten and lessen its birth-pangs'(quoted in Popper,1945/2006b;94).

Consequently, the roles of the social scientist and of the social engineer for Marx were clear. The social scientist should seek to determine the precise social and economic conditions under which capitalism would collapse and be replaced by communism,and the social engineer should seek to reform society in such a way as to hasten this collapse. This, as we have indicated, requires the social engineer and the social scientist to take a *collectivist* and *holistic* approach to understanding society:an approach which takes as its principal aim the piecing together of the ways in which societies (and political institutions) evolve in response to developments in the economic 'base'. Marx himself provided a detailed sketch of this process,most famously in his *Preface to A Contribution to the Critique of Political Economy*. While liberals and others believed that individual consciousness shaped and determined the character of social, political and economic arrangements, Marx famously believed the opposite: that the social, political, and (most importantly) economic conditions under which one lived shaped and determined one's consciousness(by which he meant one's ideas, preferences, and values, one's understanding of the world, and of one's place within it). Human consciousness was thus, for Marx, intimately tied to the particular social and historical environment in which we find ourselves, and was determined by it. This is why we come to accept capitalism, even though it has devastating consequences for our lives and our humanity. We draw our understanding of the world, our ideas, our ambitions and commitments from the network of social relations in which we are located, and these are in turn determined by economic forces. Hence, the capitalist system itself determines what we know and what we do not know about the world, and thus stifles criticism: capitalism robs us of our humanity, alienates us from those things which make us human, commodifies our productive labour power, and encourages us to think of ourselves as isolated individuals in relations of competition with one another, each with our own interests and preferences and 'rights', rather than cooperative members of a shared community, and in doing all these things, capitalism renders it impossible for us to gain the requisite critical distance from our circumstances to reflect upon them meaningfully or to criticize them. The role of the Marxist social engineer, then, is to help encourage those circumstances in which human beings might come to realize the many and varied ways in which the capitalist system brutalizes them and undermines their humanity. The continued development of capitalism will(to put it in Hegelian terms)reveal the inconsistencies within the essence, and its flaws will become more obvious to the people who live within it. When these inconsistencies become so obvious as to be untenable, and so clearly unjust as to be unconscionable, human beings will rise up and seek to change the system, thus ushering in a new historical period of communism. For Marx, then, there is a role for political and social action, but it is a very restricted one, limited merely to the establishment of conditions under which the working class might fully grasp the extent of their oppression, and seek to do something about it.

For Popper, then, Marx's claim that it 'is not the consciousness of man that determines his existence—rather, it is his social existence that determines his consciousness' represents an important critique of psychologism (which Popper praised) but also underwrites a 'conspiracy theory of society' (Popper, 1963/2007b; eg. 165), and the impotence of human beings (and politics) in the face of overwhelming historical forces beyond their control. It wrongly encourages us to think that our opinions and ideas are not really ours, and that not only our actions but our *thoughts* are determined by others, or by history itself. Not only does it negate the capacity of individuals to act freely, or to change the social and political world in which they live according to their own ideas about the world, it suggests that the deepest and most personal ideas that people might have (e. g. their sense of self, their loves, fears, hopes, ambitions) are determined by *history*, and by the historical laws of development in particular. It is not possible for individual people to exert their will on society such that they can bring about change, because the content of their will is determined by the very social, political, and economic relations that they would seek to change. All they can do is wait until the economic conditions in which they find themselves develop to such an extent that the internal inconsistencies inherent within the capitalist system are revealed; only then, when the time is right, can human beings rise up and usher in the new social and political system, as demanded by the new prevailing economic conditions. What the 'conspiracy theory of society' suggests, then, is that people cannot form their own authentic opinions and are at the mercy of the designs of powerful individuals and groups. Popper felt that this view rendered individuals invisible in the historical process, and, worse, allowed Marx to deny or ignore their expressed preferences.

Anyone who disagreed with Marx's philosophical vision could be easily denounced as suffering from 'false consciousness'; indeed the fact that they disagreed with Marx was seen as proving Marx's point, rather than undermining it, and was merely seen as testament to the power of the capitalist system to dupe the people into thinking that all was well when it really was not. Having argued as much, it thus became relatively straightforward to justify political action on the basis that it is what the people *would* want if only they could free themselves from the imprisoning ideology of capitalism, rather than what they actually *say* they want.

Popper felt that he had identified innumerable problems in Marx's philosophy, and it is simply impossible to go into all of them here. (a) it is possible and appropriate to prophesize the future development of society by revealing overarching laws of historical development, (b) in order to understand *individuals* we must first understand the social *wholes* (classes, societies, nations, cultures, etc.) in which they exist, and hence, that social science should be *methodologically collectivist*, (c) in order to understand societies (and the individuals within them) we need to grasp the fundamental *nature* or *structure* of the social whole (i. e. as determined by economic forces which are always developing), and hence, that we need to adopt an approach which is *methodologically essentialist*, (d) it is possible, and appropriate, to justify social and political reforms on the basis of whether or not they help to bring about the predestined fate of humankind (for which people may or may not express support), and (e) that individual human beings are powerless before the overarching and impersonal laws of development, which constrain them, stifle their ability to form their own judgments about the world in which they live, and determine their every thought and action.

The Open Society

Popper believed that historicist social and political thought produced a theory of the state that was thoroughly obnoxious, corrupt, and oppressive, and represented a vindication of the closed society. He also thought it was rooted in an utterly flawed methodology and a mistaken epistemology. He therefore believed that we need to reject the normative and epistemological ideas at the heart of historicism and replace them with a form of politics which is premised upon, and compatible with, his wider ideas about epistemology. As soon as we acknowledge that no group or individual (whether they be a scientist or a social scientist or a political leader) can claim to know the *truth*, we must acknowledge that no individual, institution, or social practice can be considered *infallible* or *unquestionable*. In the absence of infallible truth, it is left for individuals to work out among themselves what the role of political institutions should be, what public policies should be implemented, and what are the ends of politics. Just as science should not be understood as the pursuit of great *truths* or *proofs* but rather the resolution of problems through the elimination of *errors* in those theories which currently exist, so politics should not be understood as the pursuit of great *truths* or *ideals*, but rather the elimination of those social *problems* which afflict society, through the elimination of *errors* made by, or embodied in, social and political institutions. Popper therefore subscribed to what he called a 'negative utilitarianism': the point of social science and politics is not to encourage general pleasure or welfare, but to minimize harm and suffering by identifying the sources of such harm, and reforming them in a piecemeal way. This held for the design of social and political *institutions*, and public *policies*.

According to Popper's commitment to negative utilitarianism, and his rejection of utopianism, social and political *institutions* should not be designed so as to provide individual rulers or elites with the ability to pursue some ideal good, but rather to prevent them from 'doing too much damage' (Popper, 1945/ 2006b;142). That is, the legal framework of an open society is one conceived as a set of 'protective institutions' rather than a set of rules which enable rulers to exercise their will at any given time. State intervention in the social and economic life of individuals will sometimes be necessary, then, but these interventions can only be justified if they are the carried out by institutions which have been designed to protect individuals (and their freedom) and which have themselves grown in a piecemeal fashion as a consequence of accumulated knowledge, experience, and critique. They cannot be justified if they are the mere products of some ruler's will. The principle of institutional design underwritten by Popper's negative utilitarianism and his critical rationalism is thus one which enshrines piecemeal social engineering, and the rejection of radical change, at its heart. Reform can be concrete and enduring, but reforms must be rooted in an appreciation of what has worked in the past and what has not, and what led us to where we currently are. And the way in which we achieve our long-term ends (and these ends themselves) must be subject to critique and possible rejection in the light of all the contrary arguments that the world can provide. The point of institutions, then, is to provide a necessary check on the power of leaders and to quell the possibility of radical (and thus, irresponsible) change, by supporting important individual freedoms and an environment in which persons might engage with one another in democratic dialogue. In addition to protecting the freedom of individual citizens, and society from irresponsible changes, Popper believed that his approach had a further benefit: that the legal framework 'can be known and understood by the individual citizen'. Indeed, he felt, the system 'should be designed to be so understandable. Its functioning is predictable. It introduces a factor of certainty and security into social life. . . As opposed to this, the method of personal intervention must introduce an ever-growing element of unpredictability into social life, and it will develop the feeling that social life is irrational and insecure' (Popper, 1945/2006b; 143).

With regard to *policies*, Popper's negative utilitarianism embodied a rejection of any justification which appealed to some long-term future good, and emphasized instead the piecemeal identification and resolution of concrete social problems. The most obvious social evils that have thus far been identified and which 'can be remedied, or relieved, by social cooperation' include, he believed, 'poverty, unemployment and similar forms of social insecurity, sickness and pain, penal cruelty, slavery and other forms of serfdom, religious and racial forms of discrimination, lack of educational opportunities, rigid class differences, and war' (Popper, 1963/2007b; 497-8). It is the responsibility of the institutions of the open society to tackle these problems in a spirit of critical rationalism, and in a way which is consistent with Popper's wider claims about epistemology, the growth of knowledge, anti-radicalism, and the importance of experience.

Consequently, neither policies nor institutions should be measured according to criteria which only a chosen few can see, but according to much more procedural, short-term criteria, like whether the particular institutions or policies do the job that they are supposed to do, or whether the social problems that are currently being addressed are the right ones, and being addressed in the most efficient way. The point of politics, Popper believed, was not to draw up unsustainable blueprints, or dream of ideal societies, but to identify those social, political, and economic problems currently facing society, and to seek efficient, justifiable, and progressive solutions to these problems. Once again, social engineering should be *piecemeal* rather than utopian, and based upon a public debate about political priorities, the ends to which institutions should be aimed, and whether those institutions themselves could be reformed or replaced. Unlike utopian social engineers, who would have us believe that the only valuable form of social experiments are large-scale ones, piecemeal social engineers acknowledge the value in small-scale, short-term experiments and proposals; the

> introduction of a new kind of life insurance, of a new kind of taxation, of a new penal reform, are all social experiments which have their repercussions through the whole of society without remodelling society as a whole... the kind of experiment from which we can learn most is the alteration of one social institution at a time. For only in this way can we learn how to fit institutions into the framework of other institutions, and how to adjust them so that they can work according to our intentions. And only in this way can we make mistakes, and learn from our mistakes, without rising repercussions of a gravity that must endanger the will to future reforms. (Popper, 1945/2006a;172)

Utopianism is contrary to the scientific method and the growth of knowledge(and hence, to the identification and resolution of social and political problems)because, like the inductive model of science on which it is based, it encourages us to cling to theories in the face of evidence of their failure, rather than to embrace their failure, to learn from our mistakes, and propose new—and falsifiable—theories in their place.

Popper's conception of politics was therefore one which took individual freedom very seriously, and sought to defend individuals from arbitrary interference and oppression. Above all, it sought to free individuals from the tyranny of established and unquestionable truths, and was committed to providing all persons with the political, economic, and intellectual resources necessary to protect them against what Mill (following Tocqueville) called the tyranny of the majority. Individual freedom could not be subordinated to the good of the social whole, or sacrificed in the interests of achieving social unity, stability, or national unity. The organic collectivism and essentialism at the heart of historicism should be abandoned and replaced with methodological individualism and nominalism. No longer should individuals feel that their interests and ideals and ambitions are unimportant in the face of the overarching needs of society or the vast and impenetrable forces of history. And no longer should social and political scientists seek to grasp the fundamental *essence* of states and societies in order to work out how they should be structured and what policies should be implemented. Individuals should be afforded the resources they need to throw off the shackles of tribalism and nationalism (the 'politics of the group') and which encourage people to think of themselves as little more or less than members of some wider, and mythologized, social whole possessing a destiny of its own which trumps theirs. Individuals should be given the resources they need to develop their capacity to engage with others in debates about politics; they should be able to work out their own views about the rightful ends of social and political institutions, they should be able to express these views, and they should be able to act upon them in ways which feed into the democratic system. The authority of particular institutions or individuals is never fixed, just as the arguments and philosophical positions which provide their justification are never settled; rather, they are open to debate and question through an ongoing process of democratic dialogue conducted—as it is in science or in any other field—between equals who have adopted a critical rationalist approach to existing social and political theories, proposals, social practices, and institutions. Just as public debate about existing theories in the physical sciences establishes a form of *objectivity* among those involved, so the public debate of social scientific and political questions establishes a similar kind of objectivity or impartiality: public debates about politics weed out arguments based on duplicity, deceit or manipulation, and force those in charge to justify their actions to the people in ways that they can comprehend and find acceptable.

Popper's political vision was thus one rooted in the importance of individual freedom, democracy, and the idea that social problems could be identified, tentatively understood, and resolved through a process of debate framed in terms of a trial and error process of conjecture and refutation, in which no-one could claim to know the ultimate and final truth, and in which all current theories were falsifiable, and hence up for debate. In the absence of infallible truth, there can be no ultimate good for all individuals which can be assumed to afford legitimacy to particular institutions, practices, or people, or which set forever the problems to which institutions should attend; all we can do is approach each and every political question as rigorously and innovatively as possible, which means testing our existing social and political theories against the sum total of all that we know about the world in the interests of falsifying them.

In place of nationalism, Popper defended an optimistic internationalism—a cosmopolitan politics rooted in the uniting vision of humanity as rational and free. Plato believed that 'opinion is shared by all men; but reason is shared only by Gods, and by very few men' (Popper, 1945/2006a; 252). Hegel subordinated the importance of reason to passion and will, and hence, sought a politics of national belonging. Popper was a fallibilist about reason, and counselled against the naïve view that reasoned reflection could provide certain knowledge, and rejected what he saw as a blind faith among some Enlightenment thinkers in the ability of reason to provide social and political blueprints. However, he nevertheless united with liberals and rationalists throughout history in asserting the Enlightenment idea that the capacity for reason is possessed by all individuals, wherever they may live, and whatever groups they may belong to, and that it is this uniting capacity to reason which allows us to empathize with others, and to understand their pains: reason, 'supported by imagination, enables us to understand that men who are far away, whom we shall never see, are like ourselves... [B]y the use of thought and imagination, we may become ready to help all who need our help' (Popper, 1945/

2006b;265). No nation or state could appeal to history, or the good of the group, or traditional values, to dominate or oppress their people, and no political leader could claim refuge in the notion of national sovereignty in order to justify the violation of their peoples'individual freedoms.

Popper's commitment to freedom, reason, and critical rationalism were thus intimately linked, and held implications for domestic and international politics. Internationally, as we have said, it underwrote a liberal form of cosmopolitanism, rooted in the moral equality of all human beings, and the need for international dialogue about how best to resolve social, political, and economic problems. Domestically, it mandated the reform of social and political institutions such that they were capable of protecting individual freedoms, and safeguarding the deliberative environment necessary for individual members of society to work out together-through reasoning with one another-how best to resolve social and political problems. Reason is not, as Plato believed, 'a kind of "faculty," which may be possessed and developed by different men in vastly different degrees. Admittedly, intellectual gifts may be different in this way, and they may contribute to reasonableness; but they need not. Clever men may be very unreasonable; they may cling to their prejudices and may not expect to hear anything worthwhile from others. 'According to Popper, however,

> we not only owe our reason to others but we can never excel others in our reasonableness in a way that would establish a claim to authority; authoritarianism and rationalism in our sense cannot be reconciled, since argument, which includes criticism, and the art of listening to criticism, is the basis of reasonableness. Thus rationalism in our sense is diametrically opposed to all those modern Platonic dreams of brave new worlds in which the growth of reason would be controlled or 'planned' by some superior reason. Reason, like science, grows by way of mutual criticism; the only possible way of

"planning" its growth is to develop those institutions that safeguard the freedom of this criticism, that is to say, the freedom of thought. (Popper, 1945/2006b; 253)

Thus, we find the claim (touched upon earlier) that human reason is embodied in, and can only flourish in the presence of, *institutions* which encourage and protect it: that reason is *public* in character.

Popper therefore believed in the possibility of progress, but of a very different kind to that defended by the historicists. His idea of *scientific* progress, for example, outlined in *The Poverty of Historicism*, held that the development of human knowledge was linked to, and dependent upon, particular institutions, namely, those institutions like speech and writing, as well institutions like laboratories, universities, and research facilities, in which scientists might engage in public debate about existing theories. Consequently, it was very important indeed that, in the interests of scientific progress, the right social institutions were present, by which he meant those institutions which protected and encouraged free debate. These claims connect sharply with Popper's wider claims about the role of institutions in driving *political* or *social* progress: if we value progress, the development of knowledge, freedom, and the capacity of social institutions to improve society by rectifying those problems which afflict society and undermine the basic equality of human beings - as we should - then we must establish and protect social institutions which allow us to debate with one another about the appropriate ends of politics, to form our own judgements about politics, and to criticize the judgments of others, while all the while defending our own views against the criticisms of others and, when necessary, rejecting our theories in favour of newer, more persuasive ones. Only the 'institutional method makes it possible to make adjustments in the light of discussion and experience', he argued.

It alone makes it possible to apply the method of trial and error to our political actions. It is long-term; yet the permanent legal framework can be slowly changed, in order to make allowances for unforeseen and undesired consequences, for changes in other parts of the framework, etc. It alone allows us to find out, by experience and analysis, what we actually were doing when we intervened with a certain aim in mind. Discretionary decisions of the rulers or civil servants are outside these rational methods. They are short-term decisions, transitory, changing from day to day, or at best, from year to year. As a rule... they cannot even be publicly discussed, both because necessary information is lacking, and because the principles on which decision is taken are obscure. (Popper, 1945/2006b; 143)

Policies, if they do not do what they are supposed to do, should be dropped and replaced with ones which do. Institutions, if they prove themselves unfit to carry out the tasks required of them, should be reformed so as to be better able to meet the social and political challenges at hand. And politicians, if they prove themselves incapable of ruling effectively, should be removed in favour of ones who are better suited to public office. All of these decisions—including the prior questions concerning the appropriate role of institutions and policies and politicians—are, in an open society, decided by free and equal citizens, engaged in reasonable democratic debate with one another via institutions which protect their individual freedoms. Thus, while historicists defended essentialism, holism, utopian social engineering, totalitarianism, and the subordination of the individual to society and to impersonal laws of historical development, Popper defended nominalism, individualism, piecemeal social engineering, democracy, and the importance of each and every individual in their own right, not as mere tools to be used and manipulated in the interests of bringing about some ideal state of affairs, but as ends in themselves.

3
Reception and Influence of
Popper's Philosophy

Many of Popper's interventions in epistemology, scientific method, and political philosophy were, in their time, ground-breaking, original, and radical. His influence in these areas is significant; it is not possible to study the philosophy of the natural sciences without engaging with Popper's work, and it is arguably impossible to grasp the significance of a lot of the work in this area without being familiar with what Popper had to say. In tackling some of the most fundamental questions in epistemology and science in the way that it did, Popper's work was inspirational, and influenced some of the most notable philosophers of science in the history of the discipline. Major contributions to the philosophy of science by Joseph Agassi (Popper's student and research assistant at the LSE) and John Watkins, for example, draw explicitly upon Popper's ideas in order to defend the possibility of scientific discovery in the face of scepticism (Agassi, 1993; Watkins, 1984). Imre Lakatos sought to bridge Popper's evolutionary epistemology with Thomas Kuhn's conception of science as a revolutionary endeavour (Lakatos, 1976, 1978a, and 1978b). And for a generation of philosophers of science, Popper's work has provided the backdrop against which contemporary debates about induction, deduction, truth, and knowledge are conducted. This is not to say that they all agree with him, of course. Paul Feyerabend, for example, initially impressed with Popper's approach, later rejected Popper's theory of falsificationism as too restrictive, and argued instead for a form of scientific anarchism in place of overarching, all-encompassing methodologies(Feyerabend,1975/1993). Several thinkers, including Hilary Putnam, criticized Popper's description of falsification on the grounds that it was insufficiently attentive to the extent to which any theory could be 'immunized' against refutation; this criticism led Popper to move the idea of verisimilitude - the idea that existing theories should be replaced with ones which better approximate the truth - more centrally in his theory(Putnam,1974). W. V. O. Quine and Pierre Duhem,both proposed that the falsification of theories was complicated by the fact that it was impossible to test individual hypotheses in isolation, as each theory was inextricably part of a wider network of theories,each of which were mutually dependent upon one another (Duhem, 1954; Quine,1960). And Thomas Kuhn's *The Structure of Scientific Revolutions* published in 1962 provided an alternative account of scientific discovery as a process of revolutionary developments(or 'paradigm shifts') which, he thought, better described the way in which scientists actually worked. Popper's response to Kuhn's influential book was to suggest(in 'The Myth of the Framework') that Kuhn's claims about the incommensurability of scientific paradigms were rooted in the same fallacious assumptions which stifled the growth of knowledge and justified moral and social relativism(Popper,1994a).

Poverty and, in particular, *The Open Society* also drew praise from a broad and diverse group of thinkers from across the political spectrum. For example, socialists like Bertrand Russell and Harold Laski were keen to defend *The Open Society* for its critique of *laissez-faire* economics and its vindication of a non-Marxist form of social democracy. Meanwhile, philosophers and economists from the political Right like Hayek, von Mises, and Milton Friedman admired Popper's work and used it to bolster their critique of social and economic planning, and their vindication of free markets and political gradualism. His work on the social sciences represented an important contribution to debates among economists like Carl

Menger (1871/1981), Ludwig von Mises (1949), and Karl Polanyi (1944/2001) about the role of history, essentialism, and the state in the study of economics, but did not do so from within any specific ideological position.

Popper's influence on the development of liberal, conservative, libertarian, socialist, and social democratic thought in the twentieth century can—and has been—drawn by many philosophers and historians (e. g. Magee, 1973; Miller, 1994; Shearmur, 1996). The fact that his political thought has been adopted and defended by so many very different thinkers is a testament to its ingenuity and enduring appeal, but also presents a conundrum which goes beyond Popper and into the methodology of political thought more generally. Was Popper a conservative? Was he a libertarian? Was he a social democrat? Such questions are complicated by the indeterminacy of *isms* in general, and of conservatism and libertarianism in particular, as we will see in the next section. But they are also complicated by Popper's unwillingness to define many of his foundational commitments, and the tensions inherent in his dual role as scholar and polemicist. Popper's language and tone in *The Open Society* angered many enemies and led many potential allies to dismiss his work as unscholarly. Popper was certainly not one to suffer fools gladly. In *The Open Society*, we must recall, Popper accuses Plato (probably the most respected and venerated figure in the history of Western civilization) of, among other things, hating freedom, deliberately misrepresenting the philosophy of Socrates for his own selfish ends, advocating the deliberate slaughter of racially inferior members of society, and coming up with the rule of the 'philosopher king' in order to provide a justification for why Plato himself should hold power. He calls Fichte a 'fraud' and a 'windbag', and describes Aristotle (probably the second most respected and venerated figure in the history of Western civilization) as 'not a man of striking originality of thought' (although he did 'invent logic', for which Popper believed he should be thanked). He variously described the philosophy of Hegel as ' bombastic and hysterical', 'indigestible', and 'outstanding in its lack of originality'. Indeed, 'as far as Hegel is concerned,' he claimed, 'I do not even think he was talented... There is nothing in Hegel's writing that has not been said better before him' (Popper, 1945/2006b; 35). Furthermore, in a number of places, Popper cites approvingly Schopenhauer's description of Hegel as a ' flat-headed, insipid, nauseating, illiterate charlatan, who reached the pinnacle of audacity in scribbling together and dishing up the craziest mystifying nonsense' (quoted in Popper, 1945/2006b; 36). Clearly, to Popper, Hegel was little more than a ' clown '; a hopeless apologist for Frederick William of Prussia, who adopted a deliberately baffling written style in order that he might confuse his readers into thinking that originality lay where it did not.

It is therefore hardly surprising that following the publication of *The Open Society* in 1945, many leapt to defend Plato, Aristotle and Hegel, claiming that Popper had made huge and grievous errors in his interpretation of their works and its implications. Plato scholars, in particular, were aggrieved. Despite the emergence of a number of works criticizing Plato for his antipathy towards democracy (e. g. Fite, 1934; Crossman, 1959; and Winspear, 1940), there existed a broad consensus among classical scholars and historians that Plato represented a voice for humanity and reason. Popper's vicious attack was genuinely shocking, not merely in respect of what he said, but the way in which he said it. Most classicists responded with polemical reviews, and two—John Wild and Ronald Levinson— even wrote monograph length defences of Plato against Popper's critique(Levinson, 1953; Wild, 1953). The problem, it seemed, was not only that Popper had misread Plato and Aristotle, but that he had accorded them insufficient respect. John Plamenatz, for example, described Popper's treatment of Aristotle as exhibiting the manner that ' an unkind man sometimes adopts towards someone whom he believes to be his intellectual inferior; and, as is usual in such cases, it tells us more about the contemnor than the object of his contempt'

(Plamenatz, 1952/1967; 267). The dominant feeling among classicists was (and still is) that Popper's strident, often polemical, prose missed many nuances and intricacies in Plato's thought which would have complicated Popper's interpretation. They pointed out, for example, that a closer, more sympathetic reading of *The Republic* showed that Plato's eugenics was not straightforwardly 'fascist' in the way that Popper maintained, that classical Athens was not as obviously progressive or open as Popper suggested, and that Popper's idealization of Athenian imperialism was unrealistic and based on inaccuracy. There is also little evidence to support Popper's claim that Socrates was committed to critical rationalism, individualism, and equalitarianism, as Popper defined them, and many rejected the claim that Plato was a historicist in the sense that Popper implied, arguing that Plato's theory of the Forms appealed to philosophical ideals rather than historical ones.

Popper's critique of Marx has been similarly criticized for being too narrow and simplistic. For example, he discussed neither Marx's *Economic and Philosophical Manuscripts of 1844*, which came out in German in 1932, and which many take to be one of Marx's most important works, nor the *Grundrisse*, which did not appear in German until 1939. Furthermore, Popper failed to engage with the work of other important Marxists such as Gramsci and Sorel (who rejected the notion of inevitable change), and although in 'the early 1920s, Lukacs frequented the barracks where Popper was living... Popper seemed unfamiliar with *History and Class Consciousness* (1923) and the controversy surrounding it. He knew of Rosa Luxemburg and witnessed the council movement in Vienna, but there was no mention of them in *The Open Society*. He ignored the Austro-Marxists: Adler, most of Bauer, Hilferding, and Renner. One could hear echoes of Bauer's political essays, but that was all' (Hacohen, 2000; 440-1). Despite his professed respect for Marx, Popper seemed unwilling to extend him the courtesy of debating his ideas in all their complexity, or in dealing with the various ways in which his ideas had been interpreted, refined, and restated by his followers. Rather than present Marxism as a dynamic, evolving creed which animated many intelligent and committed people, and which was the subject of great debate inside and outside the academy, Popper attacked Marx as a false prophet of historicism, and seemed uninterested in wider debates or applications of his conclusions. His critique of Marx thus seemed rather abstract and austere, cut off from the rich tradition of thought in which Marx's work was embedded.

Many critics also took issue with the substance of Popper's critique. They argued, for example, that Popper falsely attributed to Marx a view that politics was impotent in the face of economic change (e. g. Cornforth, 1968). They also suggested that, among other things, he misunderstood the relationship between Marx and Hegel and underestimated the importance of individuals and classes in the collapse of capitalism. However, Popper at least tried to provide a coherent critique of Marx which was balanced with a broad appreciation of Marx's intentions and motivations: to alleviate poverty, and to understand the character of capitalist economics and society such that its principal evils might be transcended. Popper's furious denunciation of Hegel (to which he devoted a mere 80 pages out of *The Open Society's* 900), on the other hand, seems to be as driven by indignation as analytical rigour. It is by no means as thorough as his treatment of Plato and Marx, despite his claims that Hegel represents the 'source of all modern historicism' (Popper, 1945/2006b: 30), and hence, the source of the principal threat facing the practice and study of politics in the modern era. Hegel scholars then and since have had little time for Popper's views, and have not taken them seriously. Critics were quick to point out that instead of engaging directly with Hegel's writings, Popper had appeared to rely almost entirely on a single edited anthology — *Hegel Selections* edited by J. Loewenberg — as his source: a book which was intended for students and contained not a single complete work. Similarly, in order to establish Hegel's link with the Nazis, Popper drew heavily on the work of Aurel Kolnai, quoting substantially from his book *The War Against the West*. But many of Kolnai's claims were(and remain)very controversial. Popper, however, simply stated them as the truth, often quoting them out of context. There appears to be little or no evidence that Popper checked the reliability of these claims for himself, or drew his own independent conclusions as to their viability(see Popper, 1945/2006b; 354). Furthermore, critics suggested that in the interests of establishing a more or less clear development from Hegel to Nazism, Popper seemed to confuse and simplify the intellectual relationship between diverse thinkers like Husserl, Scheler, Heidegger and Jaspers — exaggerating the links between them, ameliorating differences, and spuriously drawing together disparate themes and ideas. Moreover, he repeatedly defended the work of thinkers like Schopenhauer and J. F. Fries against the proto-Nazi Hegel, seemingly unaware that both Fries and Schopenhauer had at one time or another expressed anti-Semitic views(Kauffman, 1959). Defenders of Hegelianism like Walter Kauffman and Charles Taylor united with many others in suggesting that Popper had profoundly misunderstood Hegel's metaphysics, and misinterpreted Hegel's defence of the state as justifying a policy of racial purity(Taylor, 1958).

More broadly, Popper was accused of leaving his central target — totalitarianism — underdetermined and undefined. Just as it appeared he had little interest in engaging with the wider literature on Hegel, Plato, or Marx, Popper also appeared to have little interest in discussing wider work on totalitarianism, or in defining totalitarianism in anything more than the broad-est possible terms. This is important because Popper's under-standing of totalitarianism differed radically from that of many modern writers. Most theories of totalitarianism existing at that time emphasized its uniquely modern character, in particular its links with modern industry and technology (e. g. Arendt, 1951/2004; Brzezinski, 1956). Popper, on the other hand, suggested that totalitarianism had existed in one form or another in the writings of thinkers as historically distant as Plato and Heraclitus. In making these claims, Popper seemed to feel it unnecessary to engage with the steadily growing literature on the nature, origins, and character of the totalitarian state (e. g. Aron, 1957). Instead, Popper left his conception of totalitarianism — and, hence, the central enemy of the open society — vague. Similarly, although in *Poverty* Popper spends a great deal of time reconstructing historicist arguments in the most favourable light (in the interests of 'building up a position really worth attacking' (Popper, 1957/2005; 3)) it is striking that virtually all the references intended to corroborate his assertions about 'what historicists think' are to one book: Karl Mannheim's *Man and Society*. Popper clearly thought that Mannheim's approach to social and political science was mistaken, however it is not clear how accurate or fair Popper's interpretation of Mannheim is, or how easily Mannheim's views can be seen as a template for other historicists throughout history, from Plato and Heraclitus to Hegel, Marx, Mill and Comte. Once again, critics have suggested, we see in *Poverty* (as in *The Open Society*) an unwillingness by Popper to engage with specific arguments by specific thinkers, and a tendency to lump many different thinkers together in order to damn them all at once.

Defenders of Popper like Bryan Magee have sought to counter the common charge of unscholarly methods by emphasizing the intentions behind *Poverty* and *The Open Society* and the context in which they were written. Popper, we must recall, described *The Open Society* as a 'fighting book'. He wrote it quickly whilst in exile in New Zealand, having left a war torn Europe threatened by Fascism. If his tone is a little too strident in places, or if his treatment of certain venerated historical thinkers is unfair or partial, supporters say, it is because Popper was driven by a moral determination to rid the world of the ideas which gave birth to the evils which threatened the world at that time. Popper wrote *The Open Society* in New Zealand amid fears that the Japanese would reach them in a matter of months. Europe was under threat from domination by the Nazis. There was simply no time to read the complete works of Hegel and Marx, or to engage in extended debate about the philosophical, historical, or linguistic complexities introduced by contemporary scholars of Plato, or contemporary Marxists or Hegelians: the world needed a defence of the open society and quick. One might well concede that such an endeavour had a place. However, it does not sit easily with Popper's wider views about the growth of knowledge and the proper conduct of academic debate. Magee has suggested that Popper was not interested in cheap-shots, and that his approach was always to construct the strongest and most positive account of his opponents' theories before demolishing their core points(Magee, 1973). On such a view, Popper thus could be said to practice what he preached by adopting the norms of critical rationalism in his own work. He certainly claimed that this was his intention in *Poverty* and his work in the philosophy of the natural sciences. Profound disagreement continues to exist, however, as to whether Popper used this approach in *The Open Society*. His treatment of Plato and Marx, though sometimes respectful, was vicious and unrelenting, and — many felt — based upon a partial and deliberately sketchy appreciation of the literature in the field. Even fewer disagree about whether he tried to show Hegel in his best light before attempting to demolish his entire philosophy: he quite clearly had no interest in doing so, and had no good word to say about him or his philosophy. Describing his treatment of Hegel some years later, Popper said that 'I neither could nor wished to spend unlimited time upon deep researches into the history of a philosopher whose work I abhor'(Popper, 1945/2006b;446). Whatever one may say about Hegel, this statement clearly violates Popper's own claims about the necessary conduct of intellectual debate, and raises the interesting question as to whether or not Popper's ideas concerning Hegel(and perhaps, Marx and Plato) can, on Popper's own terms, represent a meaningful contribution to knowledge.

Popper,Burke,and the fallibility of reason

Nevertheless,Popper's work in social and political thought has proved influential to thinkers across the political spectrum. Popper's steadfast unwillingness to be labelled as the exponent of any particular ideology meant that supporters and critics alike could draw on his work to defend or criticize a wide variety of philosophical and political positions, including libertarianism, classical liberalism, social democracy, and socialism. Popper would have recoiled at the idea that he was espousing an ideology,although he would have had some sympathy for the idea of a tradition(understood appropriately). It is precisely this anti-ideologism in Popper's thought which, for many, brings him within the conservative tradition. Conservatism,in its various historical guises, has often been at least partly characterized by its rejection of ideology. Its defenders have often seen it as more as an *approach* to understanding society and political authority, rather than a set of principles with normative content. Conservatives have, on the whole, defined themselves as prag-matists,more interested in identifying and responding to social problems by appealing to the accumulated wisdom contained within existing traditions, institutions, and values, than in appealing to principles which define some specified and ideal future.

Put this way,we can already see some of the ways in which we might want to call Popper a conservative. However, conservatism has changed in the course of its history,and it is important to understand these changes if we are to grasp Popper's association with it. Until the late 1970s and early 1980s,Conservatism had been traditionally associated with the works of thinkers like Edmund Burke. It was primarily a theory about authority and political reform. Burke famously denounced the French revolution, and the Enlightenment principles upon which it was based,as a travesty,claiming that the Enlightenment represented merely a collection of vague mistakes about human equality, reason, and the importance of freedom, and the revolution was nothing more than a violent attack on proper authority and tradition (Burke, 1790/1986). The events in France did not, he thought, mark the heralding of a new era of *liberte*, *egalite*, and *fraternite* as its defenders suggested; rather it represented a catastrophic break with those traditions in which the rightful authority of political leaders and institutions resided, and a casting aside of the accumulated knowledge and experience which might provide guidance as to how institutions should be structured, what their role might be, and who should most appropriately hold power. Burke defended political *gradualism* over political *radicalism*. The French revolution embodied the Enlightenment idea that it was possible to overthrow traditional hierarchies of power and privilege through the application of reason. Consequently, he believed, the revolutionaries were too optimistic about the power of reason to affect radical change. They were possessed of the impetuous and irresponsible notion that a just, functioning social and political order could be built, by reason alone, from scratch; that it was possible to sweep away all that had gone before and build an entirely new political system in its place, as if the old one never even existed. Burke, on the contrary, was a fallibilist about reason. He argued that the power of reason was limited: reason could not predict with certainty the outcome of decisions, and it could not alone provide the foundation for a working political system. Reason thus needed to be informed by tradition: we can only know what our political system should look like and what it should do, by working out what has worked in the past, and building upon that knowledge.

Burke also criticized the idea (common among Enlightenment thinkers) that the right to wield power is linked to reason and that, therefore, all reasoning beings should be considered able to wield power responsibly and justly. Burke was an elitist, and believed in the natural inequality of human beings.

He disagreed with the defenders of the revolution that political power should be wielded by all individuals, and rejected, too, the idea that reason (disassociated from tradition) could reliably determine in advance where political power should lie. The principles arising out of reasoned reflection alone are too abstract and too indeterminate to yield sufficient answers to complicated questions about what should be done, and who should do it. Burke again believed that these questions were more concretely resolved by an appeal to tradition; history shows that some people are fit to rule and others are not. Burke thus believed that power should be located among those few—that is, the aristocracy—that history has shown to be endowed with the necessary qualities to wield it effectively, rather than indiscriminately doled out among the general population. This is a good example of conservative *pragmatism*. The idea is that politics should not be constrained by dogmatic ideological principle, but should instead be flexible enough to deal with the realities of each and every situation as it occurs in the real world: no one, not even the greatest philosophers the world has ever known, can work out from the comfort of their armchair who should govern and who should not; rather, these questions are best answered by working out who in any particular society has shown themselves most capable of wielding power effectively and responsibly and who has not. Burke's political views thus held three important implications. Firstly, a society characterized by class divisions and hierarchy rather than the liberal, Enlightenment vision of a society bound together by equals. Secondly, an elite system of representative government in which elected politicians govern on the basis of their own (superior) consciences and views, rather than the views of those who elected them. And thirdly, a conception of social and political change as necessarily gradualist, whereby social and political institutions develop over time, in increments, in response to developments in our knowledge of the world and in our experience of trying new things and applying those measures which work, and dropping those

Karl Popper

which do not.

We can, therefore, see many ways in which Burke influenced Popper, and many ways in which he did not. Popper, of course, had little time for the idea that political rule should reside in a historical elite, or that it should be justified by the fact that some people are simply fit to rule while others are not. He also had little time for the idea of class. One of the central evils of historicism for Popper, we must remember, was that it was only interested in individual human beings in so far as they were members of *groups*: Marx was not interested so much in *people* as he was in *classes*, Hegel was not interested in *individuals* but rather in *nations*, and Plato's vision of the republic was characterized by a radical and unwavering class system (based on *race*). Popper, as we have seen, believed in the Enlightenment values of equality before the law and freedom of the individual. He also held with Enlightenment thinkers the idea that groups like class, nation, and race were arbitrary human constructs with little or no moral resonance, and that the genuine community to which we should be committed is the community of all human beings throughout the world. He therefore rejected claims made by conservatives like Burke that in order to justify change we must work out what would be in the best interests of the 'nation' or the 'community' or the 'group'. Popper believed such claims were characteristic of the closed society, rooted in outdated and pernicious ideas of historical fate, and exhibited the deliberate subordination of the interests of individual human beings to the interests of the groups or institutions of which they are members. If social and political reform was to be justified, Popper believed, then it needed to be justified by, and to, those individuals who would bear the consequences of it. And because the ultimate and final consequences of any change cannot be predicted beforehand, any change must be cautious, responsible, and based on the best evidence we currently have. And if it turns out that a particular course of action was a mistake, it must be reversible or changeable. Again, changes, and the justifications for them, must be considered *falsifiable*.

Popper believed in the capacity of individual human beings to improve their social and political lives by identifying problems and seeking solutions to them. But he was, like Burke, less optimistic than many Enlightenment thinkers about the power of reason to provide all the necessary information to construct new and complex political systems from scratch. He therefore believed, like Burke, that social reforms should be made on the basis of all the accumulated knowledge that the world currently possesses, and new institutions should grow out of those which already exist. While in the scientific realm it is appropriate for radical critique to bring about constant upheavals and shifts in thought, in the political realm, where lives are at stake, it is necessary to go more slowly, and to implement and explore changes gradually in a piecemeal fashion. Thus, Popper agreed with Burke's rejection of the French revolution, and argued, with Burke, against what he saw as the arrogant notion that all institutions should be understood as products of conscious human will. On the contrary, he united with Burke (and, as we will see, with Hayek) in suggesting that many social institutions are not 'created' but rather grow 'as the undesigned results of human actions' (Popper, 1957/2005; 59). But unlike Burke, Popper did not believe that the organic nature of these institutions justified or legitimated them. He did not defend the legitimacy of aristocratic rule, as Burke and others did; indeed, his political philosophy represents a direct challenge to any such theory. For Popper, political legitimacy was secured by testing existing institutions in their ability to achieve the ends afforded to them by the people, and in their ability to secure the social and political conditions necessary to allow such testing and public endorsement to occur. The idea that particular institutions or individuals should be rendered legitimate for reasons of historical precedent, or because they have always done so, was not merely anathema to Popper, but wrong and unjust. For Burke, tradition provided the justification of existing social and political conditions, including existing power structures, sources of authority, inequalities, and laws. For Popper, however, it represented a useful accumulation of (contestable) knowledge about the world, upon which reason might operate in order to provide guidance for piecemeal social reform.

For all their disagreements about equality, class, elitism, and the appropriate sources of authority, Popper and Burke were thus united in their rejection of radical change, and in their rejection of what they saw as blind faith on the part of other thinkers in the capacity of human reason to predict the outcome of events and decisions. Burke's fallibilism about reason led him to reject the Enlightenment aim of erecting free-standing conceptions of political life which were ahistorical and divorced from all that had gone before it. Popper sympathized, but also pointed out the error in assuming that history alone could provide an alternative source of justification for political arrangements. Both thinkers thus acknowledged the limitations on reason, although each drew different conclusions from it: Burke used it to justify an appeal to historical tradition, while Popper used it to ground his epistemological commitment to criticism and critical rationalism. And both thinkers were more interested in outlining the ways in which societies might appropriately *change*, than in outlining a thoroughgoing vision of political life. Neither Popper nor Burke were conservative in the simplistic sense that they believed change was inherently bad. Change, for Popper in particular, was not bad; after all, Popper's central problem with Plato was that he aimed to suppress human creativity and freedom in order to 'arrest all change'. For Popper, *failing* to change social or political institutions which are inefficient or unfit for purpose, or failing to reform social and political norms which are unjust, might prove disastrous. The point for Popper (and for Burke) was to determine the appropriate grounds on which change might be justified, and to work out what *kind* of changes might be considered responsible. Although he shared with Burke a rejection of the kind of changes justified by utopianism, he embraced the capacity of individuals to implement piecemeal reforms based on correct rational analysis of existing and possible practices. Popper was specific about what kind of institutions and policies we should *not* pursue (i. e. historicist ones), but deliberately vague about what kind of policies and institutions we *should* adopt, precisely because such things could not be predicted in advance without collapsing into utopian ideologism. Given that we cannot know for sure the consequences of adopting particular policies or institutions (even our favourite ones), we should avoid stipulating them in too much detail at the outset, and secure instead the conditions in which we might work out what institutions and policies would best meet the identified needs of individual members of society at any one time.

Radical politics, radical philosophy

In the years following World War II, conservatism had begun to take on a broader meaning, and many writers — who had little or no relation to Burke's classical conservatism — were labelled conservative. This process of re-labelling was largely driven by their critics. The debate as to whether Popper was or was not a conservative, for example, has been largely driven by his critics, primarily from the Left, who have interpreted his commitment to individualism and a broadly market-oriented economy as representing establishment views, and exhibiting an unwillingness to challenge the ideological dominance of liberal capitalism. Although in many respects *The Open Society* represented a powerful statement of the social democratic consensus that had reigned in Europe since World War II, Popper was nevertheless lumped together with other 'cold war liberals' like Isaiah Berlin and Raymon Aron who defended liberal individualism and markets in the face of communism in the 1950s. Berlin in particular shared Popper's concerns about the encroaching threat of totalitarianism, and identified the same enemies to democracy as Popper; his inaugural lecture (and most famous essay) 'Two Concepts of Liberty' traced the philosophical roots of totalitarianism to those thinkers like Hegel and Rousseau who had defended a 'positive' account of liberty, and others essays including 'Historical Inevitability' bore all the hallmarks of Popper's work.

During the 1960s and 1970s, Popper was considered hopelessly out of date by many on the Left for remaining committed to a *politics* of individualism rather than embracing the radical politics of social movements and protest, and a *philosophy* of enlightenment through critique and rational reflection. His continued defence of liberalism, gradualism, and the futility of radical planning at a time when so many inside and outside the academy were turning towards a more 'progressive' collectivist politics premised upon radical social change put him in the conservative camp. Critics suggested that the many of the ills that beset British and American society, for example, were too important and ingrained in prevailing ideals to be tackled tentatively in a piecemeal fashion. The American civil rights movement and the campaign for women's rights, for example, both embodied a political will to tackle fundamental problems quickly, and to take direct action which bypassed the usual channels, which many believed were the source of the problem itself. Popper's 'institutional approach' and his appeal to political gradualism through piecemeal social engineering appeared reactionary and seemed to set him against those who fought for important rights and equalities. His claim that responsible change was tentative and gradual, the implicit assumption that people should not step outside of conventional democratic debates in the interests of affecting change, and that people should work with existing institutions rather than against them seemed to suggest that campaigners for civil rights and others causes were making a mistake in speaking out against the status quo, and should raise their concerns more reasonably, through those channels which had shown themselves to be effective. Similarly, his claim that all knowledge claims are necessarily conjectural struck many as a capitulation to existing social and political injustices; while the certainty of some claims may well be questionable, they conceded, can we not know for certain that, for example, women are equal to men? Or that black people should not be denied the rights possessed by white people? Or that gays and lesbians should not be intimidated or forced to hide their sexuality for fear of ostracism or abuse?

Central to the radicalism which characterized politics at that time was a sense that, for all their claims to be on the side of all individuals equally, traditional liberal democratic political institutions and mechanisms prioritized the voices (and hence, the interests) of mainstream majorities over those of minority groups. That is, behind the liberal rhetoric of equal treatment, freedom, individuality, and the capacity of all individuals to participate fully and meaningfully in the political process, traditional liberal democratic politics merely enshrined what Mill called the 'tyranny of the majority'. Many felt that more needed to be done for those gays and lesbians, black people, immigrants, and others whose interests were being systematically over-ridden by the majority. Their answer was a new politics of identity, of social movements and protest; a recognition of the fact that if members of marginalized groups spoke together as one voice, that voice would ring louder than if they all spoke separately. The answer, then, was a rejection of traditional individualism, and of the conventional liberal concern for all those things which *distinguished* individuals from one another, in place of a new emphasis on those things which *united* people, and a rejection of traditional deference to existing social and political institutions, in place of a radical anti-establishment counter-culture. In place of a rather abstract, Enlightenment conception of politics rooted in individuality and reason, the new activism emphasized shared identity, community, and the idea that persons could be bound together by more than a commitment to liberal principles and critical rationalism: things like shared culture, or race, or

114

ethnicity, or gender. Liberals had traditionally considered such distinctions to be pernicious and irrelevant: something to be transcended. Popper agreed. But the new activism suggested that they could be sources of great social and political unity and strength and, in the context of majoritarian liberal democratic states, a means of bringing about social changes which mere individualism could never do.

Many critics therefore suggested that for all Popper's high-sounding talk in *The Open Society* of equality and the importance of open debate among political equals, his stubborn commitment to individualist politics and his rejection of the importance of social groups (as a throwback to the tribal politics of the closed society) represented little more than a description of the problem itself: a political system which prided itself on breaking down the barriers which separated people but which, in practice, was exclusionary and elitist, by placing de facto power in the hands of the majority. This problem was only exacerbated by the vision of democratic deliberation upon which Popper built his theory. Premised as it was on his wider epistemological claims that knowledge grew out the dynamic process of conjecture and refutation, critique, and trial and error, many wondered how such a political vision could ever hope to yield the kind of agreement and consensus necessary in politics. What Popper seemed to envisage was a society which evolved slowly on the basis of a tradition of rationalist critique, but which was characterized by ceaseless debate, refutation, conjecture, the proposal of bold political initiatives, and their subsequent falsification. But, critics pointed out, there is more to democracy than talking. For a democracy to function effectively, it needs to be able to make decisions, to act, on the basis of reasonable agreements among citizens, lawmakers, and politicians. The concern—which we find in its most radical form in thinkers like Carl Schmitt-is that democratic debate becomes disassociated from democratic decision—making, and that while the people discuss issues amongst themselves, the most important decisions are in fact

made behind the scenes(Schmitt, 1923/1988,and 1927/2006).
Popper's idealized conception of a deliberative democracy was
thus seen by many socialists and progressives sympathetic to
collectivism and the politics of identity to both *exclude*
marginalized groups from the democratic process and to
disassociate democratic debate from the process of political
decision-making. Thus it was seen by these people as a de facto
argument for elite rule,and a blueprint for conservatism.

   Moreover,Popper's unwavering commitment to the'narratives' of individual freedom and critical rationalism seemed
naïve and simplistic to many on the Left who were increasingly
falling under the influence of European critical theorists like
Adorno, Horkheimer, Habermas, and Marcuse, and of poststructuralists like Foucault. Popper's philosophical approach
was squarely in the analytical tradition of Russell and Ayer;
his critique of Marx was thus an analytical one, in which he
tried to replace Marx's universalism with a universalism of his
own, a liberal universalism rooted in individual freedom.
Although very different in other ways, postmodernists,
poststructuralists, and the critical theorists of the Frankfurt
School were broadly united in their rejection of such an
enterprise as grounded in meta-narratives of modernity which
were no longer tenable,and appealing to concepts,ideals,and
values which had lost their meaning. Critical theorists like
Habermas accused Popper of being merely a positivist: his
critique of Marx,and his vision of the open society—indeed,his
entire approach to philosophy—was seen as merely an
expression of bourgeois ideology, too bound up in its own
partial understanding of the world to capture anything
important about it, and too quick to reach for 'universal'
principles which were not universal at all(Habermas, 1976).
For his radical critics, Popper's broad claim that it was
possible for individuals to identify and resolve problems in so
many different realms of human experience in the same way,
according to the same process and method, was naïve, and
placed far too much faith in the ability of one conception of

reasoning to reveal all the hidden and significant intricacies of the natural world, social life, politics, power, freedom, and everything else. Hence, they believed that his approach actually *limited* the growth of knowledge; it missed entirely the fact that the concepts we use to understand ourselves and the world, the language we use to communicate with one another and to express these concepts are problematic, ambiguous, indeterminate, and increasingly out of kilter with the world in which they were used.

Most importantly of all, for the critical theorists and poststructuralists, Popper's argument failed to say anything about the most important thing about politics: the nature and location of power, and the explicit and implicit ways in which power is exercised in liberal democratic states. While Popper accepted Marx's dictum that 'it is not the consciousness of men that determines their being, but, on the contrary, their social being that determines their consciousness' undermined psychologism, he refused to draw the same conclusion from it as the Marxists. For the critical theorists and poststructuralists, Marx's claim that one's social, political, and economic environment can shape one's thoughts, interests, and understandings reveals the important ways in which one's social environment can represent a source of coercion. Having rejected this claim as the 'conspiracy theory' of society, Popper was able to discuss power in the traditional liberal manner, namely, as something that was possessed by the state, and which needed to be limited or constrained by laws and policies rooted in a respect for individual rights. But the critical theorists and poststructuralists argued that Marx's claims could not be so easily dismissed, and that, once we understand that one's interests and thoughts might be shaped (sometimes subtly, sometimes implicitly, in ways that we may or may not even notice) by society *itself*, rather than by particular *people* or *institutions*, then liberal arguments about individual freedom and rights simply miss the point. The aim of politics should not be merely to work out how — and to what extent — state power should be limited, and hence, what constitutional and legal safeguards need to be in place in order to protect the individual from it(as it is in liberal theory), but rather, to reveal the many ways in which power is exerted through those social and political norms which regulate our behaviour on a daily basis, to reveal who has the power to shape and determine these social norms, and suggest ways in which these dominant and insidious power structures might be broken down.

This key insight is one shared by many thinkers who do not otherwise belong among the poststructuralist or critical theory camp. Feminists in particular have criticized, and continue to criticize, the kind of Enlightenment reasoning implicit in liberal theory, and which are evident in Popper's ideas about society and the growth of knowledge. Feminists including, most recently, Seyla Benhabib, Nancy Fraser, Nancy Hirschmann, and Iris Marion Young have drawn upon poststructuralist insights in their work in order to suggest that the traditional liberal conception of power(as something which is embodied in, and can be regulated in, the public sphere)cannot explain the myriad ways in which women in particular are controlled and oppressed in the private realm, and hence, cannot form the basis of an egalitarian response to patriarchy(Benhabib, 1992; Fraser, 1997; Hirschmann, 2003; Young, 1990). The principle source of women's oppression, many feminists have argued, is not the state, but the implicit power structures embodied in the norms which regulate those relationships which liberals take to be private: the relationships between husbands and wives, for example, or mothers and children, or the norms embodied in religious or other communities of which women are members. Popper was, as we have seen, deeply sceptical of the idea that individuals are 'controlled' by their social and political circumstances in the sense that their choices(and their capacity for choice itself)are somehow shaped or thwarted by society. But it is not enough to say that such claims represent a conspiracy theory promulgated by people who use pretentious words and long, impenetrable sentences(as he did). Popper's theory provides little help in addressing this issue, other than to say that we should understand all individuals as equals regardless of gender, and discuss the problem. It says nothing about the deeper claim that many women will feel unable to engage in public deliberation, or in anything else, as free and equal individuals as a result of power structures which are invisible in Popper's philosophy, but which nevertheless serve to undermine the freedom of women to make genuinely free choices about their lives. Popper's rejection of what he calls the conspiracy theory of power in this and other contexts is, for many theorists, simply further evidence of his unwillingness to recognize the importance of groups, and the norms which characterize them.

In the face of such a radical and fundamental critique of modern society, of liberalism, and of the way in which we understand our concepts and language, then, Popper's belief that social problems can be overcome by asserting individual freedom and open dialogue seemed conservative indeed. Popper argued that change could not be radical, and that 'social experiments' should not be conducted at the level of society as a whole; he argued that we should adopt a methodologically individualist and nominalist approach to understanding society, rather than a holistic, collectivist, and organic one, given the inability of either reason or history to provide certain guides to the future development of humankind. But poststructuralists and critical theorists suggested that it is possible to be a fallibilist about reason while at the same time adopting a radical approach to understanding and resolving social and political problems. Popper argued that social scientists needed to choose between two opposing approaches to understanding society: one which acknowledged the limited capacity of reason to reveal certain knowledge about the long-term future by adopting a piecemeal approach to reforming society (and which presupposed the central importance of critique and a broadly liberal conception of individual freedom), and one which sought to understand societies in a holistic, collectivist way, and which presupposed the capacity of historical laws to determine the future development of humankind. Postmodernists, poststructuralists and critical theorists on the other hand, appeared to provide a third approach: one which shared the historicist commitment to holism and collectivism, and shared too Popper's scepticism about the power of reason to produce certain knowledge of the future. A common theme in critical theory and poststructuralism was and is that only by radically deconstructing the language and concepts embodied in any social and political system will we understand the ways in which power is exercised within it, and the ends to which this power is exerted. Rather than stand aloof from society and its most insidious problems, then, we should seek a deep understanding of these things, and of the social whole, in order to reveal those injustices which afflict the lives of individuals, shape their experiences, and yet often remain hidden. *Contra* Popper, the postmodernists, post-structuralists, and the critical theorists argued, in their own ways, that social and political science is necessarily and unavoidably radical; understanding society involves a radical engagement with its institutions, its history, and the people who compose it, and resolving its problems requires acting upon what we find. And what we find will not always respond well to piecemeal, tentative reform, but must be resolved instead by initiatives which have far-reaching, and possibly revolutionary, implications.

Popper's response to these criticisms — in as much as he responded at all — was not to give ground, but to further entrench his commitment to individualism and democratic dialogue. His political writings following *The Open Society* were characterized by a dogged support of liberal democratic virtues over those of other systems; liberal democracy is, he said, 'by far the best society which has come into existence during the course of human history... the best there has ever been—the best, at least, of which we have any historical knowledge' (Popper, 1963/2007b, 496). In response to those which suggested that his vision of the open society was too abstract and empty of the kind of substantive values which could unite the citizenry, Popper increasingly characterized critical rationalism as a substantive *tradition* to which people could subscribe without falling into tribalism (Popper, 1963/2007b). And in his 1965 essay 'The Myth of the Framework', Popper railed against the relativism at the heart of poststructuralism and critical theory. A few years earlier, in his contribution to what has become known as the Positivism Debate, Popper poured withering scorn on the theorists of the Frankfurt School. In response to Habermas's charge that Popper was merely a positivist, 'bound by his methodology to defend the status-quo' (Popper, 1994a; 68), Popper pointed out—not unreasonably—that he had devoted his career to refuting the positivism characteristic of the Vienna Circle. He also described the influence of the Frankfurt School as 'irrationalist and 'intelligence-destroying', and claimed that he was unable to 'take their methodology (whatever that might mean) seriously from either an intellectual or scholarly point of view' (Popper, 1994a; 66). They were, he said, like Hegel, caught up in a 'cult of incomprehensibility' which was both self-indulgent and irresponsible. Habermas, for example, did 'not know how to put things simply, clearly, and modestly', indeed, Popper felt, most of what he had to say was either trivial or mistaken. Adorno, he felt, had 'nothing whatever to say' and defended a philosophical vision that was merely 'mumbo-jumbo' (Popper, 1994a; 78). Similarly, Horkheimer's work was, he believed, 'empty', 'devoid of content', 'uninteresting', and 'merely a vague and unoriginal form of Marxian historicism' (Popper, 1994a; 79-80).

The charge of incomprehensibility was not, for Popper, superficial. Popper, we must recall, believed that the growth of knowledge depended upon critical debate across disciplines; hence, it was, he thought, the *moral responsibility* of anyone committed to the growth of knowledge to aim for accessibility and clarity in their work, so as to avoid being understandable only by a small group of like-minded intellectuals. In deliberately making their theories as complex as possible, Popper believed, the critical theorists and poststructuralists were doing little more than feed their own vanity and arrogance, and placing limits on the pursuit of knowledge. 'The total content of the so-called Critical Theory of the Frankfurt School,'Popper claimed,was thus: 'Let the present generation suffer and perish for all we can do is to expose the ugliness of the world we live in, and to heap insults on our oppressors,the"bourgeoisie"'(Popper, 1994a;84). Popper,on the other hand,argued for the possibility of reforming society for the better. 'We can do much more *now* to relieve suffering and, most importantly, to increase freedom', he said. 'We must not wait for a goddess of history or a goddess of revolution to introduce better conditions into human affairs' (Popper, 1994a; 80) as the critical theorists counselled. To emphasize the inability of human beings to understand the world in the face of incommensurable linguistic and cultural 'frameworks', and to systematically undermine our ability to change the world in which we live was,for Popper,a betrayal and a mistake,and belonged to the very same tradition of arrogant philosophical elitism that he identified,and rejected,in the coffee houses of his native Vienna. For critical theorists like Adorno, Horkheimer and Marcuse, for whom the deeply problematic nature of apparently simple concepts was precisely the point,Popper's response fell wide of the mark.

Popper and the rise of the New Right

By the late 1970s and early 1980s,the meaning of conservatism in public and academic discourse shifted still further. Popper claimed that one of his principal aims in writing *The Open Society* was to unite the trade unions and socialists behind the idea that totalitarianism had replaced capitalism as the main threat facing the world. By the 1980s,however,Popper's ideas would provide a rallying point for a very different political agenda. For many British and American liberals and conservatives during the 1960s and 1970s, the enemy was not merely the totalitarianism which had grown overseas, or domestic radicalism and counter-cultural movements, but the *collectivism* which had infiltrated the politics of Europe and the US. The roots of this collectivism lay in the broadly social democratic consensus established in the years immediately following World War II, many elements of which were articulated in *The Open Society*. Post-war Europe was focused on rebuilding the shattered societies and economies of European states. The state took a much more central role in the redistribution of wealth and the provision of welfare than it had previously done under liberalism, and there was a general sense among politicians and the wider society that the politics of the time called for a strengthening of unity and solidarity over individualism and competition.

Many of the ideas which characterized this consensus remained, and were strengthened, in the years between 1945 and the late 1970s. In Britain, for example, successive governments remained hospitable to a broadly social democratic programme emphasizing the public provision of welfare, state intervention in the economy, and the extension of the state into areas such as housing and the ownership of utilities. The drive to create jobs and to rebuild industry resulted in a strengthened labour movement represented by increasingly powerful trade unions. Increasingly dominant, then, was the idea that it was in some sense a responsibility of government to promote social unity through state action, to take seriously those things which bound people together(into a labour movement, into a class, into a people), and that it was possible for the state to engage in planned reform of society. For liberals, committed to free markets, individualism, and limited politics, and conservatives, committed to pragmatism, tradition, and a profound anti-socialism (or, more accurately, a profound anti-radicalism which seemed at odds with socialism), the continued move towards collectivism was a cause for concern.

Consequently, despite their many differences, liberals and conservatives increasingly found themselves speaking as one voice against what they saw as the twin evils of collectivism and radical (i. e. ideological) social engineering. Fears that the state was engaging in unrealistic social engineering, and that politics was becoming too dominated by powerful groups like the trade unions reached a crisis point in the late 1970s. At that time—a period of considerable social, political, and economic unrest—many liberals and conservatives thought that things had gone far enough. The state was seen to have over-stepped its bounds, it had become too unwieldy to make good on its reform plans; it had spread itself too thin—sought to get involved in too many aspects of peoples' lives—and, as a consequence, had acceded too much power to the trade unions and other sectional interest groups. Liberals and conservatives thus united under the banner of the 'New Right', and argued for an alternative: a return to political pragmatism, limited politics, individualism, and the freeing of the individual from the burden of a meddle-some, intrusive state. And they did so by turning to the economic and political theory of Popper's long-time friend and colleague Friedrich von Hayek.

Hayek, as we saw in Chapter 1, was a great admirer of Popper's work, and was instrumental in the publication of *The Open Society* and Popper's move to the LSE in 1946. Popper, in return, claimed that Hayek 'saved his life', and described him as a father-figure and his intellectual superior. Hayek was also the intellectual inspiration behind the New Right, and has been widely credited as the single most important figure in the resurgence of *laissez-faire* economics in Britain and the US. Popper and Hayek shared more than merely friendship: they were contemporaries, driven by a united concern for individual freedom and a rejection of tyranny, and their ideas were rooted in the same motivating philosophy: that 'man does not and cannot know everything, and when he acts as if he does, disaster follows' (Blundell, 1999: 12). Both Popper and Hayek were united in their rejection of the kind of radical change which characterized the French revolution, and were united with Burke in their support of a particular brand of philosophical rationalism in its place. Both rejected the overly optimistic view (typified by thinkers like Bacon) that reason—disassociated from tradition and theory—was capable of revealing certain and fundamental truths about the world, and hence, both united with Burke in his broad claim that a functioning political system could not be dreamed up by reason alone. '[T]he pessimists who feared the decline of authority and tradition were wise men', Popper argued. 'The terrible experience of the great religious wars, and of the French and Russian revolutions, prove their wisdom and foresight' (Popper, 1963/2007b; 503).

Popper, Burke, and Hayek were thus united with other thinkers like Bernard Mandeville, Adam Smith, and David Hume in adopting what Hayek called an 'evolutionary rationalism' over a 'constructivist' one; a form of rationalism, which acknowledged the value of accumulated wisdom and tradition in reasoning about social and political reform, rather than ahistorical, abstract theorizing (Mandeville, 1714; Smith, 1789; Hume, 1748). While constructivist rationalists-including such diverse figures as Descartes, Rousseau, and Condorcet in France, to Bacon, Hobbes, and defenders of the French revolution like Godwin, Paine, and Jefferson in Britain and America-emphasized the ability of humankind to 'sweep away existing institutions and practices and propose the adoption of completely new, untried plans', evolutionary rationalists counselled caution (Gamble, 1996; 32). An important task of philosophy, for Hayek and for Popper, was to discover the limits of reason and to determine the appropriate means of structuring and reforming society in circumstances of epistemological uncertainty. Importantly, then, it was not to replace *rationalism* with *traditionalism* (that is, to replace the uncritical optimism about reason with an unquestioned appreciation of historical tradition, as thinkers like Oakeshott argued), but rather to construct an idea of rationalism which was attentive to the wisdom embodied in tradition, but which allowed for the fact that such wisdom could not be certain or unequivocal. Hayek called this *evolutionary* rationalism, Popper called it *critical* rationalism, and it is what many believe puts them both in the same conservative tradition as Burke. Such an approach enshrined Popper's fundamental claim (discussed in the previous chapter), that knowledge often begins in *myths* and *traditions* as much as it begins in reason and, hence, it

> makes room... for a reconciliation between rationalism and traditionalism. The critical rationalist can appreciate traditions, for although he believes in truth, he does not believe that he himself is in certain possession of it. He can appreciate every step, every approach towards it, as valuable, indeed as invaluable; and he can see that our traditions often help to encourage such steps, and also that without an intellectual tradition the individual could hardly take a single step towards the truth. It is thus the critical approach to rationalism, the compromise between rationalism and scepticism, which for a long time has been the basis of the British middle way: the respect for traditions, and at the same time, the recognition of the need to reform them. (Popper, 1963/2007b; 505)

For Hayek, as for Popper, the inability of reason to provide certainty, and hence, to be capable of predicting with precision the future consequences of any particular action or decision, underwrote a political programme which rejected not only radical change but also long-term economic and social planning, in favour of piecemeal progress through trial and error.

While the similarities between the two authors - and with the New Right in general-are clear, it is more difficult to determine exactly how *influential* Popper's work was to Hayek's critique of radicalism, and social, economic, and political planning. In 1982, Hayek claimed that 'ever since

[Popper's] *Logik der Forschung* first came out in 1934, I have been a complete adherent to his general philosophy of methodology' (Weimer & Palermo, 1982; 323). He also believed that Popper's terminology would appeal to Leftists who were deaf to Hayek himself. Milton Friedman, another leading light of the New Right, suggested the adoption of Popper's theory of falsification into economics. Hayek, like Popper, argued against the tendency to split the search for knowledge into exclusive disciplines; like Popper, Hayek criticized conservatives for down playing the pursuit of knowledge (in case they discovered something that held implications that they did not like); and, like Popper, Hayek criticized conservatives and others for supporting a nationalist approach to economic policy, rather than an internationalist, cosmopolitan one. Both Hayek and Popper refused to be pigeonholed as supporters of any particular ideology. Neither thinker believed that they were in the business of peddling a particular ideological position, rather, they both felt that their ideas cut across ideologies—*transcended* them—by presenting a series of claims about knowledge and freedom which were *descriptive* rather than *normative*. Neither Hayek nor Popper claimed to be presenting a 'liberal' understanding of knowledge, rather, they claimed to be merely describing how knowledge actually does in fact grow, what can be said about it, and what we one might appropriately do with it. Having done so, both converged on liberalism (broadly conceived) as the doctrine most able to function in circumstances of epistemological uncertainty.

Nevertheless, Popper and Hayek disagreed over what liberalism entailed. In particular they disagreed over the appropriate extent of state intervention in social and economic matters. Popper's general political vision, after all, was social democratic. He was highly critical of what he called 'unrestrained capitalism', calling it 'inhumane' and 'unjust'. In *The Open Society*, for example, Popper explicitly stated that his view had 'nothing to do with the policy of strict non-intervention (often, but not quite accurately called *laissez-faire*). Liberalism and state interference are not opposed to on another' (Popper, 1945/ 2006a; 117). Popper argued strongly that unregulated free markets and *laissez-faire* economics violated, rather than protected, individual freedom by failing to protect the economically weak from the economically strong. 'Even if the state protects its citizens from being bullied by physical violence (as it does, in principle, under the system of unrestrained capitalism),' Popper stated, 'it may defeat our ends by its failure to protect them from the misuse of economic power... [U]nlimited economic freedom can be just as self-defeating as unlimited physical freedom, and economic power may be nearly as dangerous as physical violence' (Popper, 1945/2006b; 135).

 Consequently, he argued, the 'principle of non-intervention, of an unrestrained economic system [of the kind advocated by Hayek and Friedman], has to be given up. If we wish freedom to be safeguarded, then we must demand that the policy of unlimited economic freedom be replaced by the planned economic intervention of the state. We must demand that unrestrained capitalism give way to an economic intervention-ism' (Popper, 1945/2006b; 135-6). Such a project was entirely consistent with his rejection of utopianism, or so he thought. We can, for example, 'develop a rational political programme for the protection of the economically weak' without collapsing into utopianism. 'We can', for example, 'make laws to limit exploitation. We can limit the working day... [W]e can insure the workers(or better, all citizens)against disability, unemploy-ment, and old age. In this way, we can make impossible such forms of exploitation as are based on the helpless economic position of a worker who must yield to anything in order not to starve... Economic power ', he went on, ' must not be permitted to dominate political power; if necessary, it must be fought and brought under control by political power'(Popper, 1945/2006b; 136-7). Similarly, he argued, it is also ' the responsibility of the state to see that its citizens are given an education enabling them to participate in the life of the community, and to make use of any opportunity to develop their interests and gifts' irrespective of their ability to pay (Popper,1945/2006a;139). 'A certain amount of state control in education... is necessary, if the young are to be protected from a neglect which would make them unable to defend their freedom, and the state should see that all educational facilities are available to everybody'(Popper,1945/2006a;117-18).

The fact that intervention'will tend to increase the power of the state... is extremely dangerous... [but] not a decisive argument against it', Popper believed (Popper, 1945/2006b; 141). Intervention must be accompanied by a strengthening of democratic institutions, and it should always be informed by his negative utilitarianism, that is, in the pursuit of fighting 'concrete evils rather than to establish some ideal good. State intervention should be limited to what is really necessary for the protection of individual freedom ', namely, the establishment and reform of social and political institutions which encourage free debate among citizens, and which are capable of enacting piecemeal reforms based upon past experience and knowledge. Hayek disagreed, arguing that epistemological uncertainty invalidated *any* attempt at social, economic, or political planning.

Popper's politics cannot be understood to be wholly conservative, then, but rather as containing elements which influenced, and were influenced by, conservatism. Similarly, his views can obviously be seen to have influenced libertarian thinkers, but they do not fit easily in this tradition either. Libertarianism has been particularly influential in the US, through thinkers like Ayn Rand and Robert Nozick, who argued for a reduction in the size and scope of the state in order to establish for all individuals as significant a realm of private choice as possible, free from coercion, and a general support for individualism, the minimal state, and private property rights (Nozick,1974;Rand, 1943). But also powerful in libertarianism are the themes of experimentation and risk; of change and, in particular, the capacity of free individuals to exert their will on society in ways which bring about new and innovative ways of doing things which are often profound and radical breaks with the past. These themes seem controversial with regard to both Popper and Hayek, both of whom were sceptical of radical change and risky social reforms. Indeed, Hayek was sceptical of American libertarianism for precisely this reason: that it seemed to be rooted in a constructivist account of rationality rather than an evolutionary one, and as such fell into the same trap of exalting reason over tradition as the Russian and French revolutionaries (Gamble, 1996). Popper shared this concern and, like Hayek, also sought to defend the importance of tradition in politics and society: libertarianism seemed wedded to a vision of society as united only by the self-interest of its individual members. Popper—perhaps in partial response to his radical critics—increasingly emphasized the role of tradition in uniting individuals together. Also, it is crucially important to distinguish between Popper's methodology (his epistemology) and the political/practical outcomes yielded by this epistemology. His epistemology was very radical, and appeared in line with a broadly libertarian view. The development of human knowledge in the realms of science as well as politics emerges out of the often 'reckless' pursuit of truth by individual human beings who, on the whole, attempt to impose order on the world and their lives by trying to explain them. Ideas rise and fall in an ongoing process of critique and rational reflection, rather like companies in a market economy: 'Science, and more specifically scientific progress', he argued, 'are the results not of isolated efforts, but of the free competition of thought' (Popper, 1957/ 2005; 143). Theories that are able to withstand the rigors of intellectual competition remain candidates for the truth, those which are not, are abandoned. However, the practical outcome of this dynamic process is, in fact, political gradualism. Societies should develop slowly, as a consequence of many piecemeal challenges and interventions made by individual human beings all waking their own way in the world, against a background of existing knowledge and tradition. He believed that people should be free to make their own mistakes and take risks-indeed, the growth of knowledge depends upon such people. But he did not believe that the state should justify social reforms on such a basis. Social and political reform needed to be tentative, gradual, and risk-averse, not radical and risky.

A final word on ideologies

It is ironic that Popper's political vision, articulated in *The Open Society* and various later essays, represented a powerful defence of the social democratic consensus that had reigned in Europe from 1945 to the 1970s, yet was used by people who called themselves libertarians, liberals, and conservatives to destroy precisely that consensus. Despite arguing for the role of limited social planning and state intervention in the economy, Popper's epistemology, filtered through Hayek and Friedman, provided the philosophical backdrop to the rise of the New Right and the destruction of political collectivism. He advocated the redistribution of wealth and the public provision of welfare in order to protect the economically weak from the economically strong, but his ideas were widely praised by world leaders including Margaret Thatcher(who described him as her favourite philosopher), and entrepreneurs like George Soros, who has amassed a personal fortune by investing on global markets according to Popperian principles. He was, for much of his life, a socialist; he continued to respect Marx, and shared his rejection of *laissez-faire* economics, but rejected the left-wing politics of the 1960s and 1970s, and paved the way for its destruction in the 1980s. He joined many Enlightenment thinkers in celebrating the capacity of human beings to change the world for the better, but joined with critics of the Enlightenment in rejecting the notion(found among liberal and socialist revolutionaries) that reason could justify radical change.

Popper's views do not fit easily in any particular ideological camp, and so we should not try to make them. Popper himself had little time for labels, and did not engage much in debates about which camp he most appropriately belonged to. His anti-essentialism meant that he had little interest in engaging in discussions about the meaning of terms like 'conservatism' or 'libertarianism', and his antipathy towards breaking up the pursuit of knowledge into distinct disciplines or methodologies meant that he cared little for the activity of demarcating boundaries among ideas such that they form distinct ideological positions. There is some sense in this. The desire by critics and supporters to squash complex thinkers like Popper into fixed ideological positions inevitably leads to a simplification and misrepresentation of their views; people who choose to call themselves conservatives or liberals or libertarians may wish to claim Popper for themselves, but in doing so they would have to conveniently forget those often pivotal aspects of his theory which were inconsistent with their wider ideals. Popper was rightly sceptical of such an endeavour, and of the stifling consequences it had on the growth of knowledge. We might do well, when thinking about the Popper's rightful place in the history of political thought, to adopt a Popperian approach: to abandon the search for the ideological 'essence' of Popper's views(and the attendant desire to label him one thing or the other), and instead to engage with his ideas, and to attempt to defeat them through reasonable and rigorous deliberation and debate.

4
The Contemporary Relevance of Popper's Philosophy

In many ways, reading Popper's work is like peering through a window into another time: a time in which liberal democracy was under threat from totalitarianism, and individual freedom, equality, and rights were being threatened by the primal, collectivist politics of Nazism, Stalinism, and Fascism; a time in which the cosmopolitan quest for the international unity of all peoples under principles of reason and progress was being challenged by the strident forces of nationalism and war. As a philosophical and political work, *The Open Society* is very much a child of its time: animated by a strident belief in individual freedom over tyranny, and informed by a commitment to the Enlightenment values of science, logic, and reason over what Popper saw as the mysticism and exclusionary implications of philosophical idealism. And, together with *The Poverty of Historicism*, it represents a statement about society-and the *study* of society-which is rooted in a particular historical moment, but no particular political ideology.

Popper's claims concerning epistemology, society, and politics are not merely historical artefacts, however. They represent genuine contributions to social and political thought which possess an enduring significance. Popper's political philosophy represents a bold and controversial vision of what politics can and cannot achieve, and what politicians, philosophers, and social scientists should or should not do. Nevertheless, Popper's work is often neglected among contemporary political theorists, and Anglo-American political theorists in particular. It is entirely possible, and perhaps normal, for a student to gain a degree in politics without having ever studied Popper. Undergraduate courses in political theory rarely have a week on Popper, and Popper's political works are often neglected by more mainstream philosophers who-if they are interested in Popper at all-are more concerned with his theories about the philosophy of the natural sciences. One possible reason for this, perhaps, is the view that Popper's political works have been eclipsed by political events. Popper began work on *The Open Society and Its Enemies* in 1938, when Hitler invaded his native Austria. At that time, fascism were more than merely interesting philosophical puzzles to investigate-they were dominant forces in world politics, united by a commitment to centralize power in an elite class of leaders who claimed to know the interests of the people better than the people themselves ever could, and committed to using this knowledge as a justification for subjugation and tyranny. Following the defeat of Nazism in World War Ⅱ, and, later, the dissolution of the Soviet Union in the 1980s and early 1990s, these threats all but disappeared from the world stage, leaving many to feel, perhaps, that Popper's dissection of their motivating philosophies was redundant.

If this *is* the reason for Popper's neglect among contemporary political philosophers, then it is a mistake. The redundancy of Popper's critique of totalitarianism and historicism in politics is overstated, and his rejection of the closed society continues to hold important implications for contemporary politics. For while Nazism and Fascism are indeed in retreat, global politics is still cursed with many of the evils that Popper railed against. The tribalism characteristic of the closed society is still all too evident in the ethnic and nationalist conflicts which continue to blight so much of the world, and in the increased politicization and radicalization of religion in so many countries, including those governed by liberal democratic institutions. Despite increasingly popular claims among many social and political scientists, practitioners and commentators about the erosion of national and ethnic identifies in the wake of globalization, increased migration, and the spread of capitalist markets, and of the decline in the political significance of the nation state as a consequence of the rise in supranational institutions like the IMF, the World Bank, the EU, and the UN, the willingness among many people to cling to cultural or religious or ethnic identities, to fight for them, and to kill in their name seems as strong as ever. Similarly, the willingness of undemocratic leaders and regimes to use the institutions of the state to brutalize their citizens, to tyrannize them, and to deny them basic freedoms, all in the name of some greater good, represents an enduring source of misery for hundreds of thousands of people throughout the world. The open society still has enemies. They may be different to the ones that Popper wrote about, but Popper's critique of fascism and totalitarianism applies as directly and coherently to the newer, more obvious evils of religious fanaticism, authoritarianism, and nationalism that we see around us today.

Popper's political philosophy, above all else, represents a vindication of liberalism, democracy, and reason over tribalism, authoritarianism, and tyranny; it represents a strident defence of the right of each and every individual in the world not to live in fear of those who govern them, to be involved in decisions about the future direction of their political community, and to live a life that they feel to be worthwhile, freely and without unjust constraint. It therefore represents a defence of cosmopolitan individualism in the face of those in or outside of the academy who argue that political institutions should affirm or give special recognition to claims arising out of religious, ethnic, cultural, or nationalist identity. Such claims have become increasingly popular not just among certain political regimes, but among political philosophers too. The question of how states (and citizens) should respond to cultural, ethnic, and religious diversity has become incredibly important in recent years, especially among decision-makers in the US, and in European states like Britain and the Netherlands. The extent to which minority groups should be required to assimilate to the prevailing values of the majority, and how liberal states should manage the balance between respecting minority identities while encouraging common values in all individuals regardless of their particular beliefs and ideals remains incredibly vexed and controversial, and a source of deep disagreement among policy-makers, parliamentarians, and practitioners. Contemporary political philosophy, too, has been dominated in recent years by a resurgent interest among political theorists (both within and outside the liberal tradition) in the importance of particularist identities within liberal democratic politics. Certain liberal theorists like Will Kymlicka (1997) and Joseph Raz (1986; 1996), liberal nationalists like David Miller (1995) and Yael Tamir(1993), communitarians like Michael Sandel (1982) and Alasdair MacIntyre(1996), difference theorists like Iris Marion Young (1990) and Nancy Fraser (1997), and many others besides have argued for the philosophical, moral, and normative significance of communities and groups in liberal democratic politics, and have, in their own ways, criticized what they see as the naive and abstract individualism at the heart of traditional liberal political thought. Popper's social and political philosophy represents a coherent and enduring counter-argument to such a move, but it is one which is hardly ever mentioned or discussed. Some theorists have suggested that the establishment of a common politics among diverse groups is impossible because many of the values embodied in these groups will be incommensurable with one another and, hence, there will be no common ground over which different groups can communicate(e. g. Gray, 2000). Others have argued for a form of political pluralism which acknowledges the sometimes incompatible needs of different groups (e. g. Parekh, 2005). Popper shares with contemporary political liberals like John Rawls (1993) and Charles Larmore (2008), and difference theorists like Iris Marion Young (2000), the idea that it is possible and necessary for the members of diverse societies to deliberate with one another in such a way as to find common solutions to political problems. Popper diverges with many of them, however, in suggesting that parties to any such dialogue must view their religious and cultural beliefs not as truth claims, but as hypotheses or conjectures, and hence, fitting subjects for debate and criticism. Critics have suggested that in requiring members of different cultural and religious groups to submit to his view as to the nature of truth, Popper's approach to negotiating a settlement between diverse cultural and religious groups causes as many problems as it solves; it is too demanding in the sense that it requires members of different groups to understand their values, and their relationship to them, in a particular and controversial way. But in this, Popper seems no less controversial or demanding than many other liberals whose work is considered central to contemporary debates. Rawls and Larmore, for example, try to establish a model of deliberative reasoning which avoids the requirement that people adopt a particular metaphysical position towards their own beliefs, only to require parties to the dialogue to present their claims in certain controversial ways, in order that they might be accepted by people with very different views about the world. Iris Marion Young's difference theory falls into a broadly similar trap, as, indeed, do the approaches defended by Parekh and Gray, all of whom, in one way or another, require members of all groups to 'talk past their differences' and engage with one another in the construction of common principles and institutions by framing their discussions in particular ways, and constraining their deliberations according to wider and prior principles which determine the rules of conduct. Popper's rejection of the 'myth' that we need to understand individuals as embedded in mutually exclusive 'frameworks' which define their identity and make it impossible for groups to deliberate with one another or come to common agreements remains powerful, insightful, and largely ignored among most political theorists, many of whom have gone on to argue for a conception of deliberative democracy very similar to that defended by Popper almost 50 years earlier(Popper, 1994a). Popper's methodological individualism-his view that the principal subject of political analysis is the individual not the groups to which they belong-and his claim that the members of different cultures, religions, and nations can (and must) come together to deliberate meaningfully with one another in order to identify and solve social and political problems regardless of their differences is indeed controversial, but no less controversial or dogmatic than many alternative approaches which are considered canonical in the literature(see Waldron, 2004).

Furthermore, just as Popper's philosophy undermines the idea that social and political reforms in the *domestic* context can be justified by an appeal to overarching historical laws, or to idealized states of affairs derived through abstract reasoning (independent of a wider system of conjectural knowledge and theory), it also suggests the folly in looking to such justifications as a basis for *international* intervention, especially in the area of democratization. In particular, it undermines the idea-dominant among Western liberal democratic states like Britain and the US-that it is possible to establish democratic regimes in societies with no history of democracy. The idea that undemocratic regimes can be swept aside and unproblematically replaced with more democratic, more enlightened political systems has been shown to be fraught with dangers, particularly in recent years. The wars in Iraq and Afghanistan, for example, are arguably a fitting testament to the kind of limits to reason (and political radicalism)that Popper described: just as it is not for politicians or philosophers in liberal democratic societies (driven by an Enlightenment faith in the power of reason) to dream up visions of the ideal society and then reform society so as to bring those visions about, so they should not consider it their role to design an ideal set of social and political institutions and then impose them upon peoples who are not ready for them, do not understand them, and have not had a hand in their shaping. Such radicalism is premised upon a blind faith in the capacity of reason to provide certainty about the kind of institutions needed, the ends to which they should be committed, and the possible pitfalls and problems which will be encountered in the process of their establishment. In fact, Popper suggested, no such certainty is possible, and to foresee all the possible variables and ramifications of individual decisions in a way that is simply not credible. Consequently, any attempts to encourage democracy in undemocratic states must necessarily be gradual, piecemeal, and the product of real dialogue among those individuals involved.

If Popper's political philosophy is too often dismissed for its historical redundancy, it is just as often dismissed for its methodological implications. Popper's ideas were as much about (if not more about) establishing the appropriate *method* for the study of political and social life as they were about producing normative or guiding principles about the structure of society and the state. They are claims about the appropriate ends of politics, and of philosophy, and hence, they articulate a particular, original, and controversial political and methodological vision. And it is not a vision which fits easily within many of the dominant approaches in contemporary political thought. It is fitting, perhaps, given Popper's epistemological commitment to falsificationism and his rejection of inductive verificationism, that it is much easier to discuss what Popper was *not* than what he *was*.

For example, Popper could not comfortably be described as a member of the 'Cambridge school' of political philosophy-embodied in the work of historians like Quentin Skinner and J. G. A. Pocock-who hold that it is the principal job of the political philosopher to derive the meaning of political texts or utterances by locating them within their particular historical context. Popper shared with historians like Skinner the claim that, when studying political and philosophical texts, there is some value in working out what the author meant to achieve by understanding the historical context in which she wrote it. That is, Popper believed that it was sometimes important to derive the 'situational logic' of a text or argument by reconstructing the historical and intentional circumstances in which it was written or uttered (Popper, 1957/2005, pp. 136-41). However, he was fiercely resistant of the more radical claim that such a process foreclosed the possibility of saying anything more meaningful about politics or society, or that political concepts, texts, or arguments could not be subjected to ahistorical analysis. Popper believed that political philosophy was more than merely the study of the language used by particular theorists at any particular moment in history and, *contra* Wittgenstein, that the point of philosophy is not merely to derive the *meaning* of linguistic or textual statements, but to determine the *truth* or *falsity* of such statements. Hence, he believed that the point of *political* philosophy is to identify social and political problems, and to resolve them. He therefore thought that it was a central aim of the social and political sciences to determine the truth or falsity of claims about social and political matters, and to work out how, and to what extent, existing social and political arrangements might be considered, or made, legitimate.

Popper was also no postmodernist. His insistence that it was possible to use the tools of reason and objectivity to reveal knowledge about all aspects of the world, from quantum mechanics to the appropriate design of social and political institutions, seems in flat contradiction to claims made by postmodernists that such an endeavour was doomed to failure. Despite going against many Enlightenment thinkers in questioning the capacity of reason to reveal certain truths about the world, he was no poststructuralist in the vein of Foucault or Bourdieu, and despite being an impassioned critic (of rival understandings of science, of authoritarianism, of totalitarianism, of many branches of philosophy), he was certainly no 'critical theorist' in the tradition of thinkers like Habermas, Adorno, or Horkheimer, for all the reasons mentioned in Chapter 3. For Popper, criticism-understood as the testing of hypotheses with counter arguments and evidence-was the primary route to genuine human knowledge, and the only real way of attaining it. Popper abhorred the moral relativism that he believed lay implicit in postmodernism, poststructuralism and critical theory, and rejected too the political impotence that he felt they implied. His aim above anything else was to provide a mechanism by which the truth and falsity of claims (about all aspects of the world, including morality) could be evaluated, and to defend the idea that individuals could, by working together, take charge of their lives and their future, and to reject the common claim among 'radical' ideologists that all that people could realistically do was wait for change to come to them.

No Cambridge historian, postmodernist, poststructuralist or critical theorist, then, Popper is perhaps most closely associated with philosophical pragmatists and the political theorists working in the Anglo-American tradition. Yet, again, he cannot be easily slotted within either of these traditions. There are numerous reasons why Popper cannot be straightforwardly labelled a member of the Anglo-American tradition, for example. Since the publication of Rawls's *A Theory of Justice* in 1971, Anglo-American political philosophy has been dominated by the search for the appropriate definition of justice and, hence, of the just society. Unlike practitioners of the Cambridge school, Rawlsian political philosophers tend not to appeal to history in their theorizing, other than in a tangential way; rather, their aim is to draw upon the analytical tradition in order to establish the rational and normative coherence of certain first principles upon which a just social and political order might be constructed. To put it another way, the principal aim of Anglo-American normative political philosophy is to derive a conception of justice substantive enough to inform the design of social and political institutions, to define these institutions' roles and responsibilities, and to circumscribe their actions, from a process of reasoned deliberation. Institutions, policies, and decisions are thus legitimated by reason (by rationally defensible arguments) rather than particular values embodied in religious, cultural, or national traditions. Consequently, Anglo-American political philosophers see themselves as engaged in the Enlightenment project of justifying the authority of political arrangements in universal standards of reason as opposed to contingent, parochial memberships or ideals. The contractualism of liberal thinkers like Brian Barry(1995), Charles Beitz(1989), Thomas Nagel (1991), Thomas Scanlon(1999), and John Rawls's(1971) early work, the political liberalism of Charles Larmore (2008) and John Rawls's (1993) later work, and the comprehensive liberalism of thinkers like Joseph Raz(1986; 1996) and Steven Wall(1998) all stand united with the deliberative democratic approach defended by theorists like Amy Gutmann and Dennis Thompson(1996), and Joshua Cohen(1989) in suggesting that political institutions can be designed, and reforms enacted, according to principles revealed by reasoned deliberation among individual actors motivated to find agreement in circumstances of diversity, and that it is possible for reason (untainted by particular values or theories) to provide a blueprint for a just society which can be constructed from scratch. Anglo-American liberal political philosophy thus draws inspiration from the Enlightenment vision of thinkers like Bacon and Descartes, who believed that the truth could be found by excising from the mind all particularities and dispositions and looking at the world through clean eyes.

Popper, of course, agreed that political authority should be justified by reason rather than particularist identities or values, but he had little time for the Baconian or Cartesian vision of reasoning upon which the Anglo-American normative project appears to be built, believing it irresponsible, arrogant, and contrary to the growth of knowledge. He did not share Rawls's belief that the aim of political philosophy should be the derivation of principles of justice which could be used to structure and regulate social and political institutions. Such a project was, Popper thought, indicative of the blind optimism among many Enlightenment thinkers in the power of reason to sweep aside history and to construct fully functioning social and political systems as if the past had never existed. Rawls and many of his followers are, in Popper's terms, merely the contemporary advocates of the same mistaken epistemology as the French revolutionaries. Consequently, they fall into the same trap: their attempts to describe a functioning and just society will inevitably and necessarily be thwarted by the conjectural character of what passes for all knowledge, and the inability of reason to foresee all possible variables and, hence, to deal with all possible challenges. Rawlsian theories of social justice tend to be demanding and substantive - they stipulate how the benefits and burdens of society should be redistributed, for example, as well as what these benefits and burdens are. Popper's fallibilism about the power of abstract reasoning to resolve these questions once and for all, and his attendant scepticism about long-term centralized planning, provides an important check on the aspirations of many philosophers working in the Anglo-American tradition to settle the question of justice in the way that they do, and suggests that they should view their claims about justice in more humble terms than they sometimes do, as hypotheses and suggestions, rather than rationally verifiable truths.

Similarly, Popper would have had little time for the idea that the central aim of political philosophy was to define the meaning of terms like 'justice'. Hence, he would have considered the tendency among many Anglo-American philosophers to frame questions in terms of the definition of essences (such as 'what is justice?', or 'what is equality?'), that currently dominates contemporary Anglo-American political philosophy, as a redundant and futile activity. Popper was primarily interested in identifying and solving problems in a context in which it was impossible to provide ultimate and final definitions of such terms as equality, justice, or liberty, and in which we should be sceptical of leaders or intellectuals who seek to provide such things. In particular, he was interested in the power of, and limits to, knowledge, and hence, the justification that rulers might appropriately give for enacting social reforms. Given this, it is hardly surprising that Popper remains such a marginal figure in mainstream normative discourse. After all, if his epistemological claims are correct (and it is not possible for reason to reveal certain truths about the world), and if it is also true that philosophy should not concern itself with the definition of terms like justice, equality, or freedom, then an important concern of normative political philosophers working in the Anglo-American tradition is rendered little more than a pointless mistake. They appeal to a mistaken conception of Enlightenment reasoning in order to produce ideal definitions of political terms which are unhelpful because their coherence or persuasiveness cannot be proven.

Despite all this, there are a number of ways in which Popper's ideas are more congruent with those of Anglo-American political theorists than we might first think, and more than many thinkers within this tradition assume. For example, many if not all philosophers working in the Rawlsian tradition would agree with Popper that it is the principal role of the political philosopher to identify and seek to resolve genuine social and political problems. For example, while liberal political philosophers like Ronald Dworkin seek to answer questions like 'what is equality?', it is clear that they do so primarily in order to identify and resolve real social and political problems: liberal egalitarians of various stripes are principally motivated by the theoretical and practical question of how social and political institutions might measure and ameliorate unjust economic inequalities (e. g. Cohen, 2008; Dworkin, 2000). Multiculturalist liberals and political liberals are concerned, among other things, with resolving the question of how broadly impartial liberal democratic institutions might appropriately take into account the diverse interests of cultural, ethnic, and religious minorities (e. g. Kymlicka, 1997; Raz, 1996). And the increasing number of political philosophers working in the area of international justice generally seek answers to complex practical questions including the alleviation of poverty and suffering among the world's poor(e. g. Pogge, 2007). The point for these thinkers, then, is not to engage in abstract reasoning for the sake of it, but to apply the tools of what Popper called the rationalist tradition to concrete social and political problems in the world in a clear-headed, analytical way, in order that such problems might be resolved. Their definitional questions are therefore discussed in the context of, and in response to, the actually existing nature of these problems. Popper would emphasize the conjectural, hypothetical nature of any such resolutions, of course; he would indeed claim that reasoning needs to be conducted against the background of accumulated knowledge, and he would also point out that the answers provided should not be considered certain truths, but there is no reason to suppose that Anglo-American normative political philosophers could not unite with Popper on the idea that political philosophy(like any other discipline)is at heart a process of problem-solving, and that reason can provide the solutions to concrete social, political, economic, and legal problems.

Popper also shared with many contemporary Anglo-American political philosophers a rejection of teleological morality:that is, the idea that it is appropriate to determine the moral rightness or wrongness of an act or set of institutions according to the extent to which this act or set of institutions is in line with, or helps to bring about, some pre-determined conception of the good life for all. The majority of contemporary liberal egalitarians, libertarians, classical liberals, political liberals, and comprehensive liberals have united behind the claim(made by H. L. A Hart in his *A Concept of Law*, and, differently, by Rawls in his *A Theory of Justice*), that utilitarian teleology is *morally* deficient as it can lead to injustices like the oppression of minority groups, and have also joined Rawls in defending a broadly 'deontological' form of liberalism in its place. Popper ' s political philosophy strengthens the liberal case against teleological moral and political systems by providing a different, and perhaps even more powerful, *epistemological* critique of its core assumptions: that any moral theory which evaluates the rightness or wrongness of an act or decision according to the extent to which it brings about some future overarching good for all is not only morally inadequate but epistemologically incoherent, for no such overarching good can be known. Similarly, Popper's argument serves to undermine certain more radical varieties of moral consequentialism: any moral theory which evaluates the rightness or the wrongness of an act or decision according to the consequences it would have is undermined by the fact that (a) in order to know whether the resultant consequences are good or bad requires a prior knowledge of the goals to which they should be aimed (which is possible, but difficult, given the fallibility of reason), and (b) because the consequences-especially the long-term consequences-of any such act or decision cannot be known with certainty. This, we must remember, was the reason that Popper was committed to what he called a 'negative' rather than a 'positive' utilitarianism. He believed that we can and should seek to identify problems in society and propose solutions to them which bring about beneficial consequences, but we should not seek to construct over-arching conceptions of the good life and judge actions right or wrong depending on the extent to which they bring about this conception of the good life. The consequences of our actions are thus important in our moral deliberations, but state action can only be coherently employed in the interests of *reducing harm* rather than *promoting a particular political vision*.

Finally, there is one further, much more fundamental, claim which unites Popper with contemporary political theorists working in the Anglo-American tradition, namely, that normative statements about politics and society are both meaningful and possible. Remember, at the time at which Popper was writing, analytical philosophy was dominated by the logical positivism of the Vienna Circle, and the ordinary language philosophy of thinkers like Austin and Ryle. Together, these dominating forces appeared to foreclose entirely the idea that it is possible to make normative statements about such things as politics or society or morality. After all, logical positivists held that such statements were meaningless and, hence, could not be described as philosophical statements at all. And ordinary language philosophers suggested that the meaning of political concepts(and, hence, the normative justification of statements about political or social life) could not be separated from the context in which they were used: in asking the question 'what is freedom?', for example, ordinary language philosophers suggested that what we are really asking is 'in what ways do individuals in a particular context use the word "freedom"'? Such an approach appeared to rule out any attempt to provide universal definitions of such terms and, hence, meant that normative discussions about their importance (and how they might be protected or encouraged) could represent nothing more or less than a general conversation about the various meanings of the terms in question.

The dominance of logical positivism and ordinary language philosophy, and their foreclosure of normativity, led numerous thinkers like Isaiah Berlin and Peter Laslett to worry that political theory was dead(Berlin, 1962; Laslett, 1956). Popper may not have single-handedly destroyed logical positivism and ordinary language theory in quite the way he claimed to have, but he was nevertheless instrumental in breaking their grip on philosophy and making room for normativity *within* a philosophical approach informed by analytical rigour. Popper's rejection of the inductive scientific model, and his claim that science should be concerned with the falsification of conjectural statements about the world rather than the inductive extrapolation of general laws, suggested that philosophy could(and should) adopt a 'scientific' method, but that doing so did not foreclose the possibility of normative statements or deny the philosophical status of statements about politics, society, ethics, or metaphysics. Popper's epistemology provided a (controversial) way of rendering metaphysical, political, and ethical statements(and hence,normativity)compatible with the kind of rigour and clarity of purpose which defined the analytical tradition. Although his influence is often overlooked, therefore,it is nevertheless fair to suggest that Popper's work was instrumental in establishing the philosophical conditions in which other thinkers (like H. L. A. Hart and John Rawls) would produce their most notable normative works.

Furthermore, in reasserting political philosophy as the search for solutions to concrete social and political problems, rather than the quest for ultimate truths or essences, Popper helped prepare the way for pragmatists like Richard Rorty (e. g. 1989) to argue for the rejection of foundationalism in political philosophy,and for Anglo-American political theorists working in the Rawlsian tradition to make normative claims independently of any wider account of truth. In Rorty, for example,we find the Popperian claim that philosophers should not concern themselves with determining certain truths, as such truths cannot not be reliably known, and that they should,instead,seek to solve concrete political problems in the world using the historical, analytical, and philosophical tools currently at their disposal. The search for truth is not only pointless, Rorty thought, but pointlessly diverting: philosophers who seek ultimate truths will inevitably spend so much time looking for them that they will have little or no time to address the real and enduring problems faced by real people living in the world. Like Popper, then,Rortean pragmatists rejected the idea that in order to discuss philosophical ideas,we first have to derive the philosophical foundations (or essences) of these ideas and, like Popper, they argued that social and political problems can be resolved through the collective deliberations of individual actors. As Rorty argued, the real project for political philosophers is not to find ultimate and final *truths*, but to find coherent *justifications* for the claims we make about the world and politics. Popper,like Rorty,believed that it was possible to gain knowledge of the world, and of the ideas we use to describe and make sense of it, without first revealing their essences or, in Rorty's words, the foundations upon which these ideas rest. Hence, for Popper and for Rorty, the principal goal of political philosophy was to find grounds for political principles in the absence of firm foundations or clearly determined essences. Consequently, pragmatists, like Popper, asserted the importance of collective deliberation and agreement among individual actors who possess limited information but who are motivated to find agreeable solutions to common problems.

And this, it must be said, is a goal that is now shared not only by pragmatists but by the vast majority of political theorists working in the Anglo-American tradition. A growing number of Anglo-American political philosophers now share with the pragmatists and with Popper the claim that it is not the point of political philosophy to reveal certain truths about the world, but to seek justification for common political principles in circumstances in which there is profound, and perhaps insoluble, disagreement regarding questions of truth. Earlier in this chapter I mentioned the rise of multiculturalism as a political and philosophical issue, and mentioned some of the ways in which contemporary political theorists have tried to deal with this issue. Common to all of them, and to political liberals like Rawls in particular, is the idea that we live in a world characterised by radical disagreement about such fundamental matters as the origins of life, the nature of humanity, and our place in the world. We live in a world of different religions and moral perspectives, many of which are incompatible with one another, but which are nevertheless held to be incredibly important by hundreds of millions of people throughout the world. Given this, any conception of political philosophy which takes as its principal goal the settling of questions about truth, and which seeks to justify social and political arrangements and policies in these accounts of truth will inevitably fail or, at least, will remain inconclusive and partial, and unacceptable to many people. Political philosophy cannot, and should not try to, resolve questions of truth, and *liberal* political philosophers in particular should not attempt to do so, as such things are, for liberals, rightly left to individual conscience. The principal question for most Anglo-American political philosophers working today is not, arguably, what constitutes truth, but how we might derive political principles, institutions, and policies which are fair in the sense that they might be found acceptable by all those who live under them, irrespective of their more fundamental ideas about the world. This is a project that Popper believed in, and to which he made important contributions. The point of political philosophy for Popper, as wells as for pragmatists like Rorty, political liberals like Rawls, difference theorists like Young, deliberative democrats like Gutmann, and many other contemporary Anglo-American political philosophers is not to uncover the truth in order that it might provide some unifying moral basis for political authority, or for some particular arrangement of social and political institutions or some set of policies, but to build an inclusive political system in the face of radical disagreement about what is true about the world.

Popper cannot be easily associated with the Cambridge school, then, nor postmodernism, poststructuralism, or critical theory. He did not occupy the same theoretical space as Rawls or his followers, although his conclusions hold an enduring relevance in the areas in which they work. He was not a utilitarian in the way many understand the term, nor a teleologist, although he was committed to evaluating the success or failure of proposed social reforms at least partly in response to the consequences they generated. He was not a relativist, a nationalist, or a communitarian, but recognized the important (and often pernicious) hold that particularist memberships have had over so many people throughout history. He was not strictly a conservative, nor a libertarian, nor a classical liberal, but rejected long-term social, economic, and political planning and influenced many who associate themselves with those traditions. He was not a socialist, but he believed that state institutions can and should alleviate the crippling poverty that he believed many people endured. He was briefly a Marxist, and throughout his life continued to respect Marx's contribution to economic and social thought, but ultimately saw him as a danger to the aims of the open society. He supported the ideals embodied in the Enlightenment while fiercely criticizing many Enlightenment thinkers, defended a politics based on reason while asserting its limits, and championed the growth of knowledge while claiming that certain knowledge was impossible. In *The Open Society* he presented an important statement of post-war social democracy, rooted in an epistemology which would be used by many to destroy it. He was not a social contract thinker like Locke, Hobbes, Rousseau, or Kant. He did not rest his conclusions on controversial claims about human nature or the content of human motivations. He did not concern himself explicitly with many of the questions which political theorists take to be of core importance in the discipline, like political obligation, rights, and the source of law. And he did not provide a full and thoroughgoing normative theory of politics. Many philosophers vehemently disagreed with Popper's epistemological, social, and political philosophy, and consequently dismissed his work as mistaken, based upon faulty reasoning, or slipshod scholarship. Also, there are indeed important issues about which Popper said little or nothing, and which his philosophy does not seem equipped to tackle. It is hardly surprising, then, that the overwhelming majority of contemporary political philosophers, political scientists, economists, social theorists, and sociologists do not really know what to do with Popper, and it is hardly surprising that they have decided not to do anything with him. Popper was a polymath and a contrarian. He wrote on so many subjects, and excited controversy in so many fields, that it is possible for everyone to find something in his work to disagree profoundly with. The contradictions in his work, his forthright, often polemical written style, and his dogged commitment to principles which he thought were right in the face of what he called passing fads and trends make him difficult to locate in the literature, and hence he is, and remains, a marginal figure in contemporary political philosophy.

Conclusion

Popper belongs to a select group of thinkers whose name can be used as an adjective to describe theories and approaches (statements may be described as Popperian, or Wittgensteinian, or Rawlsian, for example). But there is no Popper*ism*, as there is Marxism or Platonism - no substantive ideology or normative programme around which supporters can rally. This is only to be expected, of course. Popper's rejection of historicism, his commitment to experimentation, piecemeal social reform, and the uncertainty of human knowledge meant that his work did not lend itself to the kind of world building (or destroying) that ideologies inspire. Indeed, in so far as ideologies represent sets of truth claims about the ideal ends of social and political institutions, they are, on Popper's terms, at best inherently fragile and partial. At worst, they embody the mistaken desire among their supporters to predict the future course of human development towards some ideal state of affairs-a desire which Popper saw as legitimating tyranny.

Popper did not leave us with an ideology, then. What he gave us was a method for finding out what we can and cannot know about the world and ourselves; a means of testing and evaluating the claims made by those who would rule us or seek to tell us how to live. He did not give us a list of policies to enact, or an institutional blueprint to establish. Indeed, he argued that the desire among many political philosophers and activists to provide such a thing is precisely the problem that we need to avoid. Rather, he provided a way of finding out what the appropriate policies and institutions might be, and how they might be justified. And in doing so, he provided a vision of politics and society which embraced individual freedom, equality, and reason. Popper believed that whatever their particular nature, social and political institutions should be structured in ways which encourage freedom of thought and discussion, and which protect individuals from tyranny; the tyranny of leaders who assume to know what is best for humankind, from institutions which fail to check the power of these leaders, and from domination by the 'economically strong' who are able to wield their economic power to subjugate and manipulate those who have less or nothing. He believed in the power of all individuals to seek common agreement on solutions to social and political matters through reasonable argument and empathy, and hence, fervently believed in democracy. He believed in the unifying character of reason, and that reason(appropriately understood)provided the key to breaking down the mentality of 'us' and 'them', characteristic of the closed society, and encouraging a universal concern for all human beings throughout the world, wherever they may live. His politics was consequently defined by what we might call a cosmopolitan rationalism-the idea that all people in all nations should receive help if they so need it, and that all people throughout the world might engage in productive dialogue with one another about political and social problems. He believed in the open society; a political community characterized by free thought and discussion; by democratic institutions accountable to those under them; by a spirit of cooperation not merely with one's neighbours, but with all persons for whom knowledge, experimentation, truth, freedom, and equality are important virtues; and by a rejection of all those pernicious ideas of historical fate, of common destiny, of nation, and of irrationalism which have provided leaders through the ages with the philosophical tools they need to rob individuals of their freedom, to manipulate them, to divide them, and, ultimately, to kill them. He believed in the capacity of individuals to bring about real and genuine change but recognized the need for change to be gradual rather than radical,incremental rather than revolutionary. In politics as in science,Popper believed that truth emerges out of the clash of ideas. Even the most sacred of cows, the most perfect and beautiful of theories, must be forced to prove themselves against rival theories; no theory is beyond criticism, and indeed,should it ever be conceived to be,the theory would lose its explanatory power. Just as Newton's claims about physics could not claim unassailable validity, so the theories of political thinkers and ideologues should also fall under the critical gaze of those who would seek to falsify them. Popper's methodological work in the field of epistemology, when applied to society and politics, provided a genuinely innovative approach to understanding the aims of philosophy and the state,and at once provided a new perspective on the debate about the possibility of a 'social science'. Such a thing was indeed possible, he believed, but establishing it would require an entirely new understanding of science.